THE
SMALL
BUSINESS
BIBLE

By the same author

The Complete Entrepreneur
Advice from the Top (with Lord Ezra)
Management Consultancy – the inside story (with Clive Rassam)
The International Manager (with Kevin Barham)
Leadership: The Art of Delegation
Perfect Recruitment (with Viv Shackleton)
The Manager as Coach (with Jim Durcan)

THE
SMALL
BUSINESS
BIBLE

Chapter and Verse on running
a successful small business

David Oates

**ARROW
BUSINESS BOOKS**

Published by Arrow Books in 1995

1 3 5 7 9 10 8 6 4 2

© David Oates 1995

First published by
Arrow Books Limited
20 Vauxhall Bridge Road, London SW1V 2SA

Random House Australia (Pty) Limited
20 Alfred Street, Milsons Point, Sydney
New South Wales 2061, Australia

Random House New Zealand Limited
18 Poland Road, Glenfield
Auckland 10, New Zealand

Random House South Africa (Pty) Limited
PO Box 337, Bergvlei, South Africa

Random House UK Limited Reg. No. 954009

ISBN 0 09 943921 2

Set in Sabon by
Deltatype Ltd, Ellesmere Port, Cheshire

Printed and bound in Great Britain by
Cox & Wyman Ltd, Reading, Berks

Contents

Acknowledgements

Small business is not a small subject. It encompasses a broad spectrum of topics, from macro-economics right through to the steps required to prepare a detailed business plan. In trying to cover such a comprehensive range of issues it has been necessary to draw on the expertise of innumerable specialists. To list them all would extend this book well beyond its allotted length.

I should, however, like to express my gratitude to Tony Randel, a small business adviser at Enterprise Plymouth, and George Raybould, an exporting consultant, for their invaluable advice in preparing the chapters on marketing and exporting respectively.

I also owe thanks to David Walker of the Rural Development Commission, for his advice on how to stage a trade exhibition; and to Ian Robinson, corporate financial partner with KMPG Peat Marwick, and John Wakefield, a director of Rowan Dartington, for their contributions to the section on preparing for a stock-market flotation.

NatWest and Midland Bank were both kind enough to allow me to extract material from their excellent guides to starting a small business. I am indebted to the Department of Trade and Industry for permission to refer to material in *Finance Without Debt – A Guide to Sources of Venture Capital under £250,000* and to the Rural Development Commission for allowing me to reproduce case study examples and general advice from two of their publications – *The Countryside Means Business* and *Action for Rural Enterprise*.

Lastly, this book could not have been written without the help of dozens of small business owners who were prepared to recall their successes and failures so that others can learn from their experience. They provide the benchmarks against which future budding entrepreneurs will measure the fulfilment of their aspirations.

INTRODUCTION

The Enterprise Culture

The 1980s were undoubtedly the golden decade for small business start-ups. Propelled by the liberating free-market policies of the Thatcher government, the enterprise culture truly took off. Small businesses were seen as the motor of job creation and entrepreneurs became the focus of attention. Small was unquestionably beautiful.

Thousands of would-be entrepreneurs seized the moment and took the opportunity to go it alone. For much of the eighties the small business boom continued but then came the recession and the economic climate changed dramatically. The government, which had introduced numerous schemes to encourage the enterprise culture, seemed to re-think its strategy towards small firm start-ups. Backing established medium-sized companies appeared to be a better bet in terms of job creation, especially as so many precarious small firms were going under. Small firms no longer seemed to be the apple of its eye.

Inevitably the change of climate took its toll. Because of their vulnerability and the inexperience of many of their owners, small firms suffered a high mortality rate even in the heyday of the enterprise culture. On average, one in three of the businesses started in Britain stops trading during its first three years. The recession and the determination of banks to invest in only the most promising ideas made it even tougher for small firms.

However, none of this seems to have put a damper on the

growth of new business start-ups. There have been many harrowing tales of entrepreneurs devastated by the recession, of homes repossessed and dreams dashed, but the image of the small business has nevertheless remained untarnished. Indeed, huge corporations, battered by the harsh winds of recession, are now carving up their monolithic hierarchies into small discrete units and are encouraging entrepreneurial initiatives among their front-line employees.

The small business contribution to the economy is no longer questioned. Businesses employing up to 500 people account for 99 per cent of all businesses in the European Union and 72 per cent of jobs; small firms with less than a hundred workers provide 55 per cent of employment. A survey in 1994 by the Forum of Private Business (FPB) revealed that 100,000 new jobs had been created in the UK by small firms over the previous twelve months and that nearly half the small firms polled were expanding.

With major firms delayering and flattening their pyramids in a constant endeavour to cut costs and improve efficiency, the situation is unlikely to change. If profitable companies like Unilever are making swingeing cuts in their workforces, it is hard to imagine where the jobs are going to come from in the future if not from the regenerating small business sector.

Ironically, the trend towards globalization has worked in favour of small firms. John Naisbitt, in his book *Global Paradox*, points out that the removal of trade barriers all over the world initially looked like a great opportunity for big companies, but in fact it opened the way for small companies which now have easy access to markets that in the past only large companies could operate in.

Naisbitt also suggests that computers and telecommunications have turned out to be formidable weapons for small companies to get an edge on big companies: 'In the past only big firms could afford new technology. Now, any micro-business can have the same state-of-the-art technology as IBM or AT&T. But small firms are not burdened with layers of bureaucracy and the leaden weight of bigness. Small companies can deconstruct and re-organize much faster than large companies.' He also notes that the deregulation and globalization of financial markets have given small and medium-sized companies access to capital that they never had before. Now small companies can borrow capital from all over the globe.

There have, however been setbacks in the small business sector's march of progress. The Third Market, intended as a home for dealings in the shares of young unproven companies, has disappeared from the scene and the Unlisted Securities Market will suffer the same fate at the end of 1995. The Business Expansion Scheme (BES), introduced by the government to encourage investors to put money into small and growing firms, ended up by being exploited for all kinds of esoteric ventures. It became even more discredited when in 1988 it was extended to private rented housing schemes, and was turned largely into a tax avoidance vehicle. It was superseded in 1993 by the Enterprise Investment Scheme (EIS), which offers income tax relief on equity investments in unquoted trading companies, but excludes invest-ments in private rented housing.

The new scheme appears to have been well received by would-be investors but the so-called 'equity gap' is an issue small firms have had to battle against for years. The problem has always been that banks are reluctant to lend money for risky projects, and the venture capitalists tend not to be interested in the small amounts (in their terms) that fledgling businesses require for start-up or expansion. Small business owners, for their part, are reluctant to take on debt that is beyond their means or give away large slabs of equity in a business they have nurtured as their own. After all, freedom of action is one of the main reasons why people become small business owners.

The recession only served to exacerbate the situation. The banks scrutinized business plans even more closely and were criticized for deserting their clients when they were needed most. In fact, of course, the recession helped to weed out a lot of small firms which were on a shaky path anyway and those that have survived have learned a lot of lessons which will serve them well as the economic climate improves.

In 1988, about 48 per cent of start-ups used bank finance against 20 per cent today. Some bankers believe that this reflects a reluctance to take on debt but it can probably be attributed to a combination of factors. Alarmed by the widely-publicized strained relationships between lenders and entrepreneurs during the worst of the recession, small firms are disinclined to believe they will get a fair deal from the banks. In addition, banks have declared that they are now applying more stringent vetting procedures before lending to small firms. The view is gathering pace that there should be a special vehicle in the UK for financing small and medium-sized firms. One proposal is that Britain should set up an equivalent to Germany's *Kreditanstalt fur Wideraufbau* (KfW), which uses its size and sound credit rating to borrow from the money markets at favourable interest rates and lend on to small and medium-sized firms.

Throughout these difficult times, the small business cause has been vigorously championed by some valiant lobbying groups, such as the Forum of Private Business and the Federation of Small Businesses. They have tried to reduce the red tape burden on small firms but the problem never entirely goes away. For instance some small firms regard the quality management scheme known as British Standard 5750 and its international equivalent ISO 9000 as unduly bureaucratic and expensive to operate, but larger firms are increasingly demanding that their suppliers meet these standards and small businesses are left with little option but to take them up, whether or not they regard them as necessary.

Likewise, lobby groups have made little headway in promoting solutions to the late payment problems that still plague many small firms. Inevitably, in a recessionary economic climate the problem has become worse as everyone tries to hang on to the money in the bank for as long as they dare. Small firms are at the end of the payment chain and if the big firms they supply fail to pay on time this puts a strain on the small firms' cash flow. This in turn causes the small firms to delay payments to their suppliers. It is a vicious circle.

The government is trying to reduce the red tape burden on small firms. In early 1994 Michael Heseltine, president of the Board of Trade, promised 'the biggest bonfire of controls that has taken place in modern times in this country'. As a start, he targeted for abolition 450 regulations that had been identified as ludicrous by seven businessmen's taskforces.

Heseltine also committed himself to protecting small companies against the potentially exorbitant costs of complying with new laws and promised to avoid exposing them to damaging new measures: before legislation, small firms will be asked what they think of the proposals. Needless to say, Heseltine's war on red tape has been greeted with considerable enthusiasm, but there is also scepticism. Will today's good intentions be remembered when tomorrow's legislation is drafted?

The government is also trying to help in another way. Towards the end of 1994 it curtailed the Enterprise Initiative Scheme which had provided funds for small firms to use the services of consultants. However, it has taken steps to preserve the unique expertise that had been created by the scheme's contractors, and a national consultancy brokerage scheme is being set up which will operate through such agencies as the Training and Enterprise Councils and a newly established network of one-stop shops called Business Links.

However, the extent of the government's current commitment to small firms is difficult to gauge. Small firms ministers have been changing jobs with bewildering speed and it is hard to see how such brief tenures of office can allow small firms ministers to get to grips with the real issues or have a significant impact. The decisions which really affect small firms are taken in the Treasury, the Inland Revenue and Customs and Excise, all of which have other priorities.

It is an ill wind that blows nobody good and the recession has not been all bad news. Plummeting property values have been a blessing in disguise to small firms who found it hard to find affordable work units during the boom years. The growth of short-lease 'managed workshops' with shared reception facilities has also helped to alleviate the problem of finding accommodation for start-up entrepreneurs.

The technological revolution has helped to further the cause of small firms. The electronic aids available to budding entrepreneurs are now so extensive that they can choose to set up shop wherever they like. Armed with a personal computer, a modem, fax, a conference telephone – and perhaps even E-mail – such entrepreneurs can be in touch with the world at the press of a button. The fact that they happen to be working from the wilds of Scotland or the Lake District for the most part presents no barrier to their enterprise.

In fact, they do not even need to invest in such modern gadgets personally. Telecottages with centralized facilities to serve a whole community are cropping up like toadstools all over Britain and provide the latest information technology aids for the price of a shared investment. Not surprisingly, the Rural Development Commission (RDC), which is trying to halt the economic decline of rural communities, is welcoming the trend with open arms.

Small firms have become part of the fabric of both urban and rural life. Small business entrepreneurs are fêted in society. Children learn the mechanics of running a business at school – and sometimes set up their own mini-businesses to put theory into practice. A multitude of award schemes recognize small business achievements. It could be said with some certainty that small firms have made their mark.

Yet a testing time lies ahead. Trading *out* of a recession is in many ways as demanding as trading *in* one. It is easy to be swept away by an upsurge in the economy and to discard all the valuable lessons learned during a period of stringency. It is hoped that the advice in this book will prevent small business owners from stumbling into some of the pitfalls that helped to fuel the recession in the first place.

CHAPTER 1

Self-Assessment

A survey published in 1988 at the height of the enterprise culture in Britain threw some interesting light on the characteristics of the country's top 100 entrepreneurs. The study was conducted by Sue Birley, professor of entrepreneurship at Cranfield School of Management and Liz Watson of consultants Arthur Young. Most of the 100 entrepreneurs who came under their scrutiny grew up in families in which the father had some type of small firm or self-employed experience. Remarkably, none of the entrepreneurs had fathers with managerial experience in a large organization.

By contrast, a similar survey of American entrepreneurs revealed that some 48 per cent came from the professional or managerial classes. The 100 British entrepreneurs studied included such well-known personalities as Richard Branson, Andrew Lloyd Webber and Alan Sugar, but most of them were not household names. Only two of them were women (Anita Roddick of Body Shop fame and Pamela Fisher of P&P Micro Distributors).

46 per cent of the companies they ran were in the service sector. The rest were in manufacturing (42 per cent) and retailing (12 per cent). The oldest firm had been around for fifty-nine years, the youngest for four years. The annual turnover of the firms ranged between £15 million and £300 million.

To qualify for the study, the owner managers had to hold at

least 20 per cent of the equity. On average they owned a 44 per cent stake. Three owned 90 per cent and two were sole owners.

According to the study findings, a first-class education does not seem to be a prerequisite for the British entrepreneur. It was revealed that 45 per cent of the surveyed group left school at sixteen and did not pursue any further qualifications. In the US, by contrast, 72 per cent of high flyers have a first degree and 52 per cent a post-graduate degree. 'In Britain, the education sector has yet to provide the correct environment for the potential high flying entrepreneur,' noted Birley and Watson.

Another intriguing discrepanacy between the US and the UK was thrown up by the survey. Where in the UK the entrepeneur had gained further qualifications, the skills and knowledge acquired tended to form the basis of the company. In the US, on the other hand, there was no apparent relationship between education and the nature of the entrepreneurial firms.

The majority of the UK entrepreneurs studied, whose ages ranged between twenty-one and forty-eight, spent their 'incubation' period working for small firms that employed up to 200 people. Of the rest, 23 per cent had previously worked for medium-sized firms employing between 200 and 500 people and 33 per cent came from large firms. Again, this pattern was in stark contrast to US experience, where only 33 per cent of entrepreneurs came from firms employing less than 500 people.

For the most part, Birley and Watson found no trading relationship between the entrepreneurial firm and the 'incubator' firm. The knowledge and experience gained, therefore, was only of limited value. By contrast, 43 per cent of American entrepreneurs start in direct competition with their previous employer and 63 per cent have an identifiable ongoing relationship.

British entrepreneurs seem to be more concerned about questions of business ethics. 'I didn't set up in competition to my previous employer because it would have been unethical and pointless to try and destroy what I had built up there,' commented one of those questioned for the survey.

The predominant characteristic of the entrepreneurs surveyed by Birley and Watson seems to have been positive thinking. Noted one interviewee: 'The introduction of EC regulations forced us to re-design the product.'

The same trait seemed to shine through the motivational characteristics of the British entrepreneur. Drive to win, optimism, determination and self-confidence were some of the most cited attributes.

The study showed that the entrepreneur relies most heavily on those close to the business – banker, accountant, lawyer, customers and other business contacts – for advice and assistance in the formative stages of setting up a company. Surprisingly, professional advice from such organizations as trade associations, enterprise agencies and chambers of commerce, which is often offered free of charge, did not appear to be used or greatly valued.

Asked to name the qualities for success, the entrepreneurs ranked 'concern for results' as the most important, closely followed by 'integrity' and 'ambition'. 'Conformity', 'appearance' and 'social adaptability' were rated the least important traits.

The clearest message to come out of the study appears to have been that the climate that pervades big business in Britain is not conducive for growing entrepreneurs, despite the boom in buyouts, which by their very nature are run by former corporate executives. Once the mould of corporation man is set it is obviously one that is hard to break out of. The qualities of entrepreneurship are more likely to be awakened in those who come from a small business background.

Layoffs

The recession that set in during the years following that study has obviously changed the balance somewhat. The wholesale layoffs by big firms has inevitably persuaded many former 'company' men and women to try their hand at self-employment. That does not mean, of course, that they will succeed or that they will ever join the ranks of the country's top 100 entrepreneurs. Past experience indicates that successful entrepreneurs are nurtured by a different training ground. Only time will tell whether the changing economic climate will produce a different cadre of budding entrepreneurs who turn their big company skills into small company successes.

Hard decision

The decision to go into business for yourself should not be taken lightly. You can be sure it will change your life completely. Six months after taking the plunge you may well fondly look back on more sober times and wonder why you decided to sacrifice so many of the things that had been important to you – like peace of mind, the opportunity to spend time on your favourite hobbies and the possibility of playing with your children whenever the mood took you.

The impact it will have on your personal life can be gauged from the fact that an organization has been set up in Gloucestershire called Support for Spouses in Business to help husbands and wives of entrepreneurs. The aim is to give partners practical training in helping their 'other halves' to run their companies and provide tips on avoiding family rifts.

Becoming an entrepreneur is not for the faint-hearted. It will take over your life, use up most of your time and energy and play havoc with your cash flow. Office hours will have no meaning any more. You will eat, sleep and live your business, certainly in the early stages of start-up.

The first question to ask therefore is whether you are the right kind of person to suffer such an onslaught on your private life and on your powers of endurance. Of course, nobody really knows what they can achieve until they have tried. But you can examine your life up to now to find some clues.

Are you in all honesty a sticker? Have you in the past undertaken major challenges either at work or as part of a leisuretime activity and failed to make the grade? Have you ever walked out of a very difficult management course, for example, declaring it is not for you? Have you ever decided to enter a marathon race only to find that you had to pull out after the first few miles? Do you give up the challenge easily? If the answer is yes, you probably ought to think twice about becoming an entrepreneur. It will be the longest marathon you have ever contemplated and there will be no going back once you have set things in motion. You may well have invested all the capital you can raise on a single belief that you can succeed where many have failed.

Personal checklist

Occupational psychologists have devised all kinds of tests and questionnaires that can help reveal to you the sort of person you are and whether you have the aptitude or not for coping with the major challenge of running your own business. But the answer really lies in your own heart. Do you want it badly enough to make all the inevitable sacrifices it will entail?

National Westminster Bank has compiled a very helpful guide to starting a business, which includes the following personal checklist:

- I am self-disciplined and I do not let things drift
- I have the full support of my family
- I am ready to put in seven days a week, if necessary
- I can get on well with people
- I can make careful decisions
- I can cope under stress
- I do not give up when the going gets tough
- I can learn from mistakes
- I can take advice

- I am patient and I expect a long haul
- I can motivate people
- I am in good health
- I am enthusiastic
- I know about the risks
- I have specific aims

NatWest suggests that if you can honestly live up to these fifteen characteristics, you are most likely to have what it takes to be a successful entrepreneur. But even if you fall short of perfection, at the very least you will know what your strengths and weaknesses are. It is a good idea to get your friends and relatives to assess you on the same criteria. You will almost certainly find their views are at variance with your own. But again you will increase your self-awareness which is a key to understanding whether you have what it takes to start a small business.

Redundancy

A lot of people first seriously consider starting their own business when they are made redundant. Being without the prospect of employment is not in itself a good reason for deciding to go it alone. It may however be the final spur for something you have been planning for a long time. In that event you may well have been preparing yourself subconsciously for some years and the time may well be ripe to have a go.

But if you are the wrong person to go into business for yourself you will only be inviting disaster if you see it as the only alternative to the dole queue. People who are made redundant often quite naturally feel low in spirit. That is not a good time to be setting out on the most arduous adventure of your life. Enthusiasm and dedication are two of the most vital prerequisites for running a small business. After all, you are going to have to sell yourself, first to your bank manager or to a venture capitalist and then to your customers. You will need to have confidence oozing from every pore.

NatWest contends that it is essential before setting up in business to be clear about what your aims are. Are you doing it to make more money? Do you want to be involved in something that interests you? Are you seeking independence? Have you lost your job and are seeking a new way to make a living? Thousands of new businesses fold because their owners fail to identify their business or personal goals.

It is helpful, in NatWest's view, for the would-be entrepreneur to copy big business and draw up what is grandly known as a 'mission statement'. It may sound a bit like overkill, but, as NatWest points out, it is surprising how useful a business mission statement can be in keeping you pointed in the right direction. If you have a firm idea of your aims and where you want to go, you are more likely to succeed.

Examples of a business mission, suggested by NatWest, include:

- To offer a first-class business and personal minicab service throughout Anytown, exclusively using Mercedes cars
- To be the leader in the business and at the top end of the personal minicab market, and to have a high-profile local business within two years
- To make 40 per cent profit on the money used to start the business
- To expand the business from five cars to ten cars within three years.

The right time

There is a right time for everything. It is pointless to consider setting up in business if you are already heavily committed to family and social responsibilities. Running a business is not something you can do from the kitchen table in your spare time. It requires a hundred per cent dedication if you are to have any chance of success.

Pauline Ralph very wisely waited until her children had flown the nest before she started her successful business in North Devon. Right from childhood Pauline had enjoyed making things, usually from scraps of wood with a cheap fret saw. When she eventually had children of her own, she delighted them with the dolls' houses and model farms she made.

By the time her children had grown into teenagers, she began to think of how she might turn her toy-making skills into a viable business. She finally hit on the idea of making thatched cottage music boxes. The original design has since spawned around fifty different cottage models that sell all over the world. The business became so successful, Pauline's husband eventually left the security of his job as managing director of a textile firm to join her full time in the enterprise.

Pauline Ralph is typical of a new breed of women entrepreneurs with bright ideas and the tenacity to see them implemented, who are determined to exchange the drudgery of the kitchen sink for the exhilaration of commercial enterprise. But not all women who set up in business do so because their children have flown the nest and they are searching for something stimulating to fill their days.

When Valerie Burrell re-married, she felt it unfair to expect her second husband to finance the education of her children from her first marriage. A keen home knitter, it occurred to her she might be able to raise the necessary funds by turning her hobby into a cottage industry. She advertised for outworkers and six like-minded women applied and provided the nucleus of a business that was eventually recording an annual turnover of hundreds of thousands of pounds.

Johanna Sheen was spurred into action when her husband announced he intended to give up his lucrative job as an advertising executive to attend a full-time course at the London Business School. She knew she was going to have to do something urgently to supplement their income. The grant her husband would receive towards the course would fall far short of supporting the standard of living to which they had grown accustomed.

Johanna decided the answer was to start her own business, but she had a very young baby daughter, so it had to be a product line she could produce from her home. After several abortive experiments she discovered her forte. It was making pictures from pressed flowers grown in her garden, which she managed to turn into a thriving business. Her original designs in elegant picture frames eventually sold in their thousands in Harrods and other leading stores. She also opened up a flourishing export business.

Personality change

Necessity and a desire for fulfilment precipitated these women entrepreneurs into starting their own firms, but it was determination and resilience that kept them in business. Most small business entrepreneurs will tell you that they have had to undergo a partial personality change to survive in business. It certainly helps to be an extrovert to succeed, but those who tend towards being introvert find that they have to undergo a metamorphosis.

Aggression is not a particularly pleasant characteristic, but it is a trait that certainly helps people to get by in business. You need to be aggressive in selling your ideas and you often need to be aggressive in persuading your customers to pay up according to the terms of your invoice.

Unfortunately, late payment, particularly during a recession, is an endemic part of business life. Shrinking violets who fail to challenge their customers will soon find their cash flow suffers and the viability of their business is seriously undermined. If you don't get on top of the problem, it will get on top of you. It is easy enough to put it off to another day. That will simply mean that the erring customers will think that they have got away with it and put you to the bottom of their priority payment list.

Many small business entrepreneurs shy away from tackling

this issue, because they find it hard to be treating the customer as king one moment (when trying to win a new order) and having to demand overdue payment the next. Often in businesses that are run by husband-and-wife teams this problem is shared to avoid schizophrenia. One partner does the selling; the other does the money chasing.

One-dimensional

All these peripheral aspects of running a business tend to be overlooked in the early euphoria of a start-up. Most would-be small business entrepreneurs go into business because they have a particular talent – usually for making something or providing a service. They tend to overlook that there is a lot more to business than that. Even if they are aware of what is required, these one-dimensional entrepreneurs assume that the other aspects will take care of themselves provided they are outstanding at what they do best.

They tend to overlook that however brilliant their product idea or service is, it won't sell itself. It will require marketing acumen to reach the targeted customers. It will require start-up capital to fund the production facilities and the office space, even if that initially is in the entrepreneur's own home or back garage. Telephone bills and electricity costs will escalate. They will need to know how to organize the inevitable administration involved and if they take on staff, how to supervise people.

Of course, there is a learning curve in any new venture and flexible people pick things up fast, but you need to ask yourself just how versatile you are. If your honest answer is that you really just enjoy making things and you don't really want to be bothered with all the rest, you will probably be better off working for somebody else who can provide the supporting business disciplines.

As an entrepreneur you will need to be a jack-of-all-trades, able to turn your hand to any aspect of the business, certainly in the early stages when both financial and people resources are scarce. One-dimensional entrepreneurs who assume that marketing, financial matters and administration will take care of themselves are doomed from the start.

Only you know whether you have got what it takes to run a small business. If honesty tells you that it is not something that is likely to sustain your interest and your determination, don't give it another thought. If on the other hand you feel that you have the courage to grasp the nettle and the motivation to tackle one of the most exhilarating challenges anyone can undertake, then it is worth the gamble.

Make no mistake, it *will* be a gamble. We none of us know what inner resources we have until we are put to the test and there will be many unforeseen setbacks along the way. You only have to read the newspapers to realize how many small businesses go under, particularly in an unfavourable economic climate.

But if you have the willpower – and a lot of luck – your business idea might just be the acorn that grows into an oak tree.

KEY POINTS

- Carry out an honest assessment of your personality to decide whether you have what it takes to become an entrepreneur.
- Are you a sticker or do you give up the challenge easily?
- Make a list of your strengths and weaknesses and get friends and relatives to do the same.
- Redundancy in itself is not a good reason to set up in business. It could, however, be the final spur.
- Be clear about what your aims are. Are you doing it purely for money or to seek independence, for example.
- Thousands of new businesses fail because their owners don't identify their business and personal goals. Consider drawing up a 'mission statement'.

- Pick the right moment to start your business. It requires one hundred per cent dedication. You cannot afford to be distracted by other issues.
- Be prepared to change certain aspects of your personality. You may need to become more aggressive than you are used to being.
- Be alert to the dangers of the one-dimensional entrepreneur. It takes more than a single talent to run a business.

CHAPTER 2

Selecting the Business To Be In

Deciding which product line or service to set up in is one of the most critical issues for the aspiring small business entrepreneur. There are a multitude of factors to take into account. Manufacturing versus services. Niche markets versus run-of-the-mill products and services. What about taking the franchising route? Or you could consider a buy-out or a buy-in. A lot of businesses are built around an invention.

The devil you know

The most obvious choice is to base your business on something you already know a lot about. If the expertise that has served you well as an employee can be turned into a business idea, the transition should be far less traumatic, provided you take account of the dangers of the one-dimensional entrepreneur referred to in the previous chapter.

If, for example, you have been working for a furniture-making firm and you are a skilled carpenter, setting up a small business in the same field should not be too difficult. It might be unwise to manufacture exactly the same kind of products. If the company you used to work for made you redundant because there was insufficient demand for its products, you would probably be tempting fate to set up in competition with it.

If an established company is having difficulty surviving in its chosen markt place, what chance is a fledgling new company which still has to go through a learning curve likely to have? It could, of course, be that the company that formerly employed you was not producing its products at a price the market was prepared to pay and that a small business with lower overheads would be able to produce similar goods more cheaply. But the chances are that if a company of long standing is struggling, you will be inviting disaster if you try to set up in a similar product line.

It would probably be better to consider other products which demand similar skills, but for which there is likely to be a more ready market. Carpentry is a skill that can be used for making a wide variety of products, from kitchen cabinets to grandfather clocks. The trick is to find a product that is in high demand. If you combine high skill with high demand you start off with a fighting chance, even if you are lacking the other talents necessary to run a successful business.

More of the same

If you decide to build your small business around a skill you are already familiar with, whether it is making something or offering a service, there is a strong possibility it will be in an area where you will have a large number of competitors. That will mean you will be up against companies that are already well along the learning curve and have mastered most of the tricks of the trade. You will be competing against people who know their business backwards.

There is a very simple way to find out how desirable your potential product or service idea is. In the case of a product, visit your high street shopping centre and look around the stores. If you find your planned product idea is in great abundance and selling at a price you are unlikely to be able to undercut, you should probably think again. In the case of a service, telephone a selection of likely users and find out if they are satisfied with the suppliers they already have to get some idea of the competition you are likely to encounter.

If you discover a good deal of dissatisfaction it may well be the case that you can provide a better service and that you will have no difficulty finding grateful customers. If, on the other hand, the firms or individuals you contact seem perfectly happy with their existing providers, you will probably want to opt for something different.

In the event that you decide to set up in a business that is commonplace, you will really need to bring something extra to bear. If, for example, you decide to make kitchen cabinets, you will need to include something in the design that makes yours stand out from all your many competitors. Or you will need to provide some special service, maybe connected with the method of installation, that sets you apart from the crowd.

NICHE MARKETS

Of course you are on much safer ground if you can serve a niche market, provided you have established you will be meeting a real need. You will have hardly any competitors – none if your service is unique. You will have a captive market once your customers come to rely on your goods or services – until of course others spot your success and try to climb on the same bandwagon. But at least you will have a head start, as opposed to going into a commonplace business where you have to make up lost ground on established firms.

A Westcountry firm called Equisports has carved out a useful niche market for itself by specializing in saddles for women, selling under the brand name 'Lady Rider Saddle'. The company decided to specialize after discovering that women have different pelvic widths from men. Explains Maurice Napper, a director of the company: 'Over the years it has been apparent to ladies that conventional saddles made for men left a lot to be desired in terms of comfort and contact. All men are basically the same pelvic width whether they are short, tall, fat or thin, but women's pelvic widths are different. The need for a new saddle shape to suit women riders was obvious. Now we are making saddles in four widths to fit women riders with different pelvic shapes.'

The niche market specialization has resulted in the company receiving enquiries from all over the world, including the United States, Canada, Switzerland and Sweden.

Building on experience

One of the best ways to identify a niche market is through personal experience. When Anna Achilleos' husband created an olive pâté to add variety to her vegetarian diet, friends and relations enjoyed the savoury taste too and Anna was inundated with requests for it. It soon became apparent that her husband had created something for which there was great demand and which could not be found in existing food shops. It became the basis of a highly successful company called Chalice Foods, which now exports savoury foods to Europe (see case study at the end of this chapter).

In an entirely different field, Dan Wagner was working for an advertising agency and discovered it was a laborious task carrying out exhaustive research for client accounts. He hit on the idea of an on-line computerized database to serve the advertising industry. After a bumpy start he eventually created a business that made him a multi-millionaire (see pages 108 and 183).

Eddie Bagley, a former British Aerospace quality technician, who lost his job as the result of the closure of BAe's commercial aircraft site at Hadfield, Herts, on Christmas Eve 1993, turned his hobby into a business by going into the production of concrete garden ornaments. His decision to specialize in Japanese style ornaments was influenced by his enthusiasm for koi carp. As he explained to Lewis Rushbrook, in an article for the Small Business Focus page of *The Sunday Times*: 'I've kept koi carp for six years and was always surprised at the poor quality of poolside ornaments for koi carp enthusiasts. I began making my own and, with the interest people showed, a full-time business seemed viable.'

Julie Wright and her father also hit on their business idea as a result of personal experience. Julie's father, an engineer by training, was dismayed at the number of used printer ribbons she was discarding in the normal course of her work. He invented a re-inking process which meant that the ribbons could be used over and over again. Not only did the idea save an enormous amount of money for their clients; it also helped reduce the mountains of ribbons that had to be destroyed. It was an idea that provided a very worthwhile service and at the same time appealed to the growing number of people showing concern for the environment. It was a niche market with more than one dividend.

A home made product

When my wife and daughter decided some years ago that they would like to set up a small business together, there was considerable debate about the niche market they would like to create. Eventually, they recalled that many Christmases ago we had bought our children some furry glove puppets but had searched in vain for a substantial puppet theatre to go with them.

In the end my wife and I had made our own theatre out of scraps of wood we found in the attic. Although it lacked the professional touch, we were pretty pleased with our creativity, which had cost us very little. It occurred to my wife and daughter when they decided to form their own business that if we had experienced difficulty finding a well-crafted puppet theatre there might be many other parents who had undergone the same experience.

Research at leading toy stores showed that years later this was still the case. There were no substantial puppet theatres to be found anywhere. The next question was: why not? This was a crucial question if they were going to invest money into a start-up company. Was there a lack of puppet theatres because there was no market for them or was it because the leading toy makers could not produce puppet theatres at an affordable price?

A survey of relatives, friends and local primary schools provided part of the answer. There was no question that people would like to buy their children a puppet theatre – the key issue was 'affordable price'. My wife and daughter decided that operating from home, using outworkers, their overheads could be kept low and that in this respect they had a distinct advantage over major toymakers which had all the normal heavy costs of a leading manufacturer.

What my wife and daughter had not foreseen was that there was a recession around the corner and that an upmarket product, as this was bound to be because of the handicraft involved, was not the best of ideas when everybody was intent on reducing their spending on everything but the essentials of life.

INVENTIONS

The best example of a niche business is one based on an invention. An invention by its very nature is providing a solution that nobody has ever come up with before. The inventor is bound to have the market all to himself, assuming he has patented his idea. But it is notoriously difficult to raise investment capital for business ideas based on an invention. Bank managers are particularly wary of them.

The problem is that it is almost impossible to demonstrate that an invention will sell well until you have made it in quantity and launched it on to the market. Bank managers are reluctant to lend money because inventions *per se* have no track record. You cannot present any reassuring business plan illustrating market potential and forecasting likely sales because there is nothing already on the market with which to compare the invention.

The Martek case study at the end of this chapter illustrates graphically how difficult it is to obtain the funding to turn even the brightest of inventions into a small business.

In many ways inventors are the last people to consider going into business for themselves. They are often so obsessed with the brilliance of their creation that they assume that once they have some financial backing the world will beat a path to their door. They are probably the worst example of the one-dimensional entrepreneur. They often overlook the fact that there is a lot more to running a business than launching an innovative product or service on to an unsuspecting public.

Probably inventors would be better sticking to what they are best at – coming up with bright ideas. The problem is that in order to get their bright ideas produced, inventors often have little choice but to start their own companies or enter into a joint venture agreement with a contractor which involves putting up their own capital.

Trying to get leading manufacturers to take up their inventions almost always proves to be a fruitless task. The problem is neatly summed up by Tony Randel, a small business counsellor at Enterprise Plymouth with special responsibility for innovation: 'Big companies don't like mad inventors knocking on their doors.'

The dilemma for big companies has always been that it is virtually impossible to distinguish between hair-brained ideas and a gold-plated winning formula without committing inordinate amounts of time and resources to evaluate them. They would prefer to rely on the less speculative option of developing in-house creativity.

For some years help for the beleaguered inventor was provided by a national network of innovation centres, funded by BP and jointly sponsored by Business in the Community (BiC). Assessment panels, made up of patenting and licensing agents and marketing and design consultants, sifted through inventors' ideas to identify those with commercial promise. Where appropriate the inventors were advised on how to set up a small business to exploit their brainchild.

The scheme was backed by the Prince of Wales, president of BiC and closely involved in an annual award for innovation screened by BBC TV's *Tomorrow's World*. BiC is the umbrella group of the UK's 300-plus local enterprise agencies on to which the innovation network had been grafted.

When BP eventually withdrew its financial support, the future of the scheme was in some doubt. However, the vacuum is steadily being filled by the Department of Trade and Industry (DTI) which is providing funding for the appointment of technology and innovation counsellors via its new Business Links network.

Randel at the Plymouth enterprise agency is convinced such schemes play an important role in getting inventions to the market place that otherwise would have languished for want of big company support. He reasons: 'When we vet the ideas and turn them into a marketable package we are able to achieve more success than an individual is likely to.'

Enterprise Plymouth has been turning the conventional approach to the problem on its head. It has introduced a programme for helping small businesses find new products to expand their portfolio by introducing them to inventors.

British Technology Group

For years struggling inventors have turned to the British Technology Group (BTG) to provide know-how on how to turn new technologies into commercial money-spinners. The company is not widely known, but most people will have used one of its products at some time.

BTG had its origins in the National Research Development Corporation, set up in 1948 by the Labour government as a way of encouraging British inventions to be commercialized in this country. Its creation was spurred by the experience with penicillin, discovered in Britain but developed by American companies.

In 1981, the corporation was merged with the National Enterprise Board to create BTG, and a decade later it was privatized in a management buy-out backed by twelve institutions, led by CINVen, with eleven universities as shareholders.

BTG takes inventions developed by academics or within companies and puts funds into developing them to the stage where they can be patented and licensed out. It then devotes its resources to defending the patents on the products and ensuring licensees pay the full royalties due.

SMART

The DTI runs an annual inventors' competition for individuals or firms with fewer than fifty employees. Known as the Small Firms Merit Award for Research and Technology (SMART) it offers grants of up to £45,000 to turn research projects into novel, soundly-based ideas with a good prospect of commercial success.

But many people feel that in the country that gave the world television, the jet engine and radar, the support for innovation in the UK is still woefully inadequate. The Japanese government, for example, has set up around 200 innovation centres where promising inventors can go and try out their ideas. By contrast, innovation centres in the UK receive very little public funding.

FRANCHISING

The franchising option, which involves building a business on someone else's tried and trusted idea, has steadily gained favour over the years. The concept has been around for some time and has proved to be a winning formula for many. The franchisee enjoys the challenge of running his or her own operation, just like any other entrepreneur, but operates under the protective umbrella of an organization with a proven concept. It could be said that franchising provides the best of all worlds – freedom of action with a degree of built-in security.

The turnover of the UK franchising industry grew by 10 per cent to £5 billion in 1993, according to a survey conducted on behalf of the British Franchise Association (BFA) and sponsored by NatWest. Peter Stern, head of NatWest's franchise section, noted that encouragingly, 87.5 per cent of UK franchisees reported that they were trading at a profit, compared with 77.5 per cent in 1992.

Brian Smart, the BFA's executive director, estimates that nearly 190,000 people are directly employed in franchising. In 1993 alone 20,000 jobs were created in the sector. The average turnover of the franchisees surveyed in 1993 ranged from a few thousand pounds to several million pounds, reflecting the diverse opportunities available throughout the sector.

A proven concept

The reason why so many first-time business people are opting for a franchise is that they are 'investing in a proven concept, because franchises are established businesses', according to Smart.

The range of franchises on offer has also broadened enormously. Prospective franchisees now have a choice that spans small jobbing firms in carpet cleaning and mobile car tuning at the bottom end of the scale to major retailers and fast food restaurants at the top end. There is hardly any sector of commerce or the service industry that is not now covered by franchising opportunities. There is even a private detective firm operating through franchisees.

A major advantage is that banks are more likely to provide loans for a franchised operation than for unproven new start-ups. The reason is obvious. Franchises are already up and running and in most cases well established in the market place. Most clearing banks now offer specially tailored franchise packages and will usually provide up to 70 per cent of the required finance.

The clearing banks monitor the progress of the main franchise firms and in order to qualify as a member of the BFA, a franchise company has to undergo stringent vetting, so anyone hoping to become a franchisee will be on pretty safe ground if he or she contacts the BFA first.

The cost of taking up a franchise varies enormously from around £10,000 for a small jobbing franchise up to around £350,000 for a major fast food franchise in London's Oxford Street, for example. In most cases the franchisee pays a once-only fee for the use of the company's name (around £3,000 for a small operation) but he or she is also purchasing a whole range of back-up facilities, which can include stock and shop fittings (in the case of a retail outlet), the benefits of national advertising, training and research and development.

The BFA warns that franchising is not normally a way to make a fortune. Although one major fast food chain can probably boast a number of millionaires among its franchisees, this is very rare. A franchisee can normally only expect to begin making a profit between eighteen months and four years after start-up, depending on the nature of the franchise. Cautions Brian Smart: 'It's hard work; you've got to be self-motivated; and it can mean working long hours. When franchisees do fail it is often because they have become disillusioned by not making enough money soon enough.'

There are other sacrifices necessary in order to buy the comparative security of a franchise that may not come easy to the person with a true entrepreneurial spirit. The franchisee will have to sign an agreement with the franchisor that will restrict the former to doing things according to established practice. It will, for example, almost certainly restrain the franchisee from introducing new product lines from other sources or changing the shop's decor to suit his or her own tastes. Franchisors will insist that all products and services are obtained through them. The main aim of a franchise is to achieve uniformity, so that customers are assured of receiving the same level and quality of service wherever they travel throughout the country.

The BFA advises potential franchisees to check out any legal agreement with a solicitor and to talk over the financial implications with an accountant. Adds Smart: 'They ought to visit the franchise company and its offices to see the whole set-up and get a feel for it. They should have no hesitation in asking to see the company's accounts. They should get a list of the company's existing franchisees and visit a number of them at random and ask how they are getting on. The aspiring franchisee should make the choice about which to contact, not the franchisor.'

The BFA

The BFA was formed in 1977 and maintained a UK code of ethics until 1989 when a European code was agreed between national franchise associations and the EC. The BFA now accredits UK franchisors against wide-ranging criteria, which include:

- *Viable*. A financial record showing a sound business
- *Franchisable*. A record of at least one successful franchised outlet and no significant record of failures
- *Ethical*. A franchise agreement and structure conforming to the European code of ethics
- *Disclosure*. Offer documents and brochures which reasonably represent the performance of the franchise system.

The BFA has some 120 franchisor members with more than 10,000 franchised outlets under its wing. It has accredited more than fifty professional advisers (lawyers, bankers, accountants and consultants) who provide valuable advice for would-be franchisees.

The Association publishes an information pack available at £18 and a franchisor manual at £31.50. It also sponsors two national franchise exhibitions – at London's Olympia in the spring and at Birmingham's NEC in the autumn. These provide a shop window for aspiring franchisees to select from the wide variety of options on offer.

The BFA receives around 20,000 enquiries a year from would-be franchisees. There are more people waiting to become franchisees than there are opportunities available so to win the franchisor's approval, the applicant needs to be convincing. There is little point, for example, someone with a shy and retiring nature applying for a franchise that requires a high level of selling power. But franchisors don't normally insist on any previous experience in a chosen field. In fact, they tend to prefer the applicant to be new to the field of operation. It means the franchisee will start with an open mind and is more likely to accept the franchisor's way of doing things.

TRADING OPTIONS

There are three main trading options when setting up in business:

- *Sole Trader*. There are no particular formalities for starting a business as a sole trader and terminating the business, should you need to, is comparatively straightforward. You will have control of the operation, to run and develop it as you wish, and any profit will be yours. But you will also have full responsibility for any losses or debts – a sole trader's liability is unlimited.

- *Partnership*. This is an effective and common form of trading. Although it is possible to start trading as a partnership without any formal agreement, a written contract is strongly recommended. This will provide a framework for the running of the partnership and will clarify what would happen should a major problem arise, such as the resignation or removal of a partner or, even worse, should the partners fall out with one another. While the introduction of a new partner may bring extra capital, should any losses or liabilities arise from the actions of your partners you will be liable because, like a sole trader, a partnership has unlimited liability.

● *Limited liability.* The great advantage of 'incorporation' is that, provided the shareholders and directors of a limited liability company do not cause it to trade fraudulently or wrongfully, their liability to creditors of the business will not extend beyond the amount of their share capital. Thus, if a business fails, a shareholder's personal assets would not be sequestrated to cover the company's debts, even if the company's assets are insufficient to meet the sums owed to creditors.

If you have to borrow money to start up the business, however, you will usually have to provide a guarantee to your bank, which may demand that this is backed by a charge on your personal property. In addition, trade creditors often seek personal guarantees, so the advantage of limited liability can be reduced. If, however, the nature of the business is extremely speculative and financially risky, or if the business's borrowing requirements are modest and the expected turnover substantial, a limited company is invariably the best form for trading.

There were numerous examples during the recession of business owners, protected by limited liability, walking away from their debts when their companies got into financial difficulties and perfectly legally setting up new companies, often in similar product lines or services. This practice naturally incenses creditors who feel aggrieved to find someone who owes them substantial amounts of money, trading under another name as though they were not responsible for their past actions. However, a lot of companies that do go on to trade successfully would probably never have been launched but for the protection of limited liability.

What are the other advantages of incorporation? If additional finance needs to be raised, this can be done by alloting shares to outside investors. Creditors may be more willing to give credit to a limited company than to a partnership or sole trader because its status can give an impression of greater stability and permanence.

Establishing the company

The quickest, and probably the least expensive, route to forming a limited liability company is to buy one 'off the shelf'. This option is suitable for most businesses, but the Memorandum and Articles of Association stating the company's objectives and constitution may need to be altered to suit the purposes of the new business. Although more expensive than a shelf company, a 'tailor made' company may be preferable and will take about two weeks to be incorporated.

If you do not choose the 'off the shelf' route you will need to have the Articles drawn up and documents prepared for Companies House to show the appointment of at least two officers and the location of the 'registered office'.

Most limited liability companies are required to have their accounts audited by an external firm of chartered accountants and filed at Companies House. However, in July 1994, new legislation came into effect as part of the government's campaign to reduce the red tape on small firms. Under the new law, companies with an annual turnover of less than £90,000 are completely exempt from statutory audit requirements. Companies with a turnover of less than £350,000 can replace the audit with a 'reporting accountant's examination', a less expensive and time-consuming procedure.

The small business lobby groups welcome this change as a step in the right direction, but they argue that it does not go far enough. They believe that the statutory audit places an undue burden on small firms and that it should be abolished for all companies with a turnover under £1 million.

All limited liability companies must prepare and file an annual return. Proper books of accounts must be maintained and decisions of directors should be made at board meetings and be properly minuted.

Considering the options and selecting the right structure at the outset is vital, if problems are to be avoided later on. It would be a sensible precaution to seek the assistance of professional advisers.

Picking a name

The name you pick for your company will help establish its identity and should give potential customers a good idea of the line you are trading in. It obviously makes sense to include something in the name that specifically describes your brand of product. But you can add to that a descriptive word which should set the tone of your company and indicate whether it is upmarket or is trying to appeal to the everyday do-it-yourselfer, for example.

My wife and daughter gave considerable thought to what their toy company should be called. In the end they chose 'Parthenon Toys' for a number of sound reasons. First, the price of the products were inevitably going to be high because the puppet theatres were going to be hand-crafted and the glove puppets individually designed. This meant that they would be upmarket and would appeal to customers who had higher than average disposable income. Parthenon is a classical name that gives the impression of quality and durability, a desirable signal when charging premium prices.

Second, the Greeks were said to have invented the theatre and the name Parthenon linked the new firm's products to an ancient tradition. As the aim was to be part of a reported trend back to traditional toys, and away from the cheap, plastic materials that have pervaded the market in recent years, it was also important to pick a name that conveyed long links with the past.

Third, the word *Parthenon* provided excellent alliteration when combined with 'puppet theatre'.

What the budding entrepreneurs overlooked, however, was the problem so many people would have with spelling the word Parthenon. At the first international toy fair they attended at Earls Court in London, they arrived to find the name mis-spelled above the provided exhibition stand. Apparently, the famous Greek building is not as well known as they had imagined. But they have never regretted the choice of name, which certainly distinguished their company from others in the field.

An intriguing discovery has been made by Prufrock (alias Richard Woods) of the *Sunday Times*. The more unusual the company name, the more it is likely to go out of business. Woods quotes some bizarre examples to support his first law of company names: 'Another firm bravely called itself *It's Daylight Robbery Ltd* – unfortunately the getaway car must have stalled because it, too, is now in liquidation. The name *No Trading Ltd* proved only too prophetic, and a firm called *Gone Fishing Ltd* went on permanent vacation in 1992. *It's a Dog's Life Ltd* rolled over dead in 1993 and *The Very Interesting Company* is now only of interest because it, too, has been dissolved.' To rest his case, Woods even found a firm called *The Funny Name Company Ltd*, which is no longer a laughing matter.

On a more serious note, there are a number of rules and regulations attached to company names. Some good advice in this area is provided by *The Business Start-Up Guide*, published by National Westminster Bank:

Permissible Business Names
If you are going to trade on your own or as a partner, read
Business Names – Guidance Notes before you decide on a name.
You can get this from the Companies Registration Office. It tells
you how you can name a business, and what you are not allowed
to use without permission or proper entitlement, such as the words
'Royal', 'Authority', and 'International'. It also explains the
regulations you must meet if you are going to trade under a name
which is not your own.

You must display certain information about your business name
in a prominent place, where you work (even if you are working
from a shed in your garden). This information must also be on all
business letterheads, invoices, receipts and so on. It is up to you
what style you use, but it must include your business name, your
own name and those of any co-directors or proprietors and your
permanent business address. You can get examples from the DTI,
Guidance Notes Section, Companies Registration Office.

Company Names

If you decide to form a limited company you need to know about the
rules and regulations explained in the booklet *Company Names –
Guidance Notes*. You can also get this from the Companies
Registration Office. Restrictions on names and the rules on what
information you must give are the same as those for individuals and
partnerships going into business. But you must also make sure that
there will be no objection to the name that you choose. This could
happen if the name you want is the same as or similar to a name
already being used. This is a fairly important point, because if you are
told to change your name, it could cost your business a lot – and not
only in money.

Patents, copyrights and trademarks

Copyright and patent laws protect your ideas from being exploited
by a rival business. They also prevent someone using your
'intellectual property' without your permission.

If you have invented a real money-spinner which could be
developed into a product, you might want to apply for a patent. If
you do, you will find it a very complicated procedure. It is strongly
advised you talk to a patent agent. The Chartered Institute of Patent
Agents or the Patent Office will be able to help you. Even if you have a
patent, there could be a long and expensive battle trying to stop other
people using it.

Another legal protection is 'copyright', which is the creator's or
legal owner's rights in creative works like paintings, writings,
photographs, advertising artworks, videotapes and TV commercials,
even when these are made for a client. Remember this if you are using
artwork or creative work of some sort. Unlike patent protection,
copyright happens automatically.

When you have decided on a name for your new firm or product or
you have designed a logo, you can apply for the trademark to be
registered. This will give you greater legal protection. The Institute of
Trade Mark Agents and Trademarks Registry can help you.

Trading Laws

The law is there to protect the buyer and the seller but who it protects
the most depends on the type of business transaction. It is worth

checking with your solicitor to find out what impact the trading laws could have on your business.

Whatever your business, there are three trading standards which are most bound to affect you:

- If goods are faulty, customers can have a full refund or part of a refund. Or you can agree to repair or replace the goods. A notice which says 'No Refunds' is not legal. In some cases displaying such a notice can be a criminal offence.

- Goods must always live up to the claims you make for them. Fashion boots described as waterproof must keep out rain and protect people's feet against puddles. If you label goods falsely, you could be prosecuted and buyers would be entitled to their money back.

- Goods must meet certain safety standards. If a child is injured or poisoned by a toy, or there is an accident with a faulty kettle, you could be prosecuted and a large claim could be made against you for damages. Although these safety standards are not part of the law, if you are in the kind of business where this could happen, it would be wise to get insurance cover.

KEY POINTS

- Your chances of success are greatly increased if you base your business on something with which you are already familiar.
- But you need to bring something extra to the party in order to compete with established companies in the same field.
- Research the market place to find out how prevalent your product or service idea is and whether you can compete on price.
- If you go for a niche market be sure you will be meeting a real need.
- An ideal way to identify a niche market is through personal experience. If you or your friends have difficulty finding a product or service to meet your needs the chances are thousands of others will be facing the same problem.

- Inventions can create niche markets, but it is difficult to raise capital for products that have no track record.
- Inventors can be the worst example of a one-dimensional entrepreneur.
- Seek the advice of enterprise agencies and other experts on whether your product or service idea has commercial potential.
- Consider the franchising route. There is security from going into business with a proven idea.
- Consider the three main trading options of sole trader, partnerships and limited liability.
- Pick a name for your company that reflects the product line or service and helps to promote its assets.

CASE STUDY
Chalice Foods

Chalice Foods is a small company, now based near Welling-borough, Northants, that manufactures olive pâté spreads and dressings for health food and grocery shops and leading stores such as Waitrose, Selfridges and Harrods. It was founded by Anna Achilleos and her husband, Achilles, a Greek chef, who used to work at the Food For Thought, a well-known London vegetarian restaurant. Anna, the extrovert, is the driving force behind the company, while her husband works quietly behind the scenes dreaming up recipes and filling endless jars with his special ingredients. But they both, insists Anna, who is English and has an uncanny resemblance to Anita Roddick, have the same attitude to enterprise: 'We want to do something that actually improves the quality of life for people. We want to be in a business that helps to make the world a better place. It's a very strong ethos in us.'

Such a strict company ethos made her task of starting a company without any previous experience all the more difficult. For example, when it was mentioned in a national newspaper article that she needed £40,000 to buy equipment and rent factory space to get her company on a solid footing, Anna was besieged by potential investors. Instead of gratefully taking the money, she vetted every single one of them during lengthy interviews. Only one passed her acid ethical test. Reasons Anna: 'You've got to have integrity all the way through a company; you can't just have it part of the time, because if you haven't got integrity in one area, it will seep through.'

It hasn't been easy for Anna to carve a niche for her company in the commercial world. She admits that, like most would-be entrepreneurs, she was very ill-equipped for the practical side of running a business. But her instincts and intuition seem to have served her well. She observes: 'Mainly it's creative people who start businesses. They're not financial people; they're creative people and they happen to end up putting that creativity into a business for one reason or another. I have never actually met a successful business person who started out to do what they're doing. It always happens by accident and it did with us too.'

Anna's happy accident was that she is allergic to dairy products. Her husband decided to create an olive pâté for her to provide a variation to her vegetarian diet. It was so delicious that all the couple's friends kept asking where they could obtain it and it proved so popular that Anna became increasingly convinced that it could be the basis of a small business. Before she knew it, she was delivering her special brand of pâté regularly to around twenty health food shops.

All this only added to her husband's problems. He was making the olive pâté in his spare time at the Food For Thought restaurant; the more jars Anna sold the more he needed to produce. That was not the worst of it. The Kamata olives they were using were particularly difficult to de-stone. No machinery existed tht could do the job properly. In the end, Achilles adapted a piece of standard equipment to do the task. His invention was so novel that it later appeared on BBC TV's *Tomorrow's World*.

After that, Anna decided to put the whole operation on a more professional footing and hired a leading PR company – at a bargain price – to promote her products. It was also clear that her company needed a financial adviser to help raise funds to buy equipment and rent a small factory. Chalice Foods had already approached a management accountant a year previously, but Anna's disenchantment with the help he was supposed to be providing grew by the day. 'The only thing he ever did for us was to make an absolute mess of our Inland Revenue returns. He held up the progress of the company because if we had known that he wasn't going to do anything, we would have done it ourselves, but he had been recommended to us and he kept saying we shouldn't worry.'

The experience left Anna with a very jaundiced view of

accountants. The relationship wasn't entirely abortive, however. Concedes Anna: 'He did get us a £10,000 overdraft facility at one point with a bank manager he happened to know. Maybe I could have got that myself, but at the time I didn't have the confidence.'

David Setchell, an independent certified accountant, who subsequently became auditor to Chalice Foods, finds it difficult to understand why Anna's experience with accountants has been so unfortunate: 'My feeling is that she was very naïve in that she thought that by handing over a heap of papers to somebody, that would be that. She probably didn't realize that the people to whom she was handing over all the documents would not know her business like she knows it.

'Everything just needed to be tightened up, but it's difficult to keep the books, keep the customers happy, go out and sell and look after production at the same time. There aren't enough hours in the day. On the other hand, you can't really afford to employ somebody to do any of those things for you. People just don't realize how complicated it is, starting up a business.'

Growing demand

Anna may have lacked financial acumen, but her instinct that the olive pâté had good market potential was proving to be sound. As the business grew, so did the demands on Chalice Foods' financial resources, but Anna's antipathy towards financial advisers showed no signs of abating. She became very dissatisfied with the NatWest bank manager who had given her the overdraft facility: 'He never listened to me. When I went in to see him he did the talking and I did the listening. I thought that was a complete waste of time.'

The solution was to switch branches, but it took longer for Anna to dissociate herself from her original accountant: 'All he did was hamper our business. At one point he introduced me to my auditor. I didn't even know I had a separate auditor. This went on for several years and it cost me a lot of money. It's an important lesson not to take on an accountant until you really know who he is and what he is going to do for you.'

It soon became apparent that the £10,000 overdraft facility was totally inadequate. Anna estimated that Chalice Foods needed a capital infusion of around £40,000. An article in the *Financial Times* at the end of 1989 about her fledgling company seemed to be the answer to her prayers. She was contacted by a lot of people offering to invest in Chalice Foods, some even wanting to buy the company.

Only one of the enquiries came from the kind of investor who would seem to benefit Chalice Foods. The understanding was that he would invest £40,000 for a 25 per cent stake in the company. At the last moment, though, he changed tack and said he would be prepared to put £10,000 into the company in return for a 33 per cent stake and that the rest of the money would have to be obtained from a bank under the government's Loan Guarantee Scheme (see page 87).

Even though they had signed an agreement on a factory, Anna and her husband were not prepared to give up such a hefty stake in their company for such a small investment. Recalls Anna: 'We were determined this guy was not going to get us into a corner. Somehow we would get the money from the right person. So I just started talking to everybody I knew and ringing people up.'

The communication blitz did the trick. An investment group she contacted put her in touch with Lucius Cary who runs Seed Capital, a venture capital company specifically set up to invest in small firms. After a three hour discussion with Cary, who mainly invests in engineering firms, a cheque for £40,000 arrived in the post within ten days in return for 25 per cent of Chalice Foods' equity. Anna had got the deal she wanted.

Mediterranean diet

Chalice Foods subsequently raised a further £25,000 under the government's Loan Guarantee Scheme and obtained a £12,000 business development loan from NatWest. In 1992 Chalice Foods received an injection of £100,000 from private investors to help fund ambitious expansion plans. To offset the effects of the recession, Anna and her husband explored the possibility of expanding the range of their savoury products and of moving into export markets. Recalls Anna: 'One of the areas we discovered was the Mediterranean diet. There was a big interest in the UK following a TV programme about how much better it is than other diets.'

This persuaded Anna to launch a broader range of olive products, including fast-selling Mediterranean dressings in Italian-style bottles and, ironically, Chalice Foods has since found a ready market for its delicacies in Mediterranean countries.

Since the injection of £100,000 from private investors in 1992, Chalice has come a long way. It is now a recognized brand name found in most major supermarkets.

With the advent of the recession, Anna and her husband adopted a two-prong business programme: to build the Chalice brand in the UK and to develop the export and food service sides of the business. This strategy enabled Chalice to achieve a turnover of £1 million in 1994.

In the UK the development of a clear identity has played an important role in securing recognition of the brand. Anna employed designer Lynn Oxford specifically for this project. The Chalice name and symbol has been designed to reflect the Mediterranean flavour of the range. As a result, Chalice now boasts a total of eighteen products and there are new product introductions in the pipeline.

In order to diversify the business and spread the risk, Anna has concentrated the business in two areas: retail and food service.

A communications blitz has achieved major multiple listings in the retail sector and excellent leads in the food service business, which were expected to come to fruition in early 1995.

The development of the export market has also been a great

success with the extraordinary achievement of exporting Mediterranean foods to Mediterranean countries. Anna's efforts here have not gone unrecognized. In 1993 she won awards for export development from The London Enterprise Agency and the Inner London North Training and Enterprise Council.

Other company innovations include developing Chalice's relationship with its customers by the formation of a special consumer club – Chalice Gourmet Club. Through this, Anna and her husband are able to gauge customer response to new products, as well as assess customers' shopping habits.

In June 1994, Napier Brown Holdings Ltd., a major food company, bought a substantial share in Chalice. This new partnership has enabled Chalice to expand. The company now employs fifteen staff. In July 1994, Chalice relocated from London to Irthlington, where it established its head office and a 22,000 sq. ft. factory. Other group benefits include the use of inter-company resources, such as marketing support and recruitment advice.

Anna has great ambitions for the future. She plans to see Chalice receive recognition as the leading brand name for gourmet Mediterranean food with a turnover of around ten million pounds.

CASE STUDY
Martek

Some years ago, Tom Ketteringham was carrying out some home repairs when his drill bit broke. It set him thinking that there must be thousands of people who, faced with the same situation, throw the bit away since re-sharpening drill bits was then a laborious process, virtually impossible for the amateur handyman.

Ketteringham, an engineer by training and a compulsive inventor, concentrated his mind on an idea that would make it possible to re-use blunted drill bits with minimum effort.

What Ketteringham set out to invent was a drill bit sharpener that operated like a pencil sharpener. He now runs a successful £1 million turnover company in Cornwall called Martek, which churns out tens of thousands of such sharpeners a year, together with a range of other products based on similar principles.

It took Ketteringham two and a half years to arrive at a prototype he was satisfied with, as it involved overcoming complex engineering problems to fulfil the simplicity-of-use goal he aimed for. He decided to make the device from plastic to keep the costs down, but even so he was told that it would cost around £160,000 just to make the tooling to produce the prototype.

It meant starting again from scratch. Ketteringham was told that if he made the sharpener in two halves it would cost a lot less to produce, and solving that problem led to a more efficient sharpener. 'When I realized I could make the sharpener in two halves, I saw that I could also alter the angles. So one thing developed from another. By trying to get the product down to a sensible cost, I was able to improve it.'

When the sharpener was entered in inventors' competitions, the results were beyond Ketteringham's wildest dreams. It won the gold medal at an international contest in Geneva and the top award at a similar competition in Paris; it took the Blue Riband award for bright ideas at the 1986 Ideal Home Exhibition in the UK. All the signs were that his idea had a bright future.

But the banks and financial institutions were far from convinced. When Ketteringham needed £1,500 to patent his invention, still in a very crude form, a friendly bank manager offered to lend him the money. But when he and two associates decided to form a company to produce the drill sharpener and needed around £45,000 for tooling-up costs, the banks and venture capitalists didn't want to know. The would-be entrepreneurs came up against the classic paradox, that financiers are reluctant to invest in a product that has no proven track record.

The three colleagues first approached a local bank seeking capital under the government's Loan Guarantee Scheme, but their request was turned down on the grounds that the project was too risky. Undeterred, the aspiring entrepeneurs approached City investors. By now, they had attracted the attention of several major power tool manufacturers which were keen to buy the rights to the invention, but the three were determined not to sell out.

They were, however, prepared to give up a 30 per cent stake in return for equity capital, but they came up against another immutable fact of life. Venture capitalists are not interested in injecting small amounts of capital into companies. Reflects Ketteringham: 'If we had wanted £250,000 we could probably have got it. At that time, quarter of a million pounds was easier to get than £50,000.'

Near desperation, the Martek entrepreneurs finally struck lucky after a short article appeared in a local newspaper. Within weeks they had received several offers from small private investors and had raised £34,000 in return for non-voting shares. It was enough to launch the company.

After working out of a garage for a while, the directors moved to a small industrial unit in Cornwall which they quickly outgrew. Martek then moved to a 1,600 sq. ft. factory near Redruth, from which it still operates today.

Ketteringham and his colleagues learned some important

lessons with their first marketing efforts. They soon realized it was the end user they had to convince rather than the corporate buyers. They rapidly concluded that Martek should aim to create a demand among the buying public, so the hardware stores would be compelled to stock their products. They concentrated their marketing efforts on trade shows such as the Ideal Home Exhibition.

The same principle held good with overseas markets. Martek has never had to advertise its products. By attending international trade fairs, it has managed to attract all the consumer interest it needs – and the retail interest has followed. One of the companies that came knocking on Martek's door was the Japanese group Marubeni, best known for its Komatsu heavy equipment subsidiary. Observes Ketteringham: 'The big tool distributors of this world didn't want to sell our product, so we had to prove to them there is a market.'

Delayed payment

Martek's exporting success led to another problem – ensuring that it had enough cash to cover production costs. Some countries tend to delay payment for several months and this can put a severe strain on small and medium-sized companies. At one time the company was owed a total of £70,000 by customers in the US, Australia and Spain who were overdue with their payments.

When Martek needed additional finance to fund expansion, it had to take a new tack. This eventually led it to the engineering company in Switzerland which manufactures all the grinding stones used in Martek's products. The relationship was formed when Martek could not persuade any UK company to supply grinding stones to the required specifications. The Swiss firm had a reputation for manufacturing specialized grinding stones for blue-chip engineering groups and it agreed to supply Martek, but the costs were high.

As Martek grew and it became obvious that it was a company

of some substance, a number of UK engineering firms came out of the woodwork and offered to undercut the Swiss group. Martek then informed its Swiss suppliers that it could obtain the grinding stones more cheaply in the UK and offered it the option of lowering its prices. Martek threatened that if the option was not taken up it would be forced to switch suppliers. But the Swiss company held its ground, arguing that it could only lower prices by reducing standards, which it was not prepared to do. It had a reputation to maintain.

The Swiss suppliers, however, offered another option. They would buy a one-third share in Martek in return for an undertaking that the Cornwall company would buy bearings exclusively from them. This was an offer that Martek could hardly refuse, given its need for more working capital. One director had decided to leave and was prepared to sell his one-third share. The Swiss company's buy-in provided Martek with the capital to underwrite its expansion plans. Everyone seemed to win.

An event then occurred that could not have been foreseen. A second director left the company and, without telling Ketteringham, sold his one-third stake to the Swiss group, leaving Ketteringham a minority shareholder in the company he had founded, with control in the hands of an overseas parent.

To complete the story, the Swiss group later approached Ketteringham to acquire his stake in the company. It offered to take over all outstanding debts and bank overdrafts if he was prepared to convert his stake in Martek into non-voting shares. The offer meant that the founder would be free of all the financial liabilities involved in running the company and could concentrate on what he enjoys most – inventing new product ideas. The offer was too enticing to refuse.

Ketteringham retains the patent rights, which he swears he will never part with, although he is certain the Swiss group would dearly love to buy them.

At first sight it might seem a sad end to the story. But

Ketteringham displays no signs of resentment; rather, he considers himself very fortunate. He is still first and foremost an inventor at heart, and he views the situation philosophically: 'I have probably only a few years before retirement. That's the wrong time to have the hassle of owning a business. If I owned the company what would I do with it when I retire? I've got two daughters who are not interested. That means I'd have had to sell it anyway.

'I'm lucky. I'm still chairman of the company and I'm doing something I've always wanted. The Swiss look after the pennies which makes things a lot happier for me. When times are tight I no longer wake up in the middle of the night wondering whether I shall be in the same bed tomorrow night with a roof over me.'

CHAPTER 3

Buy-Outs and Buy-Ins

BUY-OUTS

One of the most popular routes to self-employment is via a management buy-out (MBO), where managers raise the capital to purchase a business or division from their company, which they then run independently. It has several distinct advantages. The business, which is already a going concern, stays in the hands of the managers who are accustomed to running it. They will continue to operate a company with which they are already familiar and comfortable rather than launching an unknown quantity. The main difference is that they will be able to do it with a greater degree of independence.

The parent group, for its part, is only too happy to see the division it is anxious to shed – often for operational reasons – handed over to former employees. It eases the conscience and avoids the trauma of announcing redundancies.

The buy-out boom of the past decade or more has been fuelled by the venture capitalists who have been drawn like moths to a candle at the prospect of investing in a low-risk sector of the business market. The big attraction, observes one venture capitalist, is that 'you're getting more experienced management and better quality management prepared to take risks, which wasn't the case a few years ago. There's an awareness now that instead of working for a large industrial company for the rest of one's life and being concerned about pension rights, managers can personally earn a lot of money in a very short period of time by participating in a buy-out.'

Management buy-outs look like being one of the favourite routes to self-employment for some time to come. In many cases the parent group does not decide to dispose of a division because it is inherently unsuccessful. It may simply be the result of a corporate decision to rationalize or to hive off businesses which no longer fit the core business strategy. Set loose to be run as a separate entity, however, the division may well prosper without the constraints, and possibly heavy overheads, imposed on it by the former parent group. From the motivational point of view, the former managers, now turned entrepreneurs, are more likely to put extra effort into a venture that has their own capital riding on it.

Fast-track to wealth

As David Clutterbuck and Marion Devine point out in their book, *Management Buyouts* (Hutchinson), management buy-outs provide an opportunity for managers to get rich quick. They quote the examples of the managers and employees of National Freight who bought their company for £53.5 million in 1982 and saw the value of their investment rise 2,700 per cent in four years. Similarly, managers at Stone International, saw an exceptional return on the £250,000 they put up to buy their energy and electrical equipment group from the receiver in 1982. When the company was floated two years later their 25 per cent shareholding became worth £7.5 million.

Clutterbuck and Devine estimate that there are hundreds of buy-out millionaires in Britain. Few of these managers, suggest the authors, would have taken the risk of setting up their own business, even if they had had the capital to do so. Building on a business they know, and a team they are familiar with, is a much safer way of creating personal wealth. Even so, the authors doubt if money is the prime motivator for those participating in management buy-outs: 'Equally, if not more, important is the challenge of really taking charge. Often the managers will have been frustrated by the restriction of being within a large group. They talk of being prevented from making investment decisions they considered essential, of the burdens of a huge central bureaucracy and of being tied by conflicts of interest with other parts of the company.'

BUY-INS

Despite a chequered history, the management buy-in (MBI) has made something of a comeback in the past few years. MBIs have the same ingredients as the better-known MBOs. They involve the combined forces of the venture capitalist (or a group of investors), which provides the bulk of the finance, and a management team that takes an equity stake and, frequently, options to reward performance. But whereas the managers of a buy-out are formed from the existing management team, in a buy-in they are drafted in from outside.

According to one estimate, MBIs represented 17 per cent of all private company acquisitions in the water-shed year of 1991. That signalled a major resurgence of interest in a technique that had fast been losing favour.

In the second half of the 1980s, as the enterprise culture gathered pace, an increasing number of company managers became enthused by the idea of owning their own business. They were spurred on by the success of MBOs in which teams of intrepid managers transformed small investments into millions of pounds. But many ambitious managers were thwarted – the companies or divisions they worked for were not up for sale.

Kevin Reynolds, a director of County NatWest Ventures Ltd., observes: 'It was this combination of frustrated managers eager to do an MBO and a venture capital industry with funds to invest that gave birth to the MBI.'

But initial enthusiasm gave way to dismay as MBIs suffered a far higher failure rate than MBOs. Says Reynolds: 'Many managers have had their dreams shattered, as they not only failed to make millions, but actually lost their original investment.'

Reynolds attributes the disappointing past performance of MBIs to two main factors. First, venture capitalists tended to assume that an MBI involves the same risks as an MBO. However, the great advantage of an MBO is that the members of the management team have usually been operating together for some considerable time and know the company well. With an MBI, the target company tends to be purchased 'as seen', substantially increasing the risks.

Second, most MBI companies were purchased at the height of the 1980s boom. Premium prices were funded with high levels of debt that became difficult to support when the recession took hold and interest rates soared.

Three types of company particularly lend themselves to buy-ins:

- Family businesses where there is no obvious successor to the chief executive
- Companies where the business has outgrown the founder
- Ailing companies that need increased resources and management change.

Family-owned

The majority of the buy-in deals backed by 3i, the venture capitalists, involve family-owned businesses. A good example is the £2.2 million buy-in in 1992 of Innisfail laundry. The MBI was led by Keith Ellarby, a former group finance director of Spring Grove Services Ltd., a leading garment rental firm.

Innisfail laundry was founded over ninety years ago and had

been in the ownership of the same family since 1943. With the imminent retirement of managing director Cecil Jeffs, the family was keen to find an individual who would buy the business as a going concern, preserve its independence and retain its eighty-six employees.

Ellarby had been one of the casualties of a management shake-out at Spring Grove and had decided that rather than seek another financial director post he would sooner start his own business. That took him to 3i, which helped him search for an appropriate buy-in. Recalls Ellarby: 'I was looking for something that was traditional with a good family background, not something that had been put together simply to be sold.'

Another advantage is that the owners of family businesses will often sell at a reduced price to a buy-in team rather than strike a better deal with an established group that could end up shutting down the factory. The reason is quite simple. The former owners often retire in the area and are anxious to avoid facing the wrath of the local community if such an eventuality were to occur.

The buy-in in 1992 of Granelli McDermott, a Cheadle-based ice-cream manufacturer, provided the ideal solution to a succession problem at this third-generation family business. It was founded more than a hundred years ago by Louis Granelli, who introduced the delights of traditional Italian ice cream to the Manchester area. The family owner wanted to retire but there was no natural successor.

The Granelli buy-in team had a surfeit of experience in the food industry. Chris Storrar, who led them was an ex-Mars senior manager who was instrumental in setting up Appleford, the Lyons-Tetley owned manufacturer that gave the world *Cluster* cereal bars. He was backed up by Keith Jamieson, a former Lyons-Tetley managing director as chairman.

Hiving off non-core activities

The recession threw up new opportunities for MBIs. It put large companies under pressure to raise cash and reduce borrowings. One way of doing that was to hive off non-core activities and loss-making divisions, providing a fertile buy-in source.

Mike Emery of Hartcliffe Ltd. had previously run his own small design company and had headed up a diversification department for a leading packaging group. He seized the opportunity to lead a buy-in when he heard that the Gateway supermarket chain wanted to divest itself of its in-house printing operation. His previous experience had given him 'a taste for acquisitions and exploring opportunities'.

This buy-in appealed to him because it 'primarily revolved around people and being part of a team that is able to develop a concept quickly in the market place, plus the chance to apply new skills and techniques to the printing industry, which tends to be pretty sales and production led'.

Alan Lewis, a regional director of County NatWest Ventures, believes the recession has been 'a good time for buy-ins because companies are available at more realistic prices and there are some quite talented managers loose in the market'. He points out, however, that venture capitalists have to be vigilant during a recession; some interested managers are totally unsuitable. 'Some of those available in the market might be tempted to try some sort of buy-in when actually they should be looking for a job. Some people do it, not necessarily because they are desperate, but because it's something on a list of various options they have available to them, whereas actually they haven't really got an aptitude for it.'

Guildford Man

But whatever the climate for buy-ins, venture capitalists realize that successful transactions call for managers with special qualities. One venture capitalist describes the ideal buy-in manager as 'Guildford Man'. He – few women are involved – is aged around forty and will have built up a strong skills base during his thirties. He will have acquired good general management experience as head of a major subsidiary or a group of subsidiaries, but is getting impatient about his move up to the main board.

Research by 3i shows that the next generation of buy-in managers will come from the ranks of experienced managing directors who are seeking greater job satisfaction and who are prepared to invest around £100,000.

When asked what motivated them to undertake an MBI, 37 per cent said job satisfaction and 26 per cent said independence. Only 24 per cent mentioned wealth. Keith Ellarby supports this finding. He insists that financial gain was not his main motivator. 'I could have gone off and got myself a nice, quiet, pleasant financial director's job and continued to have a reasonable – if not very good – standard of living.'

He first got a taste for running his own show at Spring Grove where he enjoyed a high level of autonomy. 'Once you get that flavour, you get used to it and you enjoy it. The major factor as far as I'm concerned is the freedom to run my own business – to make my own decisions and stand or fall by them.'

Mike Emery of Hartcliffe, however, would argue that the prospect of good financial returns has to be part of the motivation: 'Anyone who says they aren't doing it for the money is a liar because you're risking a fair amount of your own capital. But my experience of life is that if you are successful at what you're doing, the monetary and other rewards will come automatically.'

Skeleton in the cupboard

The most serious problems faced by buy-in managers surveyed by the Centre for Management Buy-out Research at Nottingham University included: 'Skeleton in the cupboard type problems ranging from misleading or inaccurate accounting information and changes in the operating and business environment since the last audited accounts, to the condition of stock, plant and equipment.'

One consolation seems to be that few buy-in managers meet with any resistance from incumbent personnel. Says the report from the Nottingham Centre: 'Evidence indicates that in many cases the arrival of new management, which is focused on solving problems and returning the target company to health, ends a period of uncertainty and is generally welcomed by the majority of employees.'

Funding

There is no shortage of available funding for MBOs and MBIs. Nevertheless, venture capital fund managers, wary of the business failures of the late 1980s and early 1990s, are cautious about where they invest their money and need to be convinced of the applicants' ability to meet essential criteria.

In an article in the June 1994 issue of *CBI News*, Stephen Curran, chief executive of Candover Investments, noted that his company usually looks at four key elements when assessing an MBO or MBI. First is the quality of management: 'The ability to write a succinct, yet comprehensive, business plan is a good guide. Usually, if management is unable to produce such a plan, they lack the necessary characteristics we seek. We also require management to make what is for them a significant equity investment.' Second, Candover looks for a stable market place, where there is a realistic prospect of growth in profits. Third, it looks for a reasonable price. And fourth, it looks for 'the ability of the company concerned to generate cash to service and pay down the relatively modest level of debt which we introduce into our financial structure. The ability to generate cash is a function of a number of different variables, including the ability to shrink working capital, the level of capital expenditure required and the existence or otherwise of tax losses. Generally, we do not rely on asset disposals to reduce acquisition debt.'

BIMBOs AND VIMBOs

Because of the high risks attached to MBIs, combined management buy-outs and buy-ins – popularly known as 'BIMBOs' – are increasingly favoured. The theory is that they blend the best of both worlds. There is an infusion of blood from outside the company that combines with existing senior managers who know the ropes and can quickly expose any skeletons in the corporate cupboard.

Geoff Westmore, a corporate finance partner at Coopers & Lybrand, the leading consultancy group, told the June 1994 issue of *CBI News*: 'A BIMBO is the ideal transaction where the current under-performance of the business can, in large part, be attributed to a lack of strategic direction. The buy-in candidate provides the strategic direction and vision to take the business forward while retaining the skills of the existing management team.'

Another step beyond the traditional buy-out or buy-in is the VIMBO, or vendor initiated management buy-out, a trend that is expected to strengthen in future.

Whereas buy-outs have traditionally been put together by venture capitalists working closely with management teams first and corporate sellers second, the growth of the VIMBO will see venture capitalists spending as much time wooing potential vendors as they do management teams.

This process should be given added impetus both by predictions of venture capitalists having fat wallets and by scarce opportunities for investment in MBOs.

KEY POINTS

- Management buy-outs have become a favoured route to self-employment.

- Buy-outs reduce the risk of failure because they are run by a team of managers who are used to working together and who are familiar with the business.
- Venture capitalists are attracted to management buy-outs because it means investing in a management team with a proven track record.
- Buy-outs can provide an opportunity for managers to get rich quick.
- Despite a chequered history, management buy-ins seem to be back in fashion.
- Management buy-ins involve the combined forces of a venture capitalist and an outside management team that takes an equity stake.
- The ideal buy-in manager is aged around forty and will have built up a strong skills base during his thirties.
- A Bimbo combines the advantages of both a management buy-out and a buy-in.

CHAPTER 4

Support for Small Firms

Going into business for yourself is undoubtedly a major challenge, but there is no shortage of small business support agencies in the UK to help you on your way. Some of them are sponsored by central government, but increasingly they are regional initiatives combining the resources of local government and the private sector. There are, for example, some 300 local enterprise agencies spread throughout the country offering free advice to small businesses. They normally have access to the kind of expertise that small firms lack. Among a host of other organizations offering advice and support is the Rural Development Commission (RDC), which helps to set up companies in rural areas.

Few of these support agencies offer substantial financial assistance, although most of them give advice on where to go to get it. Some will even accompany the inexperienced small business entrepreneur on the first visit to the bank manager. There is, however, a considerable amount of grant money available from the Department of Trade & Industry and via special European funds, but this is largely contingent on setting up in job-starved regions of the country.

A view has prevailed for some years that the proliferation of so many aid organizations results in a duplication of effort and confusion among those who could best benefit from the services. It was partly in response to this concern that, in 1994, the government started establishing a network of one-stop shops, known as Business Links, in key regions of the country. Some 200 Business Links are expected to be in place by the end of 1995. Wales and Scotland have long enjoyed the advantage of such one-stop shops, having their own development agencies which combine all the services small firms might need.

Business Link is a partnership between local authorities, enterprise agencies, the Rural Development Commission, CBI, the Institute of Directors, regional tourist boards, local colleges and universities and a host of other representative bodies, including chambers of commerce and the Federation of Small Businesses. With such an extensive pool of expertise accessible through one contact point, small businesses should at last be in no doubt about exactly where to go to satisfy their every need.

When the network is fully operational, small business owners should be able to access a wide range of business support services covering everything from export to employment, legislation and raising capital, to marketing techniques. Business Links can also refer clients to training courses, in-depth consultancy services, lawyers and accountants. While open to any business, the main focus is to guide firms with potential for growth.

Personal business advisers, some of them on secondment to Business Link from leading high street banks, are on hand to work with individual companies to help diagnose problems, develop action plans and monitor progress.

There is a lot to be said for grass-roots agencies, serving their local communities. To some extent, local enterprise agencies (LEAs) have tried to fulfil this role in the past, but often such agencies are under-funded and rely on a handful of volunteers to keep them going. Some of them face a struggle for survival similar to that encountered by the small firms they are supposed to be helping.

The creation of Training and Enterprise Councils (TECs) – another grass-roots network – has helped to alleviate the problem. TECs are well-funded and usually have the manpower resources many LEAs lack. Prior to the advent of Business Link,

TECs have often been the first port of call for the aspiring small business entrepreneur. When TECs have not been able to provide the specific help being sought, they have often passed enquirers over to local enterprise agencies.

DEPARTMENT OF TRADE AND INDUSTRY

Assisted Areas

The Department of Trade and Industry (DTI) offers financial assistance to companies setting up in areas of industrial decline, designated as Assisted Areas (ie Development Areas or Intermediate Areas).

The main incentive in Assisted Areas is Regional Selective Assistance, available for investment projects which create or safeguard jobs. Firms can apply for help towards projects, such as new plants or factories, or expansion of existing operations.

Intermediate Areas also qualify for Regional Innovation Grants which help firms with fewer than fifty employees with grants up to a maximum of £25,000 for projects which lead to new or improved products or processes.

Regional Selective Assistance

Regional Selective Assistance is a project grant based on the fixed capital costs of a project and on the number of jobs the project is expected to create or safeguard. The level of grant is negotiated as the minimum necessary to enable the project to proceed.

All manufacturing industries are eligible, *except* those which are subject to special European Community restrictions: currently, these apply to man-made fibre and yarn, shipbuilding and ship repair, vehicles, iron and steel, some fisheries and certain agricultural products. Some service projects also quality.

Criteria for Assistance

All applications for Regional Selective Assistance are considered against the following criteria:

- *Viability*. Your project should have a good chance of paying its way.
- *Need*. You must show that you need assistance in order to go ahead with the project on the basis proposed (eg without the grant the project could not go ahead at all or only on a smaller scale).
- *Regional/National Benefit*. Your project should contribute to both the regional and national economy. Those service sector projects which serve only a local market do not generally qualify for this type of assistance. Any adverse effect on employment in other firms will be taken into account.
- *Employment*. Your project should either create new employment or safeguard existing employment in the Assisted Areas.
- *Private Sector Finance*. You will normally be expected to find most of the finance for the project from your own resources or other private sector sources.

It is strongly advised that you do not commit to a project until you have applied for assistance and received an offer. It is very difficult to establish that you need support if you have already started work on the project.

Grants

Grants can take two forms:

(a) *Job-Related Grants* will normally be paid in three equal instalments linked to the creation of jobs and progress with the project. The first instalment is usually paid when one-third of the total jobs linked with the project have been created. For small projects which are completed quickly, the grant may be paid in one or two instalments;

(b) *Grants related to capital expenditure* are normally paid out in instalments related both to your firm's expenditure and progress on the project, including job creation. Eligible costs include purchase of land, site preparation, buildings and plant and machinery (new or second-hand). Certain non-recurring costs, such as patent rights, professional fees, installation and reinstallation of machinery, may also qualify. The working capital required for a project can be taken into account in fixing grant levels.

The jobs and assets in a project have to be maintained for a certain time after a project has been completed. The grant may be recoverable if employment falls below planned levels, or assets are sold, during these periods.

How to Apply

Details on your eligibility for assistance and how and where to apply for grants can be obtained from the DTI regional offices listed in Appendix A to this book. If you apply for more than £25,000 you will be asked to give the following information:

(a) Brief background information on your firm and an outline of your project, including a description of the product, markets aimed at, relationships with your firm's existing business and employment projections;

(b) Details of the financial performance of your firm, forward trading estimates and a statement of requirements and resources for at least the next three years of the project, a breakdown of fixed and working capital expenditure on the project and confirmation of sources of funds for the project.

For grants of £25,000 or less there is a simplified application form.

Help for Packaging Firm

A Devon firm, which produces packaging for a wide range of industries, boosted its business with the help of a £10,000 Regional Selective Assistance grant from the DTI. British Dalcon Plastics applied for the grant in 1993 after it became available to firms in the newly-created Assisted Area of Torbay.

The grant went towards a £34,000 investment project which has allowed the firm to increase its output considerably. It enabled the firm to purchase a high-tech thermo-forming machine, which manufactures a range of plastic packaging.

As a direct result, the firm was able to employ three more staff, one full-time and two part-time, and made plans to increase staffing levels still further. Says David Newton, the firm's managing director: 'We have experienced tremendous growth since we set up four years ago and decided that the time was right to further increase our manufacturing capacity. In addition to safeguarding jobs and recruiting new employees, the grant enabled us to respond promptly to our ever-increasing order book.'

Loans from Europe

The European Investment Bank (EIB) provides loans for capital investment projects in industry or infrastructure. Loans may be for up to half the project cost; they may be in sterling or in other currencies; they may be at either fixed or floating interest rates. Borrowers can draw loans in one or several instalments with flexibility on their timing.

The EIB will consider loan applications from small and medium-sized companies anywhere in the UK for investment projects in most industrial sectors.

Small and medium-sized companies (ie those with fewer than 500 employees and net fixed assets of less than £50 million) requiring EIB loans for projects whose total costs are below £20 million should apply to Barclays Bank, which is the only EIB intermediary at present operating in the UK, either through their local branch or the European Loans Unit, whose address is given in Appendix A to this book.

European Coal and Steel Community (ECSC) Conversion Loans

ECSC provides loans for up to 50 per cent of the fixed capital costs of productive investment projects providing new employment opportunities in coal and steel closure areas designated by the Commission. The loans are normally at fixed interest rate for eight years, with a four-year grace period on the repayment of the capital.

A discretionary interest rate of up to 3 per cent for the first five years may be granted on a portion of the loan, calculated according to the number of permanent jobs created.

ECSC loans are normally available for projects in all *except* the following sectors: retailing, healthcare, general education, housing, finance and agriculture. Projects in the leisure sector may be eligible if they can be shown to contribute to the development of tourism in the area.

ECSC loans from £10,000 to 5.25 million to small and medium-sized firms can be arranged through the following intermediaries: Bank of Scotland, Barclays Bank, Clydesdale Bank, 3i, Midland Bank, National Westminster Bank, Royal Bank of Scotland, TSB Scotland and the Welsh Development Agency.

LOCAL ENTERPRISE AGENCIES (LEAs)

Loca Enterprise Agencies are the first point of contact for many start-up businesses. There is a national network of more than 300 LEAs throughout England. Each is committed to the economic development of its own area through the provision of help to new and existing small businesses. LEAs are private sector led, and most are funded by a partnership of local and national companies, local authorities, TECs and central government.

They vary in size, but their core service is business information and advice, especially on the development of business plans. Individual LEAs may offer other services, such as business training, a business club, and help with premises or putting together a marketing plan. Each LEA has good links with other business organizations in the area, so if they are not able to help, they can put you in touch with someone else who can. LEAs should also be able to give guidance and advice on possible sources of private sector finance for start-up businesses.

THE RURAL DEVELOPMENT COMMISSION

The RDC has local business teams who can offer advice to established small businesses in many rural areas of England. (It does not give advice on how to start a business; LEAs do that.) The teams include both generalists (business consultants in the broadest sense) and a full range of specialists from management accountants and planning advisers, to experts in such traditional rural crafts as forgework, thatching and saddlery.

Assistance given by the RDC includes advice on finance, premises, production layout and techniques, planning permission, business plans, marketing and quality assurance, and help with prototype development. In the area of marketing, it helps client firms to participate in prestigious exhibitions and it provides grants towards both marketing and exhibition attendance.

The RDC can help you present your case to your bank to raise the necessary finance and, in certain circumstances, may be able to help achieve agreement from a local planning authority.

TRAINING AND ENTERPRISE COUNCILS (TECs)

There are more than eighty Training and Enterprise Councils (TECs) covering the whole of England and Wales (in Scotland, their equivalent are called Local Enterprise Companies, or LECs). Their 'mission' is to deliver quality training and small business support which meet both government targets and community needs.

TECs offer a wide range of training and enterprise services through organizations and employers in their local area. You should approach TECs for information about the following programmes, initiatives and services:

• *Business and Enterprise Services*: for example, business planning, which can help reduce financial risk (the help includes the offer of professional support at reduced rates); and business training courses, which cover everything from setting up in business to expanding an existing enterprise (offered free or at reduced rates).

• *Business Start-up Schemes*: some TECs operate business start-up schemes, which, among other things, give fledgling companies access to a network of business mentors, including banks, accountants and successful mature companies. The networks are set up specifically to nurture a new business through its first two years by guiding and advising the entrepreneur. Such schemes, which TECs run in partnership with other national and regional support agencies, are likely to be expanded with funding from the government's Single Regeneration Budget. Over £1 million is expected to be made available nationally from the fund in 1995.

• *Enterprise allowance*: TECs have taken over responsibility for the former government-run Enterprise Allowance Scheme to help out-of-work people start their own business. Schemes vary from one TEC to another, but basically applicants need to have been out of work from six to eight weeks and to have £1,000 in their bank account. They normally receive £40 a week for twenty-five weeks and a lump sum payment at the end of that period. Some TECs conduct a business plan assessment.

- *Workshops*: TECs regularly hold workshops, such as the *Focus on Small Business* initiative to give advice to fledgling entrepreneurs. These are often held in conjunction with the DTI, the RDC and local enterprise agencies. The range of subjects covered includes financial awareness, managing people, customer satisfaction, marketing and exporting.

- *Networking*: some TECs act as a catalyst for small business networking initiatives. The benefits derived from networking include finding joint solutions to overcome trade barriers which are too great to be tackled individually; pooling of specialist knowledge in areas like technology or marketing; and the opportunity to compete jointly for contracts too large for one firm to manage alone.

- *Training for Young People*: a guaranteed place on this training scheme is offered to anyone aged sixteen or seventeen who is not employed in full-time education. The scheme works towards the award of National Vocational Qualifications (NVQs), which are nationally recognized.

- *Training for Work*: an amalgamation of three former programmes – Employment Training, Employment Action and High Technology National Training. It offers unemployed adults a range of opportunities to train, or to gain work experience that is directly related to the job they want to do.

- *Investors in People*: an initiative that encourages employers of all sizes to improve their business performance by linking the training and development of their employees to business requirements. It is based on a set of rigorous criteria which together form a national standard. If employers are formally assessed and are found to meet all the criteria, they are officially recognized as an 'Investor in People'.

- *Career Development Loans (CDLs)*: an Employment Department scheme which operates in conjunction with three banks – Barclays, Co-operative and Clydesdale – to help individuals pay for vocational training courses lasting between one week and a year. The government pays the interest on the loan approved by one of the three banks for the duration of the course and for up to three months afterwards. It is then up to the borrower to repay the loan and any further interest over a length of time agreed with the bank concerned.

The Consortium of Rural TECs is a group of twenty-eight TECs working in partnership to promote training and enterprise in rural areas. Membership is open to all TECs that have a rural dimension to their areas of operations. Associate membership is available to non-TEC national organizations concerned with rural matters. By working together, consortium members gain economies of scale in research and development in areas of mutual interest, share experiences and new ideas, and use their collective strength to influence policy-makers.

SMALL FIRM LOBBY GROUPS

There are two main lobby groups in the UK fighting the small business cause. They are the Federation of Small Businesses and The Forum of Private Business.

The Federation of Small Businesses (FSB)

The FSB was formed in 1974, since when it has campaigned vigorously on behalf of all Britain's small businesses to promote their interests and to further a financial and economic climate which engenders wealth creation and which allows small businesses to fulfil their job creating potential.

The small business group claims a considerable number of achievements over more than twenty years of its existence as a result of lobbying Whitehall and Brussels on behalf of its 60,000 members. It claims in particular to have made a major contribution towards reducing the red tape burden on small firms and to have championed their cause in such contentious areas as VAT, business rates, and the quality management standard BS 5750.

In 1981 the FSB launched a unique legal fees protection scheme. This scheme covers many areas of business life when protection is afforded against uncertain and unpredictable legal and professional costs. The FSB scheme affords protection to traders faced with investigations by the Inland Revenue and the VAT man. The pioneering policy has saved members over £6 million in tax which the FSB claims would have been unjustly collected by the revenue. Members also receive protection in many other areas including health and safety prosecutions, criminal defence prosecutions, especially regarding the Road and Traffic Act, and receive compensation for jury service.

Employment disputes which may end up with an industrial tribunal are also protected by the FSB – as are property disputes, problems with data protection, personal injury matters and the cost of appealing if an essential licence is suspended, revoked, altered or not renewed. Over and above this specialist legal and professional insurance is a free 24-hour legal advisory service for all members, all year round. Some 3,000 calls a month are handled by the FSB from members seeking legal advice on both personal and business matters.

There is a network of FSB regional branches throughout the country which hold regular meetings, seminars, exhibitions and conferences on all aspects of running a small business.

FSB members sit on influential committees covering many industrial sectors; representatives serve on councils, committees and boards which include police liaison committees, water authority consumer committees, health and hospital boards, educational institutions, electricity, gas and telephone consumer bodies, rates consultative committees, industrial tribunals, ACAS and in many other areas of public and business interest.

The Forum of Private Business (FPB)

The FPB was formed in 1977 to promote and protect the interests of smaller firms. Active on many fronts, including banking, late payment of debt, rates and simplification of red tape, the FPB strives to improve the climate in which all privately-owned businesses operate.

Its 22,500 members determine FPB policy/action in a six-weekly referedum postal ballot on important business issues. A record of each member's vote is sent to his or her MP in Westminster and Strasbourg. The results form the springboard for future FPB lobbying.

The referendum research is underpinned by a quarterly survey of the membership conducted face-to-face with the business owner's by FPB market researchers. Other FPB activities include:

- maintaining contact with all levels of government in order to influence legislation and government action affecting free enterprise;
- promoting its members' views through national publicity campaigns and speaking engagements;
- monitoring current trends through detailed membership surveys.

Another major benefit of FPB membership is its member information service. Business owners may face decisions on over 3,000 different issues in any year. FPB members can use the organization's help-line to explore new avenues before making decisions. Chief executive Stan Mendham claims: 'We are known as the only organization with access to the facts across the whole spectrum of private business, which means our views are often called upon by policy-makers.'

The FPB has pursued the issue of late payment of debts most vigorously and it seems likely not to let the government off the hook until more tangible steps are taken to solve one of the most serious problems faced by small firms. The FPB described the government's 1994 White Paper on Competitiveness as a 'charter for cheats' because of its failure to take any firm action on this issue. It believes the voluntary measures advocated by the government will fail to come to grips with the problem because they 'lack the teeth to change the UK's ingrained late payment culture'.

Successes claimed by the FPB include:

- Winning greater protection for firms which suffer excessive sickness levels under the revised Statutory Sick Pay arrangements;
- A campaign for improved banking services which has persuaded the UK banks to pre-notify businesses of charges and has seen the introduction of a written banking contract by the first UK bank;
- Winning a reduction in the VAT bad debt relief qualifying period from two years to six months;
- Securing compliance cost compensation in the form of quarterly payment of PAYE/NI for smaller businesses.

The FPB has also won important savings for small firms by securing freezes and reductions on the Uniform Business Rate and it has persuaded the government to soften VAT penalties.

It also helps members to make savings and become more efficient with 'Profit Builders and Action Alerts' – DIY documents which, for example, enable business owners to reduce their bank charges or negotiate better interest rates.

Members pay a fee but the amount is voluntary and the maximum subscription accepted by the FPB is £500 per year. On average, members pay around £2 a week.

HELP FOR YOUNG ENTREPRENEURS

Livewire

Livewire is one of the principal organizations that supports young people wanting to set up their own companies and seek ways of self-employment. Over the past decade it has helped around 35,000 young people throughout the UK to go it alone.

The idea for Livewire evolved from the Shell Survival Awards Scheme set up by Shell UK and aimed at young people who had created their own work.

Livewire became a national programme in 1985. Its co-ordination was taken over by the Newcastle-based enterprise agency Project North East and in 1990 Shell extended its sponsorship and funding commitment.

Livewire operates three key programmes:

- The enquiry and link-up service
- The business start-up awards
- The business growth challenge

The aim of the *enquiry service* is to act as a gateway to youth enterprise supported by:

- promoting awareness of the option of self-employment;
- providing information about starting in business;
- linking enquirers to a quality adviser;
- providing an opportunity for people to think through the implications of starting in business and to undertake proper preparation.

A free booklet, *Unlock Your Potential* is sent to all eligible enquirers (16–25 years of age). It is full of tips on how to get organized and is intended to help them think through the implications of starting in business. It also includes an action diary and project planner to help them plan their next steps and a local co-ordinator can link enquirers to a suitable adviser.

The Livewire UK network of over eighty co-ordinators under-takes the management of programmes in each locality. Co-ordinators are employed by other organizations such as enter-prise agencies, local authority economic development units, education or careers departments, youth enterprise centres and training organizations.

The Livewire co-ordinator draws upon a range of local people and organizations to act as advisers and to provide a service through which counselling, advice, training, finance, premises and other support can be accessed easily by young businesses.

Livewire participants are given a free business plan guideline which has been specifically designed in loose leaf format so that sections can be issued as appropriate. The guideline provides substantial extra information to complement the adviser's support and to help in the preparation of a well-researched and carefully thought-out business plan.

One of those who found the Livewire service very beneficial is Maureen Fox of Fern Valley Knitwear, Galashiels: 'When I first started to think about being my own boss I collected a lot of information from a wide range of organizations. The *Unlock Your Potential* booklet from Livewire stood out from all the rest. It really made me think seriously about what starting a business involves, and challenged me to come up with answers to the many questions I began to ask myself. When I was sure that I wanted to take the next step, Livewire backed me all the way.'

The Livewire *Business Start Up Awards* scheme provides a promotional opportunity for young people who have just started or are about to start in business. It also promotes role models of successful businesses and awards cash and in-kind business support.

The annual Livewire Awards have been a constant feature in a rapidly changing youth enterprise scene. The awards presenta-tions provide an annual opportunity to celebrate with the promising young business people who are about to start in business or have started within the previous year. The events provide a stimulating opportunity for young businesses, advisers, organizers and sponsors to mix and learn from one another.

Over 80 awards presentations take place each year at county, regional and national levels leading to the prestigious Livewire UK finals, at which up to £150,000 is given in awards each year.

Entrants for the awards need to be sixteen to twenty-five years of age and submit a business plan to their local co-ordinator. Eminent independent judging panels assess both the people and their plans following Livewire judging guidelines.

The coveted title of 'Livewire Young Business Person' and a major cash award is presented to the UK's most promising young business at a high profile UK awards ceremony in London sponsored by Shell.

There were over 1,200 entries for the competition in 1994, which was won by 24-year-old Eira Guest from Manchester, whose business, Cornerstar Design Company, makes stylish clothing for professional women with a fuller figure. She received her £3,000 award from Dr Chris Fay, chairman and chief executive of Shell UK Ltd.

A total of 100 businesses, with a combined turnover of £6 million, took part in the 1994 regional finals of the Livewire competition. A survey of the participants produced some revealing statistics. For example, those businesses which undertook regular business planning had an average profit margin of 54 per cent. Those who failed to do so only achieved 35 per cent.

On the issue of funding, some 98 per cent of the respondents found their banks particularly unhelpful, not only in terms of finance, but also in terms of advice, leaving the youth enterprise network as the main, and often the only, source of funding. This would suggest that there is something of a generation gap problem when young people approach the high street banks for start-up funds. Fortunately, organizations like Livewire are there to restore the enthusiasm of young people who find themselves rebuffed by the banks. The morale of Alison Matthews, owner of a Belfast bridalwear design business, was boosted enormously from winning the Livewire UK award in 1991: 'Winning the UK Livewire award represents a tremendous vote of confidence in both the business and myself. It has strengthened my belief that what I am doing is right and will, undoubtedly, enhance my reputation with potential customers and give me more credibility with those whose backing I may need to help me achieve my future goals in business.'

Since its inception in 1989, Livewire's *Business Growth Challenge* has offered high quality management training to help owner managers of small businesses to develop the skills they need for growth and to replicate some of the management and personal development they would have received if they worked for a large company.

Business Growth Challenge focuses on existing businesses with growth potential and those which are beginning to create new jobs and aims to:

- help young owner-managers undertake personal learning to improve their management and personal skills;
- present training in a new and exciting way to stimulate business planning;
- demonstrate that there is continuing support available to enable young businesses to grow;
- provide role models of growing businesses.

Prince's Youth Business Trust (PYBT)

The Prince's Youth Business Trust, headed by Prince Charles, helps young people aged between eighteen and twenty-nine, with viable business ideas, to get started. It provides grants of up to £1,500 and loans of up to £5,000.

Some 400 of the young people set up in business by the Trust are reporting annual turnovers of more than a quarter of a million pounds. Compared with small businesses generally, the Trust-supported firms achieve a better than average success rate, according to Nigel Dumbrell, a regional fund raising manager for the Trust. Two-thirds of them are still trading after three years.

In the year ending June 30th 1993 loans totalling £4.3 million and grants totalling £2 million were given to 2,717 young people who successfully applied for aid from the Trust. Since its foundation in 1986, the Trust has helped a total of some 19,000 young people to set up 15,000 businesses through a combination of soft loans, grants, business advice and other support.

The Trust believes that the secret lies with the business advisers. Before young applicants are given a grant or soft loan they must agree to accept a business adviser who will call on them at least once a month. The applicant may call the adviser as often as they like.

There is a network of around 6,000 of these volunteer advisers working with the Trust – big business leaders, small town bank managers, solicitors, marketing men, among others. Since the Trust helps between 3,000 and 4,000 new businesses a year, the demand for more advisers is considerable.

The Trust has a London headquarters and thirty-eight regional managers, many of them seconded from industry, commerce and the government, usually for two years. Each region has its own board of local people drawn from the worlds of business and enterprise. It is the board members who decide who should have help.

The Trust is particularly concerned to help the disadvantaged –the unemployed, those from minority communities, disabled applicants, young ex-offenders and those from decaying inner cities and areas of rural deprivation. But before young people can qualify for financial help they must have tried, but failed, to raise any or all of the money elsewhere.

The PYBT is a source of last resort finance. Often, however, once a bank knows that the Trust is involved with the young person, it reconsiders its original decision and agrees to help after all – such is the Trust's reputation.

KEY POINTS

- The proliferation of support agencies for small firms can be overwhelming.
- The government has launched a network of 200 Business Links to act as one-stop shops.
- The Department of Trade and Industry offers financial assistance to companies setting up in areas of industrial decline.
- A national network of local enterprise agencies provides the first point of contact for many start-up businesses.
- The Rural Development Commission offers advice to established small firms in non-urban areas of England.
- Training and Enterprise Councils deliver quality training and small business support to meet government targets and community needs.
- Small firm lobby groups campaign vigorously on such issues as red tape and the late payment problem.
- Livewire and the Prince's Youth Business Trust helps young people to set up in business.

CASE STUDY
Cornerstar Design Company Ltd

A 24-year-old fashion designer from Manchester who produces clothing for professional women with a fuller figure, was named Livewire's 1994 UK young entrepreneur of the year. Eira Guest, trading as Cornerstar Design Company Ltd., received a cheque for £3,000, a special gold medal and the Livewire Business Start Up trophy.

Cornerstar Design Company, which is based in Ducie Street in Manchester, designs quality, stylish ready-to-wear and bespoke womenswear, specializing in sizes 16–24. Clients are mainly professional women who are dissatisfied with the clothing available in the high street.

Most clothes are sold through mail order catalogue, but Eira does provide a one-to-one service and supplies direct to designers, retailers and wholesalers. She also markets her fashions through the pan-European television shopping channel QVC, and has developed a range of corporate clothing for a car hire company.

Eira and her partner Clair Leyden, who are both in the 16–18 size range, started their business primarily because they were tired of the 'floral tents' offered by high street retailers. Eira, a law graduate, and Clair, who is an experienced fashion designer, decided to start their own business after finding themselves temporarily unemployed. Recalls Eira: 'We realized there must be a niche in the market for our designs because of the problems we had in finding suitable, fashionable, stylish clothes. Our considerable research vindicated our feelings, and we discovered that there were no other British manufacturers supplying the market.'

Cornerstar's main competition comes from Italian and German designers, but Eira believes her upmarket, executive designs have the edge in terms of quality and price. Also, she believes clients prefer to buy British when they can. Her principal brand, 'Nemesis', is named after the goddess of retribution. Says Eira: 'It's large ladies getting their own back on the fashion industry.'

The success of the venture has not come as a surprise to Eira. She projected a turnover of £120,000 with profits of at least £50,000 in the first year of operation and a turnover forecast of £250,000 for year two.

Eira plans to make Cornerstar a pan-European company, followed eventually by a stock-market flotation. A range of clothes for very thin women is another idea she plans to pursue.

CHAPTER 5

Raising the Start-up Finance

Starvation of capital, both to launch a company and, to a lesser extent, to fuel its growth once it is up and running, is one of the most serious problems facing small businesses. Bank managers tend to be a very conservative breed – all the more so in a recession. Some would argue that it is a function of their job to be that way. They are, after all, primarily guardians of their customers' wealth, which has been deposited at the bank for safe-keeping and in the fond hope that it will provide reasonable returns.

Few bank managers have themselves worked in a conventional company, let alone run one, so it is hardly surprising that they are more likely to offer backing to those who go along with tried and tested concepts, particularly as the demand for funds far outstrips the money available.

Someone planning to start up as a window cleaner is likely to receive a sympathetic hearing. It is something every bank manager can identify with. It is not difficult to demonstrate that with a certain amount of industrious endeavour a favourable – if modest – return on investment can be achieved.

If, on the other hand, the bank manager is confronted with an innovative idea, which the inventor insists is going to take the world by storm, where is the proof? How can the likely returns be calculated for a product the buying public hasn't yet set eyes on? Cash flow forecasts can only be an inspired guess at best.

Venture capitalists, on the other hand, expect to take risks. Many of them operate on the one-in-three formula. One project will go down the drain, another will tick over unspectacularly, but the third will be a shooting star that will make enough profits to wipe out the losses of the other two and make a tidy sum for the venture capitalist into the bargain.

But to achieve that goal the stakes have to be high. It is unlikely that a small firm, starting up on an initial investment of less than £100,000 is going to produce exciting returns in the short term. It will take years for such a small operation to blossom into a major success story – if it ever happens.

The Equity Gap

This unfortunate fact of life is probably one of the principal causes of what has become known as the 'equity gap'. In the main, venture capital firms are reluctant to seek injections of less than £100,000 and most of the deals they are interested in are considerably in excess of that amount.

There have been a number of attempts to plug the gap. The Midland Enterprise Fund was launched in 1994 to address the problem. It is a network of regional funds sponsored by the Midland Bank and supported by a variety of other private and public sector organizations, including TECs, local authorities and accountancy firms.

Each fund is independent and operates its own investment criteria but, generally speaking, amounts of up to £125,000 are made available for investment. The main recipients are manufacturing companies or companies providing services to the manufacturing sector. The funds purchase a minority stake in the small firms, and, where appropriate, provide loan capital. The investments are primarily in established businesses with high growth potential, although some start-ups are eligible.

Launching the fund, Tim Sainsbury, the Industry Minister, declared: 'The small firms sector has shown great vigour and dynamism over the last decade . . . If small firms are to continue to play a vital role in the economy, they must have access to the finance they need.' He added that the Midland Enterprise Fund was designed to plug the 'equity gap' by making available venture capital to small and medium-sized firms at levels not normally considered viable by investors. The experience of recent years, he said, highlighted the dangers of small businesses being over-reliant on short-term debt finance, particularly overdrafts. However, there were welcome signs that both banks and small businesses had begun to recognize the advantages of more long-term arrangements.

There is a view that small business owners should be encouraged to abandon short-termism in their approach to funding by offering them tax incentives. David Lavarack, head of small business services at Barclays Bank, has proposed the introduction of what he describes as a 'Business Tessa'. His idea would work on the same principle as ordinary Tessas (tax-exempt special savings accounts). He explains: 'It will provide a real mechanism to re-invest for small firms. They can save up to a certain amount and the interest in that scheme accrues tax-free.'

The savings would allow more money to be ploughed into development. However, a fundamental problem has to be overcome if the government is to be persuaded to look seriously at introducing Business Tessas. Although they would offer a certain amount of long-term financial security, small firms tend not to make long-term savings plans. Adds Lavarack: 'Most businesses will not look ahead as far as five years; 60 per cent of small firms do not look more than one month ahead. More often, businesses take short-term funding such as trade credits and bank overdrafts. The net result is that we have created a culture of small firms which are very unstable. We want to change this culture and have to provide the incentives to do this.'

Such initiatives are a step in the right direction, but they are only a drop in the ocean compared with the potential demand from financially-starved small firms, particularly those at the start-up stage.

Where then are the small businesses – the acorns that are expected to grow into tomorrow's oak trees – to get their capital from? The sad fact is that there is very little start-up capital around, despite all the high-blown speeches by politicians and others about small businesses being the job creators of tomorrow.

In the old days, start-up capital used to be provided by the proverbial Aunt Agatha, who invested her private nest-egg in a promising project dreamed up by a favourite nephew. Today, there is far less private capital available and what there is tends to be heavily taxed. Business angels (see next chapter) are beginning to take up the slack, but they too are only scratching the surface of the problem.

Start-up entrepreneurs are left with little alternative but to borrow the money they need from financial institutions, seek equity or launch their companies on a wing and a prayer. One estimate is that seven out of ten start-ups are launched on a very small bank loan or overdraft facility in the fond hope that the venture will be able to survive on retained profits.

To some extent, this unsatisfactory situation was recognized by the government when it introduced the Enterprise Allowance Scheme, which provided unemployed people wanting to start their own business with £40 a week for a year. The idea was that it would allow them the opportunity to plough back into their fledgling enterprises whatever profits they made.

It is a source of great frustration to many small business entrepreneurs that they have such difficulty raising small amounts of capital to create new enterprises when there are vast sums of money circulating in the City of London. The terrible truth is that under existing economic rules, small businesses are not going to attract financial support on anything like the required scale when there are so many more appealing ways of obtaining returns on investments.

Code of Practice

Towards the end of the 1980s when the recession started to bite, relationships between small firms and the high street banks deteriorated rapidly. There was a strong suspicion that the already beleaguered small firms sector was being exploited by the banks in their attempts to halt sliding profits and recoup enormous losses from bad debts in the Third World.

There was a lot of evidence to support this view. Banks appeared to introduce obscure new charges at the drop of a hat. These were automatically deducted from their customers' business accounts, often before the customers had realized what had happened. There was also an accusation that the banks were not passing on to their customers the full effects of reductions in the base rate.

My wife experienced the ill-effects of this unsavoury turn of events when she was summoned to call on a newly-appointed enterprise manager at her local bank to discuss developments in her toy company. After a fairly lengthy discussion during which she familiarized the bank manager with the current status of her company he said that a sum of £60 would be deducted from her company's business account for this consultation and that she should count herself lucky that the amount was so insignificant.

This was an extraordinary attitude to take to a business customer, particularly in view of the fact that the meeting was called at the behest of the new enterprise manager and that its purpose was apparently to acquaint him with details he would otherwise have had to glean by studying the toy company's files.

Many similar instances of heavy-handed treatment were related in articles in the national press and a huge groundswell of indignation put pressure on the banks to be less cavalier in their dealings with their small business customers. The banks subsequently issued carefully-worded codes of practice to try to reassure their customers that they would not in future be penalized in this way but many small business entrepreneurs, who already felt under severe pressure from the recession, were embittered by the experience. It is likely to be some years before relations between the high street banks and small firms are restored to amiability and mutual trust.

The Loan Guarantee Scheme

An attempt was made by the government in the early 1980s to relieve the funding problems for small firms by introducing the Loan Guarantee Scheme (LGS). The idea was that the pressure would be taken off both the banks and small businesses if the government shouldered the majority of the risk involved in investments. The scheme was particularly aimed at would-be entrepreneurs who had insufficient collateral or business experience to be able to raise normal bank loans.

Between 1981, when it was launched, and 1993 over 33,500 loans were made under the LGS, totalling approximately £1 billion. Over the same period 12,000 of these loans defaulted at a cost of around £229 million to the Exchequer, according to The Centre for Small and Medium Sized Enterprises at Warwick Business School.

Originally the government guaranteed 80 per cent of loans raised under the scheme. Disenchantment grew, however, when it became apparent that the failure rate of participating companies was unreasonably high. The reason appeared to be that bank managers were ill-equipped to make judgements about the viability of business proposals and were invariably backing the wrong horse. There was also the suspicion that they were perhaps less thorough in vetting proposals in the safe knowledge that the government carried the brunt of the risk.

To stem the losses it was sustaining the government reduced the guaranteed amount to 70 per cent and increased the premium. This simply had the effect of discouraging small businesses from considering the LGS because it was too expensive. It also put a brake on the banks which were less inclined to risk catching a cold on investments in which they now had a larger stake. The whole exercise inevitably became self-defeating since it meant that the impoverished small business entrepreneur was again being starved of badly needed funds.

A strong rumour spread that the government was about to scrap the scheme altogether, but instead it re-instated it in the 1986 Budget and reduced the premium to make it less expensive. More recently, the government's faith in the scheme seems to have gained a new lease of life.

In early 1993, with the need to help firms climb out of the recession very much in mind, the government decided to expand the LGS. In his March 1993 Budget Norman Lamont, the then chancellor, announced he would increase the maximum proportion of a debt covered by the LGS from 70 per cent to 85 per cent, raise the limit on loans from £100,000 to £250,000 and lower the dividends levied by the DTI. This time around the government has hedged its bets. The 85 per cent guarantee on loans up to £250,000 only applies to established businesses that have been trading for at least two years. For businesses that have been trading for less than two years, and which present a much greater risk of failure, the guarantee is only for 70 per cent of loans up to £100,000.

The government hoped this would stimulate a renaissance but the banks have been less than enthusiastic.

In August 1993 the *Sunday Times* Small Business Focus Page reported that small businessmen across the country were finding to their dismay that the banks were refusing to sponsor loans through the LGS. According to the *Sunday Times*, Baroness Denton, the then Small Firms Minister, carpeted the big banks for their reluctance to co-operate with the LGS. Denton threatened to publish league tables showing the extent to which each bank was supporting the scheme. 'It will also help businessmen identify which banks are sympathetic to their needs,' she was reported as saying.

Denton's determination to make the LGS scheme work was understandable. Smaller companies will be the main generators of post-recession growth and jobs, and the scheme has become the linchpin of government aid for small firms. Having covered £1 billion of loans to 33,500 firms since it was launched in 1981, the government considers the scheme to have been a success. The British Bankers' Association, however, argues that the level of bad debt carried by the banks involved in the scheme is too high.

Venture Capital

Eleven years ago, if an unquoted company in Britain wanted to raise equity finance, there were few places to go. The term 'venture capital' was then almost unheard of, even though it had taken root in the United States twenty years previously. Apart from the 3i group (then known as the Industrial & Commercial Finance Corporation), founded in 1945, there was only a handful of equity providers. For the vast majority of independent firms, the banks were their only recourse for raising finance.

The emergence, and subsequent growth, of a large venture capital industry has been one of the most remarkable features of Britain's corporate financial evolution. In the ten years to the end of 1992, British venture capital organizations have invested over £9 billion in unquoted companies and currently invest around £1.4 billion a year.

Each year over 1,000 companies, many of them management buy-outs, receive equity finance ranging from £100,000 to many millions. In return, the venture capital organizations obtain shares in these firms – usually a minority holding – which they then hold for up to ten years before they hope to sell them at a profit.

The 3i group

Today there are over 100 UK organizations which supply venture capital. The largest is 3i which is represented in just over half of all the UK deals completed annually. It was established in 1945 as the Industrial, Commercial and Financial Corporation to try to ensure that British industry had access to sufficient funds to feed its long-term growth. Using finance raised in public capital markets all over the world, 3i is a major force in the provision of share and loan capital to unquoted British companies. Until its flotation on the stock market in 1994, it was owned exclusively by the clearing banks (85 per cent) and the Bank of England (15 per cent).

Since its foundation, 3i has supported well over 9,000 companies. It invests in all the major points of change in the life of a company, from start-up to flotation. In a typical year it supports some 300 brand new or very young ventures.

Captive venture capital divisions

Another important group of equity funders is the so-called 'captive' venture capital divisions of the major banks and insurance companies. A significant contribution also comes from independent venture capital funds which every three or four years must raise money themselves so that they may start a new round of investment.

Each year any one of these venture capital organizations can look at up to 500 investment proposals from independent companies seeking finance. Typically, a venture capital house will back no more than half a dozen firms a year and they can afford to be very exacting in their choice of companies.

In 1992, 1,300 firms received venture capital in Britain. Some of these would have been start-ups or other early stage businesses, typically receiving equity packages averaging around £400,000. During the recession, venture capitalists often invested to assist firms re-financing bank debts; these deals averaged just under £1 million.

Small company share prices took a hammering during the

recession; but as economic recovery takes hold, investors will increasingly look for value while prices are still low and they are likely to consider it a good time to buy small company shares.

A post-recessionary period is also an opportune time for independent companies to raise the capital they need in order to gear up for economic recovery. A good deal for the venture capitalist should also be a good deal for a company's management team if a genuine opportunity for growth has been identified.

A survey by the British Venture Capital Association revealed that even at the tail end of a recession, 60 per cent of venture-backed companies had increased their sales by more than 10 per cent. Half of the firms had increased profit margins and the same number expected to increase staffing levels during the coming year.

High growth potential

Venture capital is most suitable for risk investment in unquoted companies with high growth potential. It can broadly be subdivided into seed or start-up capital (used to bring a research idea to the development stage), second round finance for young companies (used to expand the range of products) and development capital for established companies (used to develop an alternative product or expand through acquisition).

For the purposes of this book, the main concern is with seed and start-up equity, but much the same criteria apply at whichever stage your company happens to be. Venture capitalists are primarily interested in investing in profitable and fast growing companies. After all they are themselves commercial organizations. They will want to finance a business through a key stage of growth for, say, two to five years and then to be able to 'exit' from the investment by selling on their equity stake. If the business is unlikely to develop significantly over the next few years venture capitalists will probably not be interested. Indeed, they will normally expect your business to double its profits every three years.

A useful booklet, *Finance Without Debt – A Guide to Sources of Venture Capital under £250,000* has been compiled by accountants KPMG Peat Marwick for the DTI, which sets out the steps for attempting to obtain an equity injection.

A sale of equity can help reduce a business's interest charges, but in the long run it may prove to be more expensive than other forms of finance because the equity partner will require a high rate of capital growth and will own part of the business. An equity investor is typically looking for capital growth of 35 per cent plus. This initial cost of an equity sale may also be significant, particularly if it is necessary to issue a prospectus to comply with the Companies Act 1985 or an investment advertisement to comply with the Financial Services Act 1986.

However, an equity sale can help to give balance to a business. Businesses which have too little equity or too much debt are highly geared. Like a geared machine, they produce good results while they work but are in danger of breaking down completely if things go wrong. They are risky businesses. By selling equity you reduce the level of risk in your business and you share the reduced risk with your new partner.

In addition, the new equity may provide a sound base for raising further debt finance or to invest in research and development if retained earnings are not sufficient.

Giving up control?

It is widely believed that an equity sale means giving up an element of control and technically this is the case, but it should be remembered that other kinds of financiers can also influence the way a business is run. Your new equity partner may have different skills to yours, gained from having helped other businesses grow and might help you manage your business more efficiently. It is, however, important to choose an equity partner with whom you feel you can develop a good personal and working relationship. There will be setbacks as well as successes in the days ahead. The relationship must be able to withstand the stressful times as well as the good. You should also understand what your equity partner is expecting to gain from the deal. How quickly will he or she want to exit and will the partner be able to help finance the business through the next stage of growth? Essentially, will the partner add value to your business?

Small business entrepreneurs are often reluctant to seek venture capital. They resent the idea of relinquishing a part of the ownership of the company they conceived and built up with toil and sweat to 'outsiders' who are merely contributing financial resources. A realistic way of looking at it, though, is that it is better to own say, 70 per cent of a successful company than 100 per cent of one that is about to go under because of lack of funds.

'Do you want a slice of fruit cake or all of a currant bun?' is the way one financier puts it. Venture capitalists argue that talk of 'giving away' equity is totally misplaced. 'I don't know of anybody who has given away equity. One in a hundred perhaps. All the rest has been bought for pound notes – often at a very high price,' says one financial expert.

Although venture capitalists are more likely to back risky enterprises than banks or the more traditional lenders, they are nevertheless looking for winners and examine the prospects for success very closely before making an investment. Primarily, they are looking for firms that show signs of being well managed and which have good prospects for growth.

Venture capitalists tend to look for the three Ms – management, marketing and money. Is it the right management team to undertake the enterprise? Have they got a market place for the business they are going into? Is the financial package they are trying to put together, which may involve loans, equity, bank overdraft, factoring, leasing and hire purchase, capable of supporting the business plan?

In the case of Martek (see page 45), the financiers the

company initially approached without success probably felt happy about the management team and the financial package it was attempting to put together but they may have had some doubts about whether it had been established that there would be a market demand for the drill sharpener the company founders wanted to produce – doubts that ultimately proved unfounded.

The quality of management

One of the prime concerns of venture capitalists will always be the quality of management of a company seeking equity. However much sense the business plan makes, the critical factor is the people who are going to implement it. There are basically two types of management that come under consideration – the one-man band and the management team, where a group of people with different disciplinary skills have joined forces to launch a new venture.

Either situation can cause problems. The one-man band certainly has limitations, because there are only so many hours in the day and if the solo entrepreneur brings in part-time accountants or marketing consultants, they won't have all their loyalties devoted to his or her company. But at least costs should be kept at a manageable level.

When looking at the one-man band, venture capitalists are definitely put off by the entrepreneur who insists he can do everything himself and is convinced he doesn't need any professional help. A common problem is the entrepreneur who is obsessed by a new invention or by perfecting a device until the R&D costs outrun any prospect of their being recouped in the market place. Venture capitalists have no time for such people because their motivation is product superiority rather than the drive to build a successful company that will show good returns on the capital invested.

In the case of a management team, talented people are often only attracted if there is an enticing salary package on offer or equity in the company, which can be expensive. At the same time, there is no guarantee that, just because you have brought the right disciplines together, the people in the team will be compatible, particularly if they were previously unknown to each other.

Venture capitalists will therefore be at pains to examine the track records of the people on the business team to make an assessment of what they are likely to bring to the new venture and they also explore whether the team members have worked together before for any length of time. Some will only inject capital into businesses run by proven management teams. For this reason, the lion's share of available funds is increasingly being invested in management buy-outs and buy-ins (see chapter 3).

Venture capitalists also look for commitment, which can take several guises. It can be apparent from a willingness to take low salaries while the new venture gets off the ground. Giving up a good job to join the firm is also an encouraging sign. Venture capitalists are very wary if the directors appear to want to 'milk' the company at an early stage.

Sometimes requests for venture capital are turned down, not because there is anything inherently wrong with the submitted proposal, but simply because the venture capital organization may have enough start-up companies on its books already. Fund managers are anxious to establish a balanced portfolio that spreads the risks. However much they would like to support aspiring entrepreneurs they cannot afford to have a portfolio that is overloaded with start-ups.

Venture capitalists are sometimes maligned for taking a long time to make up their minds about a proposal. But often the fault lies with the entrepreneur. Observes one financier: 'What often happens is people don't get their act together quickly enough and what could have been quite a decent little proposal then becomes very risky indeed because the cash flow has dried up, losses have accumulated while they've been inefficient or unable to sell their products and then it gets beyond redemption.'

Venture capital organizations often insist on nominating a

non-executive director to the board as a condition of equity investment. The nominated board member is appointed to offer advice and monitor financial progress and the management of the firm generally. In some cases, the nominated director plays a more 'hands-on' role in the company if the venture capital organization feels the firm has a serious weakness in the make-up of its management team. The nominated director will then be chosen from a discipline that complements the skills of the rest of the management team.

Sources of venture capital

The chief sources of venture capital are:

Professional venture capitalists. They manage funds, usually on behalf of institutional investors, and specialize in purchasing the equity of growing businesses. They are highly selective about the investments they make and normally do not invest amounts under £100,000; although there are exceptions, particularly for seed investments in potentially high growth ventures.

Private investors. There are many wealthy individuals searching for profitable investment opportunities in the UK. (See next chapter on business angels.) Before you accept an investment you must be sure that the investor can afford to lose the money if the worst should happen and that the risk is fully understood. Many private investors have been successful in business themselves and may be willing to assist in the management of your business. Typically, they prefer to invest in a sector in which they have experience and will invest through the following schemes and organizations:

• *Firms of stockbrokers, solicitors and accountants*: many of these firms have contacts with individuals in their local areas who may be in a position to invest in profitable businesses.

• *Agencies which specialize in introducing investors to investment opportunities*: there are an increasing number of intermediary organizations which help to put business angels in touch with suitable small businesses needing capital. They include banks, financial advisers, TECs, LECs and local enterprise agencies.

● *Corporate investors*: larger companies may invest in smaller companies. This is sometimes referred to as corporate venturing. It may mean a takeover or a partnership. Typically a larger business invests solely for commercial reasons, but there are funds run by large companies who have other investment criteria, such as creating jobs in areas where the company has made redundancies.

THE BUSINESS PLAN

Before approaching a bank or a venture capitalist you need to draw up a business plan. Even if you have sufficient funds to set the business up, it would be sensible to draw up a plan for your own purposes. NatWest sets out a detailed approach to designing a business plan in its booklet, *The Business Start-Up Guide*. In it, the bank points out that: 'Trying to run your business without a plan is like floating aimlessly at sea in a fog. You will not know where you are going, any more than where you have been or where you are. What is worse, sooner or later you will hit something. Also, working out the cash you expect to make is part of the planning. It will show you whether you need more finance. If you do, it will be easier for your bank or any other organization to help you if you can give them a business plan which covers all of the information in a logical way.'

Turning up at the bank with a few scribbled notes on the back of an envelope will ensure that your mission is doomed from the start. Would-be entrepreneurs have been known to argue that they carry all their ideas around in their head and that they will be able to supply any information required by the bank verbally. This is not the way banks operate and it is certainly not the way to convince a bank manager that you are the kind of person who will be able to organize all the intricate administration that goes into running a business today.

If, on the other hand, you furnish the bank with a well set-out plan that gives a good over-view of your business and your strategy for making your product or service a success in the market place, the battle will be half won. Remember that before you sell any products and services you first need to sell yourself. You have to convince a bank manager, who has come across all sorts of hopeful entrepreneurs, that you are one of those who will go about things in the right way.

The best way to win over any bank manager is to put yourself in his or her place and ask yourself whether in their situation you would put up money on the evidence presented. Above all, be enthusiastic about your product or service. Your enthusiasm could rub off on the bank manager. But even if it doesn't, he is bound to be impressed by how much you believe in yourself and your idea.

When my wife and daughter approached an enterprise manager at Midland Bank for an overdraft to help launch Parthenon Toys, they took along with them the foldaway puppet theatre and some glove puppets to demonstrate the strong points of the products. The bank manager was able to see first hand that the toys were well made and why they were likely to appeal to the target customers. Seeing the puppet theatre in operation took some of the tension out of the meeting and helped to win over the bank manager's interest.

The right approach

NatWest has set out some very useful advice on the right approach to bank managers in its *Business Start-Up Guide*:

Preparation
Be as clear and brief as possible. Don't leave everything until the last minute. Give yourself plenty of time and send a copy of your

plan before the meeting. Be realistic. Look at things clearly and decide whether to include alternative plans covering the best and worst scenarios. Be ready to answer searching questions about the information you have put together.

The Business
Your bank may know some or all of the background information they need. However, it will be particularly interested in your business aims for the coming twelve months and beyond. Be concise and realistic about these. Your aims should be achievable and must be compatible with the figures in your cash flow forecast and operating budget.

The Market
This is one of the most crucial parts of any business plan. The lender will want to know specifically which market you are targeting and what are the unique selling points (USPs) of your product that will enable you to attack that market successfully. Are you aiming to create a niche market? If so, how big is it and will it provide sufficient returns to make your business viable. If it is not a niche market, what is the competition and how are you going to make an impact on an established market? Is yours an upmarket product? If so, how will you reach it? Have you got your pricing right?

Key Personnel
Include brief details in the plan itself. If necessary, add more details about experience, job responsibilities and health on separate sheets of paper. You need to give a clear summary of the experience people in your business have, including your own. The exercise will also help show whether any of your staff need training. Be ready to answer questions about your own abilities and skills.

Premises, plant and machinery
Any lender will be interested in your premises for a number of reasons. In particular, you will have to show that your premises are in the right location. And if you need to spend a lot of money on your premises, this must be covered in the plan. With plant and machinery, a banker will need to know how old it is, its present value and how much it will cost to replace it, its condition and whether it

can cope if you expand. Be open and realistic when you give these details.

Assets you have as security

Any decision to lend you money will be based on the prospects of your proposed business and whether it will be able to pay back the loan from profits. However, there is always an element of risk. Depending on how much risk the lender thinks there is, you may need to give security as insurance against things going wrong. Be prepared to look at what business and personal assets you have.

If the bank needs security but your assets do not cover the amount you want to borrow, it may still be able to help by using the Loan Guarantee Scheme.

Finance

The last part of the business plan should set out your financial requirements. But you first need to work out your expected cash flow, income and costs. For example, if you think you might need an overdraft, you must check the finance you need against the cash flow forecast [see page 102].

It is easy to under-estimate the amount of money you will need to get going. No bank wants you to have a bigger loan than you need, but not having enough finance is one of the most common diseases in small businesses, and it is often fatal. Carefully drawing up your cash flow forecast is the best way of estimating how much you will need. The bank is more likely to back you if you are putting an equivalent amount of money into the business yourself. This is proof of your commitment and it is only right that you should be shouldering your fair share of the risks.

The money you need to run your business day-to-day usually comes from an overdraft. The kind of money used to buy premises or plant and machinery is usually arranged through a bank loan. When you take out a loan make sure the repayment term is the same as the working life of the asset. For example, if you need a machine which you think will be useful for five years, then plan to pay back the loan over five years.

Operating Budgets

A lot of businesses do not make a profit or have enough cash at the right time because the management has not planned ahead. Too often, they do not know how much profit or loss they have made until months after the end of the financial year. And often profit is not properly thought out until there is a crisis.

Budgeting gives you a useful planning tool. By comparing your actual performance with the budget, you can spot difficulties early on and take action to put them right. The operating budget will give you a fair idea of the profit you will make. However, all forecasts are based on assumptions, so these must be specific.

Think about 'building in' money if the worst happens. This can be shown as a separate item or by building it into the individual cost figures.

Whatever you do, you must explain your reasoning. Remember, this is a plan for your trading operations. It is to do with profit and loss, not cash. Include any item that gives a profit, or is a cost against profit. Do not include any other items, such as capital expense, if this will not directly affect your profits.

You must also be clear about the difference between the various costs of running your business. Some will vary depending on how well your business is doing, some will not change:

Variable Costs. Also known as 'direct costs', your variable costs are linked directly to producing your goods and services. They are the costs of your new materials, components and so on, as well as the wages of your employees who actually produce the product or service. Normally, the amount of stock you hold will change constantly. The stock change figure in your operating budget is the net increase and decrease in stock during the month.

Fixed Costs. You will have these costs even if you don't make any sales. They include rent, rates, heating, lighting, insurance and business salaries, including your own. They are also known as indirect costs or overheads.

Depreciation is the term used for the process that takes into account the reduction in the value of an asset over its working life. It is an expense so you should charge it to the profit and loss account, and include it in the operating budget.

By looking at your different costs you can work out your break-even point.

Cashflow Forecasts

Cash is the lifeblood of your business. Managing cash badly is one of the main reasons for business failure. The time you spend working out your cash needs and monitoring cash flow is time well spent. This is because you can:

- find out when you might not have enough cash before it happens
- find out when you might make extra cash and use it efficiently
- make sure you have enough cash for any necessary capital expense
- find out how to use your resources more efficiently and reduce costs.

Like your operating budget, your cash flow forecast will be based upon assumptions. Again you must be realistic. Think about the best and worst cases and explain the assumptions you make. The more realistic your forecasts, the better any bank will like them. Unlike your operating budget, your cash flow forecast is not to do with profit and loss. It is just your best estimate of how the cash will go in and out of your bank account over a certain period of time.

Loans versus Equity

Providers of loans and providers of equity will have different motives in assessing a business plan. In its *Finance without Debt* booklet, the DTI makes the following distinctions:

- Providers of equity are looking for capital gain (normally a minimum of 35 per cent compound return on their investment) and a built in 'exit' route.
- Lenders are not seeking to make such large returns, nor do they look to assume such high levels of risk as the equity investor. This approach will be reflected in the lower cost of their funds. Since they seek lower returns, one of their prime aims will be to minimize losses, which may in turn require the borrower to provide adequate security.

The cash flow forecast is a vital part of the business plan. It will identify the amount of cash required on a day-to-day basis and, therefore, highlight the operating needs of the business for additional finance. It will help identification of how much should be:

- equity – to finance the risk element
- medium to long-term debt – for core borrowing and fixed assets
- short-term – for working capital

Both bankers and equity investors will need to be convinced about the viability of a business. This depends initially on two things – sales and management. Therefore, when approaching financiers the first priority is to prove that there is a sufficient market for the product, that it will achieve reasonable sales in the market and that management are experienced and capable enough to identify problems and devise solutions to steer a successful path.

Presentation

It is best to approach a limited number of providers of finance in the first instance, say about three bankers or venture capitalists. This gives you the opportunity to revise the plan in the light of their comments and have another attempt if it is poorly received.

You could harm your chances by distributing a poor plan widely among financiers.

The DTI advises taking four basic steps:

- Sell the idea on paper. Convey what it is that makes the project exciting in the minimum number of words and ensure that it is eye-catching.
- Consult professional advisers with knowledge of the financiers. Good contacts and working relationships are important.
- Follow up with a telephone call and arrange a meeting at which you, the management, can sell the idea and prove your ability.
- After the meeting, the detailed plan can be amended to take account of the financier's comments, particularly in respect of changes to financial assumptions such as their views on interest rates.

Raising finance takes a long time: on your side since you want to have a choice and the ability to negotiate the best deal; and on their side because they want to get to know you. It is always wise to maintain contact with potential financiers as well as your existing financiers. If your business is rejected by a venture capitalist you should stay in touch in order to build the relationship and trust in case you need help again. The funding decision is not one to be taken on poor information or with insufficient time.

The DTI advises that seekers of finance should be realistic rather than optimistic, especially with the figures in the business plan. An enthusiastic, positive approach is important – by all means present the strong points, but don't ignore the weaknesses. Sensitivity analysis is essential in evaluating key assumptions in the business plan – for example, by varying the effect on profits of varying the rate of interest payable.

Your financial requirements are obviously an important part of the business plan. However, resist the temptation to give too much detail. You should indicate the amount you require and its intended uses along with any other relevant pieces of information. Anticipate the questions that the financier is likely to ask:

- Why has no one else thought of it?
- Why will it sell?
- What price will it sell at?
- How much will it cost to produce?

The business plan must be yours, not your professional adviser's. You must be fully familiar with its contents and although your financial adviser will be closely involved in its preparation, the business plan should not be bought 'off the shelf'.

TYPICAL CONTENTS OF A BUSINESS PLAN

Executive Summary

The Business
history
current status

Products
description
regulatory requirements
research and development

Production Process
techniques
location
suppliers
capacity

Sales and Marketing
market size
competition
sales analysis by product and customer
marketing techniques

Management and Organization
management team with full CVs
organization chart
remuneration policies

Financial Information
historical results
profit and cash flow projections
sensitivity analysis
financing requirement

The Future
future prospects
exit routes for the investor

(Source: *Finance Without Debt – A Guide to Sources of Venture Capital under £250,000*, compiled by KPMG Peat Marwick for the DTI. Crown copyright is reproduced with the permission of the Controller of HMSO)

KEY POINTS

- Consider your objectives for the business honestly.
- Look carefully at the strengths and weaknesses of the management team.
- Consider how you might increase the business's resources, such as asking customers for payments in advance.
- Match the type of funding to the needs of the business.

- Present an enthusiastic plan but be realistic in your figures.
- Allow yourself enough time to negotiate properly.
- Don't be misled into thinking that growth is the only route. A period of consolidation might be essential for the success of the business.

CASE STUDY
MAID, Part 1

Dan Wagner's company, MAID plc, was valued at £89 million when it was floated on the stock market in March 1994. That was quite an achievement for a company that had started life nine years previously with debts of £130,000 and which at the time of the flotation had a modest turnover of £5.7 million and pre-tax profits of around £600,000.

But 30-year-old Wagner, a fast-talking super-salesman with a penchant for Aston Martins, has made a habit of pulling off surprises and his rise in the corporate firmament has been far from orthodox.

The first priority for most budding entrepreneurs is to raise the capital to fund the up-front costs of a new venture. Dan Wagner, with all the audacity of a self-assured 20-year-old, took the opposite route when he set out to establish an on-line information service. He decided that he first needed to prove that his idea worked, so he ran up costs of £130,000 establishing a prototype before turning to the City for financial support. Since he was on the dole at the time, the exercise had some nerve-racking moments.

The gamble paid off. Today, Wagner, is a multi-millionaire.

He founded the company in 1985 after spotting the need for a comprehensive computerized database to serve the advertising industry. A decade later, MAID (market analysis and information database), has offices in London, New York and Paris. Subscribers include not only advertising agencies, as Wagner originally had in mind, but also an impressive number of blue-chip companies. They all tap into the on-line database that Wagner's company has built up as a result of signing exclusive agreements with market research publishers.

Wagner first demonstrated his business acumen when working for WCRS, at the time an up-and-coming advertising agency. As a complete newcomer to the industry, he secured a £1 million TV advertising campaign with a jeans company, an account that had remained dormant for some time. On the strength of that success, Wagner expected a substantial increase in salary. When it was not forthcoming, he went on the dole and started laying the ground for MAID. He was confident he could secure another job in advertising if the plan failed: 'I had no mortgage, no capital base, no family, nothing really. I wasn't earning a great deal of money and it was very easy to leave and live at around the same level of poverty. If I was trying to do something similar today, I would have a very big problem, because I now have a mortgage and I have commitments and a lifestyle I may not be prepared to give up.'

The idea of MAID was one of those 'eureka' brainwaves that hit Wagner forcibly while he was working with the new business team at WCRS. He soon found that when taking on a new account it was necessary to become instantly knowledgeable about a particular product area. Acquiring that knowledge was a laborious exercise, requiring a huge amount of leg work.

Wagner's novel idea was to approach market research publishers like the Economist Intelligence Unit and Euromonitor for exclusive deals to create a comprehensive database that advertising people could instantly access via a VDU. He offered the publishers 50 per cent royalties on all the material used by MAID customers. Says Wagner: 'What I wanted MAID to be was the only database that had information on every single advertiser and every single advertised market.'

Having the idea was one thing. Convincing investors it was a sound business proposition was something else. At first he was given the cold shoulder: 'Nobody wanted to even talk to me. Everyone was sceptical of a 20-year-old ex-adman talking about trying to put together a very high-profile, capital intensive business.'

The only answer was to rent space on an existing mainframe computer to contain start-up costs to a reasonable level. Wagner negotiated a deal with the Pergamon group to rent space on its on-line system and sought advice from IME, a leading information consultancy. He also gained access to Pergamon's communications satellite. Insists Wagner: 'This was by far the best route to go, because it basically meant we were able to link up to the world. If you were in Australia you dialled a local number through the satellite and you got access to MAID in a split-second linking.'

The first breakthrough came when Wagner managed to tie up an exclusive contract for a one-year test run with the Economist Intelligence Unit. But he was still left with the problem of having to raise the finance to pay for such an expensive operation. Even though renting someone else's mainframe was cheaper than providing his own hardware, the costs involved were by no means negligible. He ran up a £100,000 bill with Pergamon before even contemplating where the cash was going to come from. Admits Wagner: 'At this point I suddenly panicked. I realized I now had to raise some money because I couldn't pay this bill. Nor could I pay the consultant's bill of about £30,000 and other bits and pieces I had racked up.'

At the time he was drawing £22-a-week dole money. But Wagner never doubted that once he had the system up and running he would find the money. His conviction that his business idea was a winner never wavered: 'I'd done a business plan and it was very optimistic. I believed that people would be queueing up at the door to buy the service.'

They didn't – and they never have. Wagner soon discovered that however good an idea is, it has to be sold to prospective clients. It was naïve to expect the world to beat a path to his door. Getting his idea across to prospective customers would take time and his financial position was worsening by the day.

'Between February and September 1985 the bank tried to foreclose on a £1,500 loan, even though it was guaranteed by a friend. It was basically what I was using to run the company at the time. If I took a director of the Economist out to lunch I would draw it out of my personal overdraft.

'It was easier to run up bills with Pergamon and IME. I gave them the impression that I had loads of capital available. They didn't bill me until the work was completed. That was the agreement. When the work was completed I had a few months to raise the money.'

Wagner approached some City contacts for help. One of them was Tom Teichman, the general manager of the Bank of Montreal's London office, who has since become MAID's finance director. He helped Wagner put together an investment plan which the youthful entrepreneur hawked around the City. By January 1986 Wagner had managed to raise £187,000. The major backer was Hoare Octagon, the high-tech investment arm of Hoare Govett.

Wagner succeeded in convincing Octagon of the high-growth potential of his brainwave: 'The interest was primarily based on the fact that the fixed costs of the business, although high, would ultimately be covered by the subscriber base and then the renewals and new subscribers would show huge profitable growth, which is actually what has happened. I think they were influenced by that and by the youthful team I had put together. I was the oldest at twenty-one.'

Ian Barton, director of Octagon Investment Management and a non-executive director of MAID, confirms that evaluation: 'Octagon was attracted to MAID because it was a subscription-based service and that means that every year you keep customers happy they will renew their subscription. So you build up a revenue stream of committed customers who pay every year and in addition they pay for their usage of the system. The advantage of that kind of business is that the costs are largely fixed. It doesn't cost that much more whether you've got one or hundreds of users. And when your fixed costs are covered, the business should become profitable.'

Octagon initially invested £113,000 in MAID through a BES fund. But the anticipated build up of revenue took longer than everyone had anticipated. So Octagon invested a further

£100,000. Its faith was justified when MAID subsequently emerged as a market leader.

In the subsequent three years there were additional private and institutional investments in MAID, bringing the total amount raised to around £1 million. This included a rights issue in July 1987 which raised a further £136,000.

Wagner is convinced that getting the system up and running before attempting to raise the funds to pay for it was the right course to take, even if it did give him some sleepless nights: 'Once the system was running, even if it had very little data on it, raising money was a lot easier. I would never have got it off the ground if I had needed the money first, because nobody would have seen the product. When they saw it they could relate to it and understand that it was a valuable service.'

This was a view endorsed by Barton of Octagon: 'We weren't put off at all by the fact that Dan had already incurred costs of £130,000 creating a prototype. For someone who wants to raise venture capital, there is always a dilemma. If you try to get the money right up-front, venture capitalists will say it's only at the idea stage. The longer you can put off having to raise venture capital the more likely – if the idea is starting to take off – you are to get it and the better the terms will be, because you've got something demonstrable.'

In early 1986 Wagner approached Michael Mander, then the chairman of Thomson Information Services, hoping to persuade him to put an additional £500,000 into MAID. Mander was obliged to turn the request down because Thomson was not in the venture capital business and MAID didn't own the data on its computer system. Mander, who has since become non-executive chairman of MAID, described Thomson's reluctance to invest in the company as 'like giving up the rights to *Gone with the Wind*.' Recalls Mander:

'My impression was that MAID had a lot in common with many small growing companies – needing the cash to develop the business, but not having the business to attract the cash.

'There were good surprises that evolved within the business. One was that it was a system that when originally designed was aimed specifically at advertising agencies in the UK. The fact of the matter is more than half the clients are not from advertising agencies. It also hadn't been anticipated that the potential overseas would be as great as it turned out to be.'

Mander, now also chairman of the Institute of Directors, has given MAID the kind of experienced backing that ensures that Wagner's entrepreneurial flair is channelled in the right direction. Says Wagner: 'His influence has been phenomenal and his influence on international contacts has been instrumental in our growth.'

But the growth didn't come overnight and in the early stages MAID looked as though it might more closely resemble a B-movie flop than a *Gone with the Wind* blockbuster.

The problem initially was that Wagner made a fundamental miscalculation from the market research he carried out. He counted up the impressive number of computers owned by British companies that were potential clients but failed to check who operated them. In fact, the majority were used by accountants, not marketing people.

So he was confronted with the classical stumbling block of start-up companies: the idea was good and MAID had a dedicated management team willing to work all hours; but the customers were not materializing in sufficient numbers to cover the overheads. How Wagner and his management team solved the problem is outlined in Chapter 8, which deals with marketing issues.

CHAPTER 6

Business Angels

Increasingly the small business equity gap is being filled by private investors – or business angels as they have come to be known. They are aptly named because they often appear out of the blue to inject badly needed capital into Britain's cash-starved small firms.

The term 'angel' was first used to describe speculators who put money into theatrical shows in anticipation of rich rewards from backing a hit. Business angels similarly are on the look out for small firms with the potential to reap good returns for those with the foresight to invest in them at an early stage in their development. Private investors are stepping in where the clearing banks and venture capitalists often fear to tread.

The high street banks, reeling under the strain of bad debts, have been reluctant, particularly during a recession, to provide loans for all but the most water-tight business propositions. Venture capitalists have always shied away from small-scale investment – the administrative headaches are simply too great compared with the likely returns. That means the onus is falling increasingly on private investors to provide the funds for fledgling small firms.

There are reckoned to be around 400,000 potential informal investors in the UK, of which 50,000 are currently active. Even so, private investment is still largely an untapped funding source in the UK compared with the US where it is reckoned to be the single largest source of external equity capital for small businesses. A recent survey by MORI, the opinion poll group, found that while 60 per cent of a sample of British entrepreneurs had heard of business angels only a trifling one per cent had actually used them.

Potential for growth

There has been very little research into the supply of informal investment in the UK, but a survey by Colin Mason at the University of Southampton throws some light on the issue. It shows that most business angels are themselves businessmen, business professionals or entrepreneurs. They have relatively high incomes, but few could be described as wealthy.

The key factors they take into account when considering an investment opportunity are the management of the team and the growth potential of the market. The business angels studied by Mason had made investments of between £10,000 and £100,000. The average investment was £22,000. The minimum rates of return targeted by the private investors varied according to their perception of the risk involved. For example, the average ROI sought at the pre-start stage was 45 per cent, whereas a return of 21 per cent was acceptable from an investment in an established firm.

A quarter of the business angels in the Southampton University study felt their investments were performing above expectations, but over a third reported performances below expectation. On average, business angels anticipated holding their investments for between three and five years, but many were prepared to be patient. Almost a quarter of them were happy to hold their investments for up to ten years.

Mason concluded from his study that the key to a vigorous enterprise economy was finding new ways to 'unlock substantial sums of money that business angels have available for invest-ment'. Yet private investment is often the last resort for small business entrepreneurs. For example, if it were not for private investors, Martek, the company that sells drill bit sharpeners to customers all over the world, might never have got off the ground (see page 45).

Untapped

A study conducted in 1994 by Oxford University's Templeton College, sponsored by Venture Capital Report (VCR), revealed that the business angel market in the UK may be much richer and larger than previously believed. But the report concluded that the market is largely untapped because of a shortage of sufficiently attractive investment prospects and it recommended the setting up of a national network linking all the existing introduction agencies.

The survey identified that 262 of the near-500 angels contacted had invested more than £60 million in the previous three years in more than 600 firms. This suggested that the total funds invested by angels in Britain may be significantly more than the previous estimate of £2 billion. The report also found that the average investment was much greater than was previously thought to be the case — £120,000 against the conventional estimate of £20,000.

Tracking down the investors

There is no shortage of small companies looking for funds and there are undoubtedly many private investors seeking firms with good prospects. But tracking down these investors and achieving the right match is a lot harder than it might seem.

Venture Capital Report (VCR), a publication run by Lucius Cary from Henley-on-Thames since 1978, attempts to match investors with small firms in need of capital. Each month it features around ten businesses, typically seeking venture capital of between £30,000 and £150,000. VCR has over 600 subscribers. They are reckoned to be the largest group of active business angels in the UK. They pay an annual subscription of £300 to receive the monthly report. Businesses are charged £350 to have their projects published and a success fee of £1,000 plus 2.5 per cent of any risk capital raised through VCR.

A similar service is provided by CX *Monthly*, a publication produced by Capital Exchange Ltd., which offers to summarize the business plans of small firm entrepeneurs and circulate them to 20,000 subscribers, including 10,000 potential corporate and private investors.

Another match-making service called LINC (Local Investment Networking Company) handles investments of between £10,000 and £250,000 and operates through a network of local enterprise agencies.

The Department of Employment has also gone into the match-making game. It uses the network of Training and Enterprise Councils (TECs) as a 'marriage broker' between investors and promising small firms. The scheme was pioneered initially in five TEC regions – Bedfordshire, Calderdale and Kirklees, Devon and Cornwall, East Lancashire, and South and East Cheshire.

VCR claims to be the most interventionist of the match-making bureaux, assessing projects at a depth not attempted by other services. This, VCR argues, filters out the non-starters and gives busy investors a warts-and-all view of businesses, including the amount of equity on offer. VCR consultants spend half a day interviewing the applicant company and then compile a five-page summary of the business proposition for publication in the report.

In the first six months of 1994 VCR attracted a record £2.4 million of investment capital for twenty-one small businesses, doubling its normal rate of transactions. Since it was established, VCR claims to have been instrumental in achieving over 200 successful matches. Its clients have ranged from inventors and manufacturers to pubs and retailers. Five of them have attained a stock-market listing.

Staffordshire Development Association, part of the enterprise agency network, has been particularly successful in achieving a relatively large number of good matches. Robert Redfern, who runs the Staffordshire agency, organizes quarterly meetings at which small firms make presentations to investors.

Redfern partly attributes his success rate to the fact that the enterprise agency is attached to the economic development wing of Staffordshire County Council. This gives him access to larger financial resources than the typical enterprise agency and it also means he is in touch with a broad spectrum of contacts.

A more recent entry in the marriage bureau stakes is Enterprise Adventure, the first on-line computer database to put small firms in touch with wealthy individuals with money to invest. The new database, known as VentureList, aims to fill the gap encountered by companies seeking investments of between £20,000 and £250,000. Peter Benton, a former deputy chairman of British Telecom, whose brainchild it is, believes the computerized system is more than simply an addition to the field. He aims to build up a network embracing, rather than competing with, existing introductory agencies. His vision is a truly national means of putting investors and entrepreneurs in touch. Benton told a May 1994 issue of the *Sunday Times*: 'For that you need critical mass. Even if you add up all the existing agencies you still haven't got critical mass. What we bring is a register of strategic consultants.'

Enterprise Adventure has grown out of the old Enterprise Initiative scheme that used to be run by the Department of Trade and Industry. In seven years a network of 8,000 business consultants conducted thousands of studies of small businesses. Drawing on their experience and the links they forged, Benton, who was once director-general of the British Institute of Management, has been striving to bring a wide range of suitable investment opportunities into the database.

John Berry, who runs a Westcountry business angels scheme on behalf of Devon & Cornwall TEC, sees a real need to formalize the match-making process: 'There are a lot of ships that pass in the night and what we are doing is finding a way of more of these ships meeting each other. It does happen through informal networks of friends and accountants or whatever, but this is a chance to actually do it formally within our given area.'

But what motivates private investors? Why are they anxious to invest in high-risk firms? Bob Morton, a chartered accountant from Leamington Spa, who has acted as a business angel for a number of small firms, is enthusiastic about the concept: 'I am sure there's a lot of private investors with capital, but the problem is that most of them are not financial people. The growth potential from a small business is far greater than from investing in a blue-chip stock-market company because you are building it up from an organic base. Everyone takes a sensible salary and all the profits are ploughed back and we build the company organically so that all the capital comes from trading profits.'

Active participation

Many business angels are seeking more than just financial rewards. Observes John Berry: 'Obviously there's a feeling that they are going to make money out of it in the end. That's got to be an objective, but probably more importantly it's what the Americans describe as *hot buttons* or *psychic income*. It's that you actually derive fun from doing it. You want to be involved in something that is growing and exciting.'

Research by LINC supports the view that business angels are looking for active participation. Says Fiona Conoley, general manager of London Enterprise Agency, which co-ordinates the LINC network: 'Our investors are typically self-made and quite young. Half of them are under fifty. Around 75 per cent of them have set up at least one business of their own at some stage and about half of that number have set up two or three. So they're very entrepreneurial types themselves. They have reached the stage where their own businesses are running well enough that they can afford to get involved in something else. It's like buying an extra part of their career without having the hard graft of starting right from scratch again.'

The degree of involvement varies enormously, according to LINC's research. Says Conoley: 'It can be one day every two weeks or maybe five days a week and we are beginning to get the sort of people who have perhaps been forced to take early retirement. They are a different kettle of fish to the people we already have on our books. They are the people who are actually buying themselves a new job.'

The need for involvement often means that business angels pick companies that are in their own neighbourhood, so they can watch progress first-hand. Suggests Berry:

'It's partly altruism, if you like, in terms of supporting things in your local community. That's one element of the fun part of it. Business angels do appear to want the companies they invest in to be accessible, so they can get involved, so that they can put their experience in as well as their money.

'What we are really pushing for is not the passive investor, but someone who can actually provide experience as well as investment. In the long term it is probably going to be the experience that's going to be more important than the actual money, because it is extraordinary what doors become unlocked when you've got somebody who's got a good track record and good business experience. All sorts of financial doors and marketing doors open, which is not the case when you're a little tin-pot company that nobody has ever heard of.'

Bill McPherson, who has made a number of investments in small firms since he left industry in the mid-sixties, likes the firms to be within reasonable reach. None of the businesses has been more than seventy miles from his London base. A pharmaceutical chemist by training, McPherson sticks close to what he knows. All his investments have been in developed retail chemists.

McPherson always takes a majority stake in the business he invests in and he likes a hands-on role in the management. He explains: 'We've always looked for run-down businesses with potential. It's either due to incompetence or illness. There are a lot of run-down businesses, but few of them have any significant potential. It's the upside that is the attraction – to buy them for a song and sell them at a good profit.'

Lucius Cary of VCR has experienced tremendous variety in the private investors enquiring into projects on his books: 'Someone who had been a subscriber for years was suddenly quite interested in one of our projects. He flew down in his helicopter and turned out to be one of the richest men in the UK. Another subscriber who came to see me had sold his farm for £2 million. He put £1 million in the bank and he wanted to invest the other £1 million in five or six things that were going to give him an interest. Then we've had some people who have had a golden handshake and they've got £250,000 and they'd maybe like to acquire a job.'

Cary, too, detects that investors are motivated by more than financial gain: 'There's a great non-financial buzz that comes from the whole thing. You battle away and you finally get your product into Tesco, for example, and suddenly it all begins to motor. I would say that no business angel subscribes purely for the financial returns. They subscribe because it gives them excitement which you can't get from stock-market investing.'

Backing a winner

Money may not be the prime motivator, but there's even more satisfaction for the business angel when he backs a real winner. In 1981 Sir John Aird, a multi-millionaire businessman who made his fortune investing in the commodities market and the building trade and a long-time subscriber to VCR, invested an initial £12,000 for a 33 per cent stake in a small company, called Matcon Control Engineering, selling a revolutionary pneumatic bin activator for the materials handling market. Today the company – now known as Matcon BULS – has an annual turnover of £12 million and Sir John's total investment of £23,000 is reckoned to be worth over £2.5 million. (See page

129). Comments Cary of VCR: 'You won't get that sort of return on the stock market.'

Angels come in many guises

National Westminster Bank, which has its own database of angels, has identified three main categories:

- The *patron angel* usually has a net worth in excess of £5 million, with £1 million plus to invest. They are often heads of long-established families, with substantial portions of their wealth in land. They are looking for good returns over long periods and may or may not take an active role in the business.
- The *entrepreneurial angel* is the most common investor. They are typically entrepeneurs who have built up and sold a business and may have £500,000 to invest. They are likely to take a close interest in any company they invest in.
- The *occupational angel* is normally a manager or executive with relatively small sums to invest, up to say £500,000. They have limited experience and are first-time investors.

The Oxford University/VCR study identified six species of business angel:

- *Virgin angels* have funds available and want to make their first investment, but have yet to find a suitable proposal. Their available funds for angel investment are slightly less than half that of active angels. Although they are generally less rich than active angels, they do not cite lack of funds as restricting their investment behaviour, but rather an absence of suitable proposals.
- *Latent angels* are rich individuals who have made angel investments but not in the past three years, principally because of a lack of suitable locally-based proposals. They tend to be significantly wealthier and more entrepreneurial than virgin angels and have more funds available.

- *Wealth maximizing angels* are rich and experienced businessmen who invest in several businesses for financial gain. They are not as rich as entrepreneurial angels, but they tend to make as many investments by investing slightly smaller amounts in each.
- *Entrepreneurial angels* are very rich, very entrepreneurial individuals who back businesses for both the fun of it and as a better option than the stock market. They are older than other angels, less inclined to co-invest, and while they usually take minority stakes, they take majority stakeholdings more often than other individual angel types. They enjoy the 'buzz' of being involved and they do not appear to be too concerned about the proximity of the business in which they invest.
- *Income seeking angels* are less affluent individuals who invest some funds in a business, often to generate an income or even a job for themselves. They typically make significantly fewer investments, are less entrepreneurial and have founded the least number of businesses.
- *Corporate angels* are companies which make numerous large angel type investments often for majority stakes. They have corporate resources at their disposal which enable them to make more frequent investments and they consistently invest significantly higher levels of funds in each investment than any of the other angel types.

The University of Southampton study revealed that business angels often fail to find sufficient investment opportunities. On average the informal investors in Mason's survey had a further £50,000 available for investment; but 'because informal investors are largely anonymous, and hence invisible, the search for an entrepreneur is often unsuccessful'. Mason quotes a leading US authority on informal risk capital, who described the process as 'a giant game of hide-and-seek with everyone blindfolded'.

What business angels seek in entrepreneurs

A guide to what business angels are looking for in entrepreneurs and their business plan has been drawn up by Hamish Stevenson, the VCR director:

● *Talented people and personal fit.* Business angels seek substantial financial gains, principally through investing in people. Hence the saying that investors are as interested in backing jockeys as they are in backing horses. Amounts invested typically range from as little as £10,000 to £2 million, as a mixture of both debt and equity. Business plans, therefore, need to give very detailed CVs of the key managers and what they have achieved. When potential angels first meet entrepreneurs they will be looking for a good personal chemistry. They will want to feel confident that the business is offering something distinctly different and that the targets and assumptions are achievable.

● *Substantial long-term gains and fun.* Investors will risk their capital and will not normally expect to receive any interest or repayments in the short term provided they believe their long-term (three years plus) stake will eventually return substantial profits. Angels generally expect their investment to be worth the equivalent of a compound rate of return of upwards of 30 per cent, and significantly higher returns are expected for higher risk investments. Angels also look for the fun and satisfaction of helping a company to grow.

● *Specifics of funds needed.* If an entrepreneur's proposal is to be effective in attracting an investor it must set out clearly what funds are needed, what they are needed for and what percentage of equity is being offered relative to the other existing shareholdings. No matter how good the people, the product or the projections, any serious investor will first want to see a current balance sheet, and in particular a detailed breakdown of current liabilities. The sooner accurate information is provided, the sooner the real negotiations can start. Angels expect to take equity stakes ranging from 25 per cent to 50 per cent, often in redeemable preference shares, which ensure that the first profits of the company are used to repay the investment capital, before management bonuses and dividends etc – and often before any salary increases.

- *Strategic vision and details of existing revenues and costs*. Entrepreneurs need to set out what is unique about the business and to provide a grand strategic vision of exactly how they will meet the forecasts. However, entrepreneurs also need to show that they have a ready grasp of their existing position, why they attract and retain their current customers, what their monthly revenues and costs are, what their margins are, and what they require to break even. Cash flow and profit and loss projections, and the key assumptions behind these forecasts, must be realistic and must be understood by entrepreneurs and not just their financial adviser.

- *Understanding of the risks and critical success factors*. The market place usually ensures that the higher the risk, the higher the potential return. Entrepreneurs' business plans must acknowledge the risks and show how they will be contained. Entrepreneurs and angels also need to have a firm understanding of, and belief in, the company and its products, as well as a good grasp of the critical success factors and why customers will purchase their products in preference to other potential competitors, and what the strengths and weaknesses of the competition are. At the outset, entrepreneurs must use existing results, details of market trends, and, in particular, customer testimonials to demonstrate the sustained need for their products to interest angels.

What entrepreneurs should seek in a business angel

Stevenson has also compiled a useful set of guidelines for what entrepreneurs should look for in a business angel:

- *Personal chemistry and enthusiastic long-term commitment*. Entrepreneurs of course need to find an investor with suitable cash resources and someone with whom they will enjoy a personal rapport. However, investors need to be more than just nice people. Also, not all business angels are acting as individuals, but as companies looking for suitable opportunities. Angels secure joint ownership and will therefore need to share a strategic vision of the company, and in particular they will need to be joint contributors in good *and* hard times. Ideally, investors need to make complementary contributions and to have a shared belief in how to achieve their vision.

- *Ready cash and additional resources.* A good investor is a decisive one, someone who follows up promises with hard cash after conducting the necessary, sensible, but not protracted, due diligence and legal procedures. Angels can provide vital strategic input and may also contribute additional resources, such as manufacturing or distribution capacity, and informal industry contacts, resulting in new customers and suppliers. Investors' contributions to the business ideally also change with the development stage of the business. At the earlier stages they can provide a free pair of hands and advice; whereas, at the later stages they can be a good sounding board when, for instance, securing additional funding or appropriate exit routes.

- *Successful track record of founding and funding businesses.* Investors who have founded their own business and 'have been there before' are more likely to empathize with entrepreneurs and be able to give relevant advice. However, ironically, sometimes because of their success, angels may need to be reminded about the original 'nuts and bolts' of running a small business without the support facilities many successful businessmen become accustomed to. Good sportsmen do not always make good coaches. Strong-minded entrepreneurs cannot work with angels who demand that their way is the only way of doing things. Also, just as angels need to know details about entrepreneurs' backgrounds, so too, should entrepreneurs ask angels if they can talk to other people that the angel has backed or founded a business with.

- *Similar expectations and fair legal agreements.* If the chemistry is right, if there is a shared vision, and the cash and additional resources are readily available, the entrepreneur and investor need to sit down and confirm their respective expectations and legal agreements. These agreements must be seen by all parties as simple, fair and workable in practice, and legally enforceable should the need arise. The angel is essentially backing the entrepreneur and his/her team and will therefore expect a legal agreement to make them accountable. This accountability will require the drawing up of fair, and relatively flexible service contracts, performance related pay, payment schedules and agreement of what actions will be taken if agreed targets are not met, and how to ensure an exit route for the investor which may also allow the entrepreneur to re-acquire 100 per cent ownership.

- *Mutual trust and respect.* Finally, the most important criterion is that there is mutual respect and trust. This trust can be difficult to create at the outset, but must be built upon. The partnership should be financially rewarding and generally satisfying for both parties. Although entrepreneurs are effectively in a position of control, a successful partnership requires a sense of joint ownership and control; otherwise both angel and entrepreneur can enforce their respective legal rights and make life unbearable for each other.

Enterprise Investment Scheme (EIS)

The business angels movement was given a boost in the government's autumn 1993 Budget with the introduction of the Enterprise Investment Scheme, which provides an alternative source of finance to the high street banks and offers tax incentives to would-be investors. Intended as a replacement for the Business Expansion Scheme (BES), which was phased out in 1994, the EIS could open the door to a capital market estimated to be worth up to £4 billion.

It allows investors 20 per cent tax relief on investments of up to

£100,000 in any one year. In addition, 100 per cent relief is available for capital gains up to £250,000 and 50 per cent on gains up to £750,000.

On top of that, tax on capital gains re-invested in another enterprise can be deferred under the rules of the scheme.

The EIS has similar aims to the former BES, but the latter tended to get side-tracked into housing schemes and a variety of esoteric projects which had little to do with helping the UK's small business entrepreneurs get off the ground.

KEY POINTS

- Private investors (or Business Angels) are increasingly helping to bridge the small business equity gap.
- Venture capitalists are reluctant to make small-scale investments that are costly to administer and promise inadequate returns.
- Business Angels tend to be businessmen, business professionals or entrepreneurs with relatively high incomes.
- They generally make investments of between £10,000 and £100,000 – sums that do not interest most venture capitalists.
- 'Marriage Bureau' agencies attempt to match investors with small firms in need of capital.
- Business Angels see more growth potential in small businesses than blue-chip companies because the former are being built up from an organic base.
- Making money is not always the prime motivation of Business Angels. They also enjoy the 'psychic income' from investing in small firms.

CASE STUDY
Matcon BULS

In February 1981, Ivan Semenenko, a Ukrainian-born entrepreneur, living in the UK, sought a business angel who was prepared to invest up to £100,000 in his small company making a revolutionary bin activator for the materials handling market. An article about the company in *Venture Capital Report* attracted the attention of Sir John Aird, a multi-millionaire businessman and a long-time subscriber to VCR, which matches investors and small companies.

At the time, the company – Matcon Control Engineering – was very small, but what Semenenko lacked in business experience he made up for in technical ability. He had been working on bin activators as a professional design engineer for the past four years and had worked for Chubb Locks and Safe Ltd., where he had risen to become chief design engineer. In 1977 he joined Solitec, a leading designer of vibrating annular bin discharge systems, as design manager. He left Solitec in 1979 to form his own company and to work on new designs. He subsequently patented a number of his innovative ideas.

The final prototype for the revolutionary bin activator that was to prove a market winner was completed in 1980. Semenenko sent a letter to thirty companies in the industry trying to engage their interest in the project and followed this up with telephone calls. This resulted in fifteen enquiries and five visits by interested parties to see the first activator being tested. Semenenko received his first two orders in January 1981, each for one small activator costing about £1,500.

Up to this point, the company had been funded by Semenenko and a business partner to the tune of about £3,500 each and they had received an injection of £15,000 from Barclays Bank under its business start-up scheme. The loan was interest free and unsecured. Barclays negotiated a 0.5 per cent royalty on gross sales for a five-year period.

This was enough funding to keep the company turning over, but Semenenko was keen to seek more investment to increase his staff (at that time only one testing technician) and to undertake overseas licences. He also planned to move into manufacturing his own products rather than contracting the work out.

Sir John Aird spotted the report in *VCR* and recognized the potential of Semenenko's invention. He invested an initial £12,000 for a 33 per cent stake in Matcon and became a director of the firm. Shortly afterwards Semenenko's business partner sold his stake to Sir John who invested a further £11,000 and became a 50 per cent shareholder. He worked part-time as Matcon's financial director and eventually became its chairman.

In October 1993 the BBC's *The Money Programme* referred to Sir John as 'one of Britain's most successful business angels', and estimated his investment of £23,000 to be worth over £2.5 million.

He was, on the face of it, an unlikely small business saviour. A true blue-blooded aristocrat, he was born at Windsor Castle, the son of a former equerry to the then Prince of Wales. He inherited an interest in engineering from his great grandfather, a famous nineteenth-century contractor who built the Aswan Dam in Egypt. For a while, he designed dams in the Sudan, but later went to Harvard Business School after deciding to switch from pure engineering to management. He went on to make his fortune investing in the commodities market and in the building industry.

Sir John has a number of self-imposed investment guidelines. He must be impressed by the people he is backing, interested in their product and they must be based close to his home. He tends to avoid pure start-ups.

In addition, he likes to leave the managing partner with as much of the equity that he or she can afford to take. He does not insist on a majority stake. As he told Richard Gourlay in an article on the Management page of the *Financial Times*: 'I feel having control is irrelevant. The entrepreneur always effectively has control whatever percentage of the stock is his. An investor can only really exert negative control – you can forbid or prevent, but it is difficult to be pro-active without the co-operation of the entrepreneur.'

Sir John's shrewd investment in Matcon stemmed from his ability to spot a bright idea and recognize its potential – the true art of being a business angel. It did not take long for Matcon to demonstrate that his faith in its potential was well-founded. Sales took off in a spectacular fashion. From 1981 to 1993 Matcon has grown steadily from one employee to a staff of seventy-eight and sales of £12 million in 1993. In 1988 the company won the largest order ever for materials control in Europe.

During its steady climb to prominence, Matcon has introduced a number of innovative products in the field of materials handling and it has become a world leader in the field of materials control. Many different applications use the same principles and Matcon now has an impressive list of blue-chip customers.

Matcon acquired BULS from the receiver in February 1990, is now known as Matcon BULS, and has expanded internationally. In 1989 it established a wholly-owned subsidiary in New Jersey in the US with five full-time employees. The US subsidiary has an additional twenty manufacturers' representatives throughout the US. Matcon started manufacturing in the US during 1992 with sales of around $4 million. It has also established a presence in Europe and Scandinavia and has established licensees and offices in South Africa, Japan and Australia.

(This case study has been extracted from *Venture Capital Report* (VCR) by kind permission of the publishers.)

CHAPTER 7

Deciding Where to Set Up

Selecting the right premises for your business takes time and effort. Premises can be critical to the success of your business and, if you make a mistake, it can be costly. In its guide to starting a small business Midland Bank advises that the following factors need to be taken into consideration:

- whether to work from home, a shop, an office, a workshop or a factory
- the size of the premises and whether they will be sufficient for future requirements
- their location, particularly if you will be relying on passing trade. Monitor the kind of customers you will attract and how many there are likely to be
- availability of gas, water and electricity
- whether you should rent or buy the freehold
- local crime rates and security requirements
- car parking facilities
- maintenance and running costs
- rent and uniform business rate
- refurbishment costs including telephones, fax machines, filing cabinets, tills, photocopiers, office furniture and computers.

Your final choice may depend on what you can afford. Grants

are available in some Assisted Areas (see page 62). Whatever premises you choose, arrange for a survey to be carried out.

Working from home

Small business entrepreneurs are increasingly taking up the option of working from home. It reduces travel costs and business overheads, but you need to make sure that the clauses in your tenancy agreement or legal title to the property do not prevent you from doing so. If in doubt, consult your solicitor. Also make sure that your house insurance is adequate. Your policy may need to be extended to cover business activities.

Some costs such as telephone, heating and lighting, incurred through working at home, may be allowable for tax purposes, and reduce your tax bill. It is also important to realize that if you decide to sell your home at some future date, the part of it used for business purposes may be liable to capital gains tax. It would be advisable to consult your accountant.

Information about the availability of premises can be obtained from:

- the economic development unit of your local authority
- estate agents and business transfer agents
- local newspapers and commercial property magazines
- science parks (usually attached to a university)
- local enterprise agencies (see page 66)

Some local enterprise agencies provide managed workshops, studios, offices and/or desk space specially for small businesses. These work places often have conference rooms, fax machines and photocopiers and secretarial pools which can be used on a shared cost basis. You are not usually locked into a long-term lease which means you can occupy the premises on a month by month basis. This allows you to move premises quickly, cheaply and with minimum legal formalities if your business suddenly expands or contracts.

Technological advances

Advancing technology is making it possible for small firms to set up wherever their owners choose. One of the disadvantages of working from home used to be the lack of office equipment. But the price of even the most sophisticated electronic aids has been dropping steadily over the years. It no longer costs a fortune to equip the home worker with the essentials of running a business.

Many homes now have personal computers that are used for other than business purposes. If you add to that a fax machine, a conference telephone, and an answerphone machine you are pretty well set up to meet every business need. Rapid advances are also being made with electronic mail facilities and even videophones, but they are by no means essential and it will probably be some time before they come within the financial grasp of the average home worker.

Such technological advances have led to predictions that teleworking will become a rapidly growing phenomenon, reducing the stresses and strains of having to travel daily to work and the other disadvantages associated with jammed highways and pollution from exhaust fumes. The revolution has not happened as fast as was expected, largely because employers have difficulty coping with the idea that employees can work unsupervised from home.

There is no such hang-up for the self-employed, however. The small firm operating from home can use the latest technology to be in touch with clients just as though he or she were on their doorstep. Location is of little consequence which means small business entrepreneurs are free to set up wherever it suits them. They can operate just as effectively from the wilds of Scotland or from an island off the coast of Britain.

This has inevitably led to an exodus from city centres to country locations where all the benefits of a rural environment can be enjoyed. It is a development that has been encouraged by the Rural Development Commission (RDC), which is anxious to maintain healthy population levels in country villages. The RDC has helped the development by offering grants to farmers and entrepreneurs to convert disused barns into work stations for single or communal use. It has also encouraged the growth of telecottages.

The telecottage

The telecottage is an idea that first took root in Sweden, but is catching on rapidly in this country. The idea is to provide a communal centre which is equipped with all the latest information technology and electronic gadgets. Business people operating from home or working in local units can then share the costs involved as well as enjoying the social aspects of meeting at a central point – thus overcoming the loneliness often associated with teleworking.

Coping with the problem of social isolation was a key feature of an experiment conducted by British Telecom in 1993 in the Highlands of Scotland. BT provided facilities for eleven women handling directory enquiry calls at the Inverness directory assistance centre to enable them to operate from their homes. Among the array of sophisticated gadgets that allowed the women to link up with the BT centre in Inverness were videophones that provided the next best thing to physical contact.

Up to now teleworking has mainly been confined to professionals, such as computer programmers and freelance journalists. The BT experiment was endeavouring to prove that, given the proper technological back-up, clerical workers can operate from home too.

BT admits that it had a vested interest in the experiment. Lessons learned from the pioneering work with the directory enquiry staff could pave the way for numerous other teleworking projects. Ticket agencies, insurance firms, mail order businesses, credit checking agencies and businesses handling large numbers of invoices are among the many organizations that lend themselves to the concept. That represents an enormous potential market for advanced BT telecommunications equipment.

Inevitably the directory enquiry women involved in the experiment experienced initial difficulties in adapting to the use of the sophisticated telecommunications gadgets, such as electronic mail and electronic bulletin boards. But according to Mike Grey, who was responsible for the experiment, they learned fast: 'We designed a system to give the operators as many different ways of keeping in touch as we could. Some of the equipment they were given was fairly leading edge and quite expensive. It's not the sort of thing we would expect anyone to copy as it stands, although the price of videophones is falling rapidly.'

BT is hoping that the experiment will help it to come up with specifications for a minimum set of facilities and services that are necessary to keep someone working happily from home and which can be produced and mass marketed economically.

The BT experiment also helped with research into the personality traits that best suit people for teleworking. This is an important consideration for people planning to set up a business from home using these kind of IT facilities. Of course, the small business entrepreneur who chooses to operate from a remote location probably has the kind of temperament that enjoys isolation and rural tranquillity. Such working conditions certainly don't favour the ambitious extrovert.

Predictions about how quickly teleworking will take off vary considerably. The Henley Centre for Forecasting has predicted that there will be somewhere between five and ten million people involved in teleworking within the next few years, although many of these will be employed rather than self-employed. British Telecom estimates that up to 20 million people could be teleworkers by the start of the next century. Part of the problem in trying to arrive at an accurate forecast lies in the difficulty of finding an exact definition of teleworking. In any event, there are already signs that teleworkers are becoming a significant part of economic life and that they are organizing themselves into a more coherent entity.

The National Association of Teleworkers (NAT) was formed in 1992 to promote teleworking more effectively and create a code of practice for the industry. Explains Richard Field, NAT's chief executive: 'We have developed a system for linking teleworkers into loose-knit consortia to bid for contracts on a much larger scale than they could hope to do on an individual basis.'

Field points out that the recession has compelled companies to outsource peripheral activities, but that they have been uncertain in the past how to approach the teleworking market place. Rural development agencies are showing particular interest in the sector. Field's own economic research firm, Cornix Ltd., has carried out a project for Devon and Cornwall TEC. He observes: 'Teleworking is being seen as a very advantageous activity for rural areas because economic activity can be increased with a minimal impact on the infrastructure.'

On the macro level, teleworking has started to leap across geographic boundaries. Says Field: 'There are already large-scale exchanges of relatively low-skilled but regular quantities of data processing being shipped through telecommunications to any-where it is cheap to do it.' He cites the example of Jamaica which has been turned into a *teleport*: 'That's like a freeport, but purely for telecommunications. They've worked out advantageous terms with telecommunications networks and they now market to the US and the UK, offering data processing facilities on a large scale. In Southern Ireland there are a number of companies processing claims for the American insurance industry and they do an overnight service.'

The technology is now in place for teleworkers to operate from almost anywhere in the world, servicing almost any part of the globe. The age of location-independent entrepreneurs has surely arrived. The world is their oyster.

Rural growth

Small businesses are flourishing in the countryside, according to the Rural Development Commission which is the government agency concerned with the well-being of people who live and work in England's rural areas. It helps create jobs by investing in new rural workshops and by providing grants and loans for social projects. It has helped hundreds of budding entrepreneurs from urban areas who have moved into small towns and villages and they in turn have helped to fuel an economic revival. The jobs they have created, claims the RDC, have protected country areas against the worst of the recession and helped to halt general economic decline in rural areas.

Between 1981 and 1989, employment in the countryside grew by 15 per cent compared to eight per cent in towns. A recent survey shows that even in the worst years of the recession, from 1988 to 1991, firms in remote rural areas created an average of four jobs each while comparable enterprises in towns were shedding labour.

The Commission has teams of skilled business advisers who assess business plans and help new enterprises through the financial and bureaucratic maze with which they are often confronted.

It has produced a free booklet entitled *The Countryside Means Business* which illustrates how well small-scale industry fits into rural life. Case studies of successful firms in rural locations all over England are aimed at persuading more people to start businesses in the countryside. Small business entrepreneurs cited in the booklet say that they believe that the country environment helps them achieve high-quality design and workmanship and say they have found flexible, motivated and accomplished work forces.

The business entrepreneurs also speak appreciatively of the availability of labour, the loyalty of their workforce and the lower crime levels. They believe their rural location helps improve their firms' image and relationships with customers.

It is not generally realized that employment in high technology businesses has grown fastest in rural areas. Observes Lord Shuttleworth, the RDC's chairman: 'The growth in the number, range and output of rural business has been an under-publicized success story. They are making a significant contribution to national output.' He believes that businesses in the countryside have the potential to be one of the main factors in Britain's future economic growth as it pulls out of the recession.

The RDC cites the success of a manufacturing firm tucked away near the toe of Britain to illustrate that distance from London is no longer an economic drawback. The Helston firm of AP Valves in Cornwall is a classic example of how one man's ingenuity can provide many others with a living. David Parker, the firm's managing director, was a Midlands' engineer who took up sports diving as a hobby in the 1960s. He soon realized that equipment developed for the Caribbean was unsuited to the colder, less clear waters around Britain.

So he made his own scuba set on a lathe in his garage and produced a breathing apparatus that was far safer than the American equipment that was on the market. In 1971 he patented the crucial part of the design, the AP valve, and in 1978 sold his hardware business near Coventry and moved with his wife and son to Helston.

Now the family firm employs forty-five full-time staff, has a turnover of nearly £2 million a year and produces a wide variety of diving components. Demand for the firm's buoyancy jacket, which provides emergency air to a diver whose normal supply runs out, exceeds the firm's production capacity.

Parker moved to Helston because he was enticed with the offer of a 15 per cent grant and a rent-free factory for two years from the RDC. 'Without that we would not have done it because we had practically no capital. For the first couple of years we thought we were dead. Now we are probably Helston's biggest employer.'

Workshop units

In rural areas, business premises are either privately owned or provided by county and district councils or the RDC. The RDC has built some 2,800 workshop units and has provided well over 800 units in partnership with local authorities and trusts.

These premises are normally available for sale or rent, mostly on easy-in, easy-out terms. In some cases rent concessions are available for a limited period. In addition, the RDC is looking at ways to increase privately-led development of workspace and sometimes offers financial assistance in its Rural Development Areas. These are areas designated by the RDC which are suffering from a range of social and economic problems.

The RDC also offers some serviced sites, ready for sale to the private sector for further development.

In some areas, local authorities and local enterprise agencies have established 'managed' workshops. These vary from place to place, but they usually offer, in addition to the basic workshop units, some central support, for example, advice, training and secretarial and other common services.

Advice

The RDC can provide general business advice or put you in touch with more specialized building or planning consultants. ADAS – the food, farming, land and leisure consultancy previously known as the Agricultural Development and Advisory Service – can provide full consultancy on building conversions.

The RDC, ADAS or your Regional Tourist Board should be able to give advice on turning a redundant building into a tourist amenity.

Conversions

Rural communities and farms have a ready stock of disused or redundant buildings. These are often suitable for renovation and conversion to new uses; for example, manufacturing (from high technology to traditional crafts), professional services, tourism and leisure and sports.

Government policy is to encourage the conversion of redundant buildings in rural areas. The buildings themselves can vary from disused railway stations to old mills and barns. Do not be put off if the building is listed on the grounds of architectural or historical importance. The procedure for obtaining the necessary building consent from local planning authorities is generally quite straightforward. In some cases you may be able to obtain grants for repairs and renovations from local authorities or English Heritage.

In certain circumstances conversion of such buildings for small firms or for tourism may be permittd within the Green Belt, especially if they are attractive to look at and can be expected – with normal repair and maintenance – to last for many years.

The RDC can provide grants of 25 per cent of the cost of conversion in its Priority Areas and some other designated areas. Other grants are available, in some areas, from the DTI.

Loans for premises, equipment or working capital

Through its loan schemes, the RDC offers 'top up' finance for property acquisition and development, the purchase of equipment, and in some cases, an injection to boost working capital. Its interest rates are similar to commercial rates, but its requirements for security can be less demanding than those of banks. For example, the RDC may be able to offer unsecured loans if the available assets of the business are already charged to other lenders. Its involvement in financing projects for rural businesses sometimes encourages other lenders.

A transformed grain store

Grey Matter Ltd., a computer software business run from a converted 100-year-old former seed store at Ashburton by Ian Rangeley, who moved from London to Devon in 1986, is another success story. Rangeley set up the company with just himself and a technical director. It now has a staff of twenty-five and a £3 million annual turnover stocking and supplying software for computer programmers. Having survived the worst of the recession, Rangeley is optimistic about the future: 'We have soldiered on through the recession and apart from one brief turndown have expanded steadily. In the next five to ten years we would like to see ourselves twice or even ten times as big.'

Grey Matter's total spend to convert the former seed store was £100,000. It borrowed 70 per cent of that from the bank and obtained a loan from the RDC (then known as CoSIRA) for the remaining 30 per cent. The RDC also made available a 25 per cent redundant building grant towards the conversion costs.

Rangeley designed and supervised the interior of the new building himself, spurning any advice from a professional architect, who he suspects would have probably wanted to 'gild the lily'. He does admit, however, that he should perhaps have consulted an architect for the design of the main staircase. He recalls with amusement: 'The local carpenter misunderstood my drawings on the back of an envelope. He put one step too few at the top flight and one step too many in the bottom flight. So if you're taller than 6ft, there is a danger of you banging your head on the ceiling!'

Despite such minor miscalculations, the 6,000 sq. ft. converted building attracted widespread admiration. It won a prestigious award sponsored by the RDC and The Country Landowners' Association. Rangeley received the award from the hands of Prince Charles at a ceremony held in the grounds of Highgrove, the Prince's country seat. The Devon entrepreneur was warmly applauded for turning a virtually redundant building into a stylish workplace and for creating badly-needed new jobs.

Building your own premises

Your district council will have information on sites earmarked for development and can advise you on the planning implications. You will need to ensure that you comply with all legal requirements, including building and fire regulations. If you propose to establish a new industry – notably manufacturing or food processing – you should seek advice from your local water company about the effluent that your industry is allowed to produce.

The Farming and Wildlife Advisory Group (FWAG) can help developers to understand wildlife, landscape and environmental issues by looking at the areas around specific sites as well as maintaining the wildlife interest on the site itself.

Direction signs

For all businesses in rural areas, adequate signposts are most important if you want business callers and casual visitors to find you. You need planning permission before they can be erected and you should contact the planning department of your local authority for information and guidance.

Farmers turned entrepreneurs

The changing economic climate has not only led to former town-dwellers moving to the country to set up in business; it has also turned many farmers into small business entrepreneurs. Common Market food mountains and EC quotas have combined to make many formerly successful farms unviable. In an effort to salvage their dwindling incomes, farmers have launched enterprises that are far removed from crop growing or rearing cattle and sheep.

They have not only made redundant farm buildings available for conversion for the influx of entrepreneurs from urban areas; they have seen ways to convert whole farms into lucrative business enterprises, ranging from tourist attractions to recreational centres and snail production for French gourmets.

In the Westcountry a consultancy has been set up to advise farmers on how to diversify into other businesses – an idea that may well be taken up in other parts of the country. The consultancy, Landowning Initiatives near Honiton in Devon, is run from an obsolete farm building and old milking parlour converted into an office.

Former Army officer and estate agent Michael Ford and his wife Caroline have turned diversification from a hit-and-miss art into something more akin to a science. After four years of running the consultancy, they and their business partners have devised a 'menu' of more than 3,000 diversification possibilities listed alphabetically.

No longer is diversification just a matter of doing a bit of Bed & Breakfast, converting a barn into holiday homes or opening yet another farm shop. Farmers and landowners wanting to make the most of their countryside assets are now tackling the diversification challenge on a much broader basis.

The range of possible schemes is virtually limitless. Projects Landowning Initiatives has worked on include turning a farmhouse on Snowdon in North Wales into a multi-lingual translation bureau; marketing venison on behalf of a group of West-country deer farmers; and turning a redundant building in an area of outstanding beauty into a small-scale saw mill.

KEY POINTS

- Choosing the right premises can be critical to your success.
- Working from home reduces overheads and saves travelling costs and time.

- Information technology is making it possible for small firms to set up wherever they like.
- Telecottages provide centralized office services in rural areas.
- Teleworking – once mainly the preserve of computer programmers and freelance journalists – is becoming available to everyone.
- Small firms are flourishing in the countryside with help from the Rural Development Commission.
- Workshops can be secured on easy-in, easy-out terms to reduce the financial pressures on start-up firms.

CASE STUDY
Bow Bangles

Bow Bangles is a chain of walk-in shops Mark Smith has set up at key town-centre sites all over Britain, selling low-price fashion accessories. Colourful pendants, earrings and other fashionable trinkets are displayed on wall racks in compact shops that are highly accessible to its customers, who are predominantly young women looking for low-cost items to brighten their appearance.

Smith, in contrast to most of his competitors, has benefited from the recession. The main reason is that few of Bow Bangles' fashion items cost more than £10. Even in the economic climate of the early 1990s people were prepared to part with such small sums to bring a little colour to their lives.

The recession has also been a great boon to Smith's expansion plans. The ambitious Birmingham-based retailer has set his company a target of 100 shops throughout the UK by 1996. In pre-recession boom times his goal was threatened by soaring shop rentals. But as the recession took hold landlords, anxious to find occupants for shopping mall developments, enticed Bow Bangles with attractive concessions. They were even prepared to pay up to £20,000 for the fitting out of new Bow Bangles' shops.

The rationale behind Smith's expansion plans is simple. The more profitable retail outlets he can create, the less onerous become the overheads of his Birmingham head office and warehouse.

Smith went to work for NatWest straight after leaving school, but soon decided a banking career was not for him. Seeking greater independence, he travelled to Israel to pick grapes on a kibbutz. On his return to the UK, he ran a market stall at the Birmingham Bull Ring, selling bric-a-brac. Here he learned the first principles of trading – make enough money to cover your overheads and to be able to buy more stock. Recalls Smith: 'The market taught me the basics of trading – what's your rent? how much margin are you going to make? what's your stock levels? – all those sorts of lessons. A lot of strong businesses have grown out of markets – Tesco's and Marks & Spencer, for example.'

Next he bought a large parcel of furniture from the receiver of a liquidated business, which he re-sold at a good profit. As part of the deal he took on a warehouse from which he sold fancy goods and toys at Christmastime. That gave him a taste for retailing proper. In 1980–81, in the grip of a recession, Smith saw the opportunity to sell cut price household goods to customers short of ready cash. He opened a general store with his father. One shop grew into a chain of five discount stores and an eventual turnover of £1.5 million.

He sold off the shops one by one. This provided him with the seed capital to launch Bow Bangles. The branches were opened in 1987 and a further five established in 1988. By the end of 1989, nineteen shops were trading across the country, from Sunderland to Luton.

Like many successful ideas, Bow Bangles happened by accident. One of the original discount stores in a Birmingham suburb was next to a greengrocers which was too small to trade profitably. The landlord offered it to Smith at a bargain rental. His initial plan was to knock through one of the adjoining walls and sell greeting cards. But someone else opened a card shop a few doors away so Smith was left in a quandary.

He eventually decided on a jewellery shop. The expensive goods did not sell, but the fashion side took off immediately. He opened another shop in the centre of Birmingham soon afterwards. Admits Smith: 'I was very nervous the day we opened that store. My worry was that the market it would appeal to would be too narrow – that the teenagers and the 20-year-olds would love it, but the older people and the kids wouldn't like it. But from the first day we had grandparents *and* young kids.'

Expanding the Bow Bangles chain was difficult in the late eighties as Smith came into competition with the big multiples in his search for prime sites. 'Landlords wanted to see three year accounts. We hadn't even got one year's accounts. They were getting blue-chip covenants in their schemes.'

Expansion, though, was rapid. Suggests Smith: 'I think we got by because the landlords looked at Bow Bangles and felt it was something that fitted alongside the fashion multiples – it's slightly different; it's a nice concept; only requires a small amount of space. Not many shops, apart from Sock Shop and Tie Rack, were after 300 sq. ft. to 500 sq. ft. units.'

Getting the design of the shops right was not so straight-forward. When Smith contacted some leading London designers he was horrified at their fees. One design house wanted £50,000 to come up with the decor for Bow Bangles. He ended up asking a friend who specialized in the design of pubs and night clubs. He did it for £1,000.

Smith helped fund his expansion with an injection of £150,000 from British Coal Enterprise (BCE), a government agency set up to create jobs in pit closure areas. BCE invested in £100,000 of preference shares and provided a loan of £50,000.

Eventually, however, Smith decided it was time to seek venture capital. NatWest, which had been providing him with an overdraft, was insisting that the company should budget to operate on a standstill basis, which did not accord with Smith's plans at all. The bank warned that it planned progressively to reduce the overdraft facility over the next few years. Smith, who had set his mind on a 100-store goal, was unhappy with the bank's apparent lack of confidence. He recalls: 'My problem was that I still had a head office base that warranted thirty shops and I was then only at twenty shops. That ultimately could have led to liquidation.'

A fellow director, who was a former bank manager, had always tried to persuade Smith to stay clear of venture capital. The director did not like the idea of handing over equity to a third party. But Smith felt the attitude of the bank left him with little alternative: 'I looked at it as a trade-off. Somebody was prepared to come on board and take a share of the risk, so they were entitled to a share of the future profit. The company was probably worth £1 million as it stood. With venture capital I would have a chance to built it into a £10 million company. The way I looked at it, 70 per cent of £10 million is better than 100 per cent of £1 million.'

Smith chose Parquest, an international venture capital fund managed by London-based Quester, to be his equity partner. It injected £250,000 into Bow Bangles for a 25 per cent stake. Smith has had no reason to doubt the wisdom of the move: 'It has given me greater peace of mind to expand the company, that I can do it from capital from the business rather than trying to borrow all the time from bankers in whom we felt we couldn't put 100 per cent of our trust.'

Simon Acland, a director of Quester, who became a non-executive director of Bow Bangles, saw considerable growth potential in the fashion company. He also detected that Smith was entrepreneurial material:

'A lot of people go into the retail business thinking it's a terribly easy business: you get a shop, you fill it with stock and you're away. It's actually very difficult and you need that rather intangible flair that Mark undoubtedly has.

'The second factor that encouraged us to back Mark was a general feeling that there's a trend towards the sort of fashion jewellery product and fashion accessory product that Bow Bangles sells, perhaps away from the more traditional gold-based jewellery.

'The third reason that we were keen to back Bow Bangles is that a recession was a very good time to be expanding a retail chain because of the deals that one can do with landlords. One of the things that impressed me when I looked in detail at Bow Bangles was the fact that they had resisted the temptation to expand when leasehold shops were changing hands at high premiums and going into properties with very high rents. The reason the Sock Shops of this world got into such trouble was because they paid huge premiums for new shops. They got into leases with high levels of rent; they bought at the top end of the market.'

CASE STUDY
Listawood Magnetics

Arthur Allen is a former maths teacher. He made a name for himself in the field of recreational maths and in doing so learned a lot about puzzles. A week in bed with a bad back led to a change of career, firstly as an education consultant with a firm publishing computer books. His first experience of industry was working for a King's Lynn firm making magnetic games and puzzles.

It was a short-lived experience. The firm went out of business in 1986, eighteen months after Allen had joined it. He decided, however, that he had learned from its mistakes and that together with his wife, Irene, he could make a better job of running a business. Setting up Listawood Magnetics, their own company, was very much a joint enterprise.

Their financial resources were meagre – only £500 between them. Shortage of assets and business experience was offset by the copyrights on their puzzles and a willingness to learn and seek advice. In March 1987 they won their first contract, to make components for a pocket magnetic edition of Scrabble, worth £17,000, and executed partly in their dining room and partly by sub-contractors.

Producing magnetized miniature versions of familiar board games, such as Monopoly, on contract to the maker now represents about 45 per cent of the company's activities. The worldwide market is dominated by Japanese suppliers, but Listawood's product is recognized as being of higher quality and competes on price and delivery times. The British company has now captured the home market and achieved considerable export sales. Some idea of the market potential can be gauged from the fact that Listawood produces miniature versions of Scrabble in seven different languages.

Another line is the production of promotional magnets of company logos and eye-catching characters. As a result of the quality of its production and competitive prices, the company now has 90 per cent of the growing UK market for promotional magnets. A 1992 rush order for four million magnets from British Telecom to promote its Talking Pages service demonstrated the company's ability to meet large orders with short lead times. It was also a tribute to the commitment and flexible attitude of the company's highly motivated staff.

Other lines include the production of mouse mats, memoboards and original puzzles.

Although assembly started in the family dining room, it was quickly extended to the village hall; then to a disused chapel and a borrowed barn in the village of Flitcham. In 1988 production moved to Harpley, eight miles from King's Lynn. Listawood leased part of the redundant farm buildings owned by Weaseham Farms and converted by them with the help of a *redundant building grant* from the Rural Development Commission.

These buildings, like so many other conversions of substantial farms, provide the space and light which is needed by a company producing a high quality product. As the company has expanded it has been able to take on an ever greater proportion of the available space. It now occupies four of the converted barns. Further farm buildings remain available for Listawood's future expansion. Certainly the value added by Listawood to the buildings is greater than through farming.

Harpley, together with the neighbouring villages, provides a natural pool of labour. The company now has over forty employees, of whom 75 per cent are women. Many of these are mothers returning to work, attracted by the firm's flexible approach to working hours. The pay-back is that there is a high quality labour force, who, as well as being loyal and committed, have the ability to learn and master the processes of screen printing, laminating and die-cutting. Even handling and setting 100-ton platen presses has proved no problem for women with no previous experience of industrial machinery. Moreover, with the company's expansion, women have adapted well to new responsibilities and are well represented at all levels of management. Irene Allen has introduced effective and well-organized business systems throughout the company's operations.

The Allens are adamant that the success of the company is a reflection of the quality of the labour force in their part of rural Norfolk and of the working environment in the converted farm buildings.

In the first six years of the company's life, its turnover went from £86,000 to £1.3 million, an exceptionally high growth rate of 56 per cent per annum. Irene Allen, the company's financial director, estimates that the capital employed is still a modest £130,000, but bearing in mind that the company started with £500 of equity, this is a highly successful story.

Initially the business was built on the extensive use of sub-contractors and their willingness, as suppliers, to give up to ninety days credit. The system worked for Listawood because Arthur Allen kept suppliers fully in the picture over any problems, in particular with cash flow, which were developing. Tolerance and support from both suppliers and banks were necessary while the company learned how to design and assemble its products. A measure of their confidence and support is shown by the fact that in 1988 one of the firm's suppliers, East Coast Plastics, lent the fledgling company £15,000 and purchased a 25 per cent equity stake.

Early in the firm's life, Irene Allen obtained an accountancy qualification and put it to good effect, not least in introducing proper management accounts and in ensuring prompt payment and tight credit control for customers. Without these strict disciplines it would have been impossible to turn the company's early losses into profits.

Listawood is determined to achieve further progress. Norfolk and Waveney Training and Enterprise Council has recently helped to finance a consultancy project on the company's objectives and to help establish its profit centres.

(Source: *The Countryside Means Business*, published by the Rural Development Commission)

CASE STUDY
Beauty Without Cruelty

Beauty Without Cruelty goes back to 1963 when it was started by the charity of the same name to produce cosmetics compatible with the ethics of the animal welfare movement. Well-known, animal derived ingredients, such as musk, are banned, together with the practice of testing own products on animals. Maximum use is made of oils and waxes from plants.

In 1980 the cosmetics business was restructured and became an unquoted public limited company after being rescued from serious difficulties by Joseph Piccioni, who had been appointed managing director in 1978.

The advent of Joseph Piccioni, with his business acumen and entrepreneurship, coincided with the growth of the green movement during the 1980s. It meant that Beauty Without Cruelty was able to cater for a large expanding market which was developing among people who, for ethical reasons, were attracted to its products.

Since 1980, the company has built up its market share, achieving an annual turnover of over £3 million by 1994. Initially, products were sold through mail order, but from the outset retail outlets were developed, both through healthfood shops and high street chemists. Eventually, the company developed outlets through multiples, including Tesco, Safeway and Superdrug until it was supplying to some 2,400 stockists in the UK.

The growth meant that larger premises were needed and the company decided to relocate production and distribution away from the South East, with its high costs of premises, labour and overheads, while retaining its head office in Tonbridge. After investigating several options, Beauty Without Cruelty chose a site 350 miles away at Millom in West Cumbria. It was attracted by Assisted Area status and because the support agencies seemed attuned to its needs. The company took a lease on a 5,000 sq. ft. unit on a Rural Development Commission estate and this was later expanded to 20,000 sq. ft., in two buildings on the same site, while extra space was created by inserting a mezzanine floor.

As a site for production and distribution, Millom does not present any particular difficulties. It is connected to the head office in Tonbridge by computer and direct telephone line, and there is contact with the main retail outlets by telephone link. The standard delivery time is three days with a facility for next-day delivery. The main manufacture of ingredients for BWC cosmetics is readily accessible and there is good liaison over research and development.

The company is one of the largest employers in Millom, with twenty-three full-time and twenty-three part-time employees, most of whom are women living there and in neighbouring villages. The general manager at Millom, Angela Hammond, finds that the staff have no difficulty in adding new skills, including shrink-sleeving and bar-code labelling, to their traditional tasks of bottling and packaging.

(This case study is extracted from *The Countryside Means Business*, by kind permission of the Rural Development Commission.)

CHAPTER 8

The Importance of Marketing

Whenever a certain bank manager receives a business plan in support of an application for start-up funds, his first action is to turn to the section on market research and marketing. If the applicant has failed to do his or her homework in this area, he sees little point in wasting time on the rest of the business plan. As far as he is concerned, marketing strategy is of prime importance. If it is not properly thought through, a company is doomed from the start, however innovative the business idea.

Inexperienced entrepreneurs confuse advertising with marketing. Advertising your products or services is only a very small part of the total marketing mix. Marketing is everything to do with producing the right product or service at the right time and at a price the customer is prepared to pay.

That may sound obvious, but it is amazing how many budding entrepreneurs fail to consider all the implications. In their enthusiasm to produce an outstanding product they can easily overlook the fact that if it is not available when the buying public needs it, sales will be minimal. For example, many products, such as fashionable clothes and toys, are seasonal. But the buyers of the major retailing outlets often select their purchases well ahead of the selling season.

Toy buyers, for example, make the rounds of the major toy and hobby fairs around the world in January and February to select their purchases for the following Christmas season. Once they have spent their budgets they are unlikely to take on new lines until the following year. By then your business may well have gone under through lack of cash flow.

It is equally important to consider how you are going to get your product to the customer in sufficient quantities to make your business viable. Someone who opened a shop to sell tropical fish in his local village, simply because it was his favourite hobby, failed to think through the impossible task he had set himself. If he had studied the marketing implications, he would soon have realized that only a miniute part of a small village population was likely to share his enthusiasm for tropical fish and that his sales were never likely to cover his overheads, let alone provide a profit. Needless to say, the shop closed within a year.

Similarly, a young entrepreneur in Wales decided there was a market for garden sundials. He had conducted a lot of research and decided there were many gardens throughout the UK alone which did not have a sundial. But he was something of a perfectionist. He set out to produce the perfect sundail, using the finest materials, regardless of cost. He did indeed produce a prototype sundial that everyone admired and which came close to perfection. What he had overlooked, however, was that in order to cover his production costs he would need to charge a price that few people were prepared to pay for an adornment to their garden. He eventually had to scale down his idealism and make a sundial that was less than perfect, but more affordable. In the meantime, he nearly became bankrupt, having to sell all his worldly possessions to keep his fledgling company alive.

Going upmarket

There is, of course, room in the market place for expensive products and there are people who are prepared to pay a high price for exquisite goods. But the entrepreneur who sets out to serve such niche markets needs to recognize that a very different marketing approach is required. If you produce common-a-day products that appeal to the mass market at a competitive price, the buying public might be expected to beat a path to your door. If, however, you make an upmarket product that appeals to a narrow customer base and is sold at a premium price, your marketing effort will need to be stepped up.

First of all, you will need to identify who this narrow band of customers is and where it can be found. Then you have to decide how to reach it. By way of retailers? By attending trade fairs? By mail order catalogue? By advertising?

If you decide trade fairs are the answer, you still need to be selective in which ones you decide to attend. If you have an expensive product, there is little point in trying to sell it on a stall at a local church fête. People don't attend such functions with their pockets lined with money. Your stand may receive much admiring attention, but this will almost certainly stop short of an actual purchase. Attending small-scale fairs is not a bad way to gauge public reaction to a new product, but you are unlikely to sell enough of an expensive item to cover your production costs.

Even when you go upmarket and attend an international trade fair in London or Birmingham, for example, you need to be careful that you select one that is relevant to your product line. If, for example, you make toys, a major gift fair might sound an ideal outlet, but toys are only a small element of such fairs. It would be far more prudent to save your money to pay for your attendance at a major toy fair, which is attended by all the leading buyers from around the world looking specifically for products in your field of interest. It is expensive to purchase even a small stall at such a fair, so you should make certain you target the ones that are most suitable for your product or service.

Tony Randel is a small business adviser at Enterprise Plymouth. He spends a lot of his time advising ex-Service personnel on how to start their own small firms. They tend to be experienced at getting things done, keeping records and personal relationships. Their main weakness is a lack of understanding of the main concepts of marketing and this is the area that Randel, himself an ex-Army man, concentrates on. Market research, he advises, is absolutely vital: 'I talk to them about a product never being all things to all people. You can buy a cup and saucer in Harrods and you can buy one on a market stall, but it is not actually the same cup and saucer. You have got to decide which segment of the market you're aiming at and feel comfortable with.'

Awareness of the competition is another vital aspect that Randel rams home at his seminars. It is only by understanding the strengths and weaknesses of the opposition that the start-up entrepreneur can decide on the right niche market to enter. Randel tells his seminar participants that every market place is encircled by a concrete wall and that all the players within it have carved up the area inside the wall into their own chunks. 'You will never break that wall down. You can beat your head against it as hard as you like. You've got to find a chink in their armour. You've got to go for a niche of some sort that they are not interested in. The start-up will never get there any other way.'

Fixing the price

Judging whether you can produce your product or service at a price the buying customer can afford is one of the most difficult issues for any budding entrepreneur. The answer will vary, of course, according to the economic climate. It is probably unwise for a first-time entrepreneur to set up a business making upmarket products during a recession, for example. It is difficult enough finding niche buyers when the economic climate is healthy. During a recession, when the buying public has precious little disposable income, the task is even harder.

On the other hand, there is a counter-argument that there is always a hard core of wealthy people, whatever the economic climate. If you can only locate them, they will still be prepared to fork out for something special. However, this requires marketing skills a fledgling entrepreneur is likely to lack.

It is easy to under-estimate what it will cost to produce and market your product or service and as a result under-price it. In the case of a product, you should take into account the cost of the materials involved, the time it takes to make it and all the overheads involved in getting it to market. You then have to bear in mind that if you sell through retailers your ex-factory price will be at least doubled in the shops for them to cover their costs. It is important not to overlook this, as the retailers' mark-up can easily make your product appear exorbitant in the eyes of the buying public. Of course, experienced professional buyers have an instinct about what will sell and at what price, but often they will only be prepared to take a sample of your goods to test them out, so most of the risk of setting up expensive production tools will fall on you.

In the experience of Randel of Enterprise Plymouth, there is 'a terrible tendency for people to think that cheapest is best' when newcomers to the business scene set about pricing their products or services. He insists: 'People have a perceived value and if you can't do it for the perceived value you haven't got a market. On the other hand, when you have a new product you want to go in as high up the market as you can, because you can always reduce a price, you can rarely raise it. A product will get from Harrods to Woolworths. It will hardly ever go the other way. Also, by going in high, you are more likely to cover your development and initial marketing costs, because you can build in greater profit margins.'

Randel talks from experience when he refers to perceived value. He once ran a small company making electronic devices that helped to prevent cot deaths. The devices were on the market at £79, but were not selling well. Parents of small babies simply could not relate the price to the critical function of the apparatus. It smacked to them of cheap imports from the Far East. Randel's company revamped the product and put it back on the market at £150 and it started selling well. Customers perceived the sum of £150 for a product aimed at saving life as a more realistic price.

The right packaging

In calculating the cost of getting your product to market, you should not overlook the cost of packaging and supporting sales material, such as brochures. Both of these can add considerably to your overall costs. Both will probably involve design houses, who tend to base their charges on what their larger customers can afford – often way out of line for the small business owner.

The best approach is to test the waters carefully. If you have an attractive product, which looks good on display, retailers will often not demand high-quality packaging. Some retailers, who are following the back-to-basics trend and the desire to reduce waste, will positively encourage the *minimum* of packaging. So why go to expensive lengths to produce highly sophisticated packaging that might end up pricing your product out of the market?

Some leading stores do, however, look for quality packaging and will dismiss as amateur any supplier who falls below such high standards. It should also be said that imaginative packaging can be a strong marketing tool and can make the difference between making a sale or not. It would, of course, be foolish in the extreme to produce an expensive upmarket product and spoil its chances of selling by wrapping it in inferior packaging.

To some extent, this is something you will need to discover for yourself. If a retailer who is likely to buy in large quantities, falls in love with your product but is put off by inadequate packaging, you would be foolish not to rectify the situation.

Sometimes it is possible to obtain high-class professional help without spending a fortune. When, for example, Chalice Foods, the olive pâté producer (see page 39), needed to revamp its brand image to appeal to a broader market, it could have been faced with an exorbitant bill from a design house of anything up to £80,000. However, the small food company found a novel answer to the dilemma. When Wickens Tutt Southgate (WTS), a design consultancy, contacted Chalice Foods after seeing it featured on a TV programme, the food company persuaded the design house to come up with an innovative image for a new range of peanut butter and waive its normal fees in favour of a royalty agreement. Recalls Paul Southgate, a director of WTS: 'There are two criteria we use for assessing whether we want a piece of business or not. One relates to whether there is a creativity opportunity. That criteria was met in spades. The other criterion is whether we can make any money out of it. In Chalice Foods' case we thought it was only a creative opportunity.' However, they accepted the challenge.

Unfortunately, the new range of peanut butter never took off in the market place, but at least the owners of Chalice Foods had not invested a huge amount of money in a costly experiment.

Buyer's market

In a buyer's market – which the recession has undoubtedly been – retailers have been increasingly laying down the rules for what is acceptable. Some will insist on all your products passing strict national and international quality and safety standards, for example. Achieving these can often be an expensive exercise. You need to make up your mind if the quantity of sales you are likely to make will justify this high overhead. Maybe you have enough customers who are less demanding to carry your company for the next year or so.

Obviously, achieving high quality and safety standards is a desirable goal and something that can enhance your marketing strategy enormously. But few – if any – small firms can afford to achieve everything in the early stages of their development. There has to be a large element of suck-it-and-see and a gradual build up based on your increasing sales turnover.

Sometimes your marketing efforts will be met by obstacles that are frustrating in the extreme. You may feel you are making all the right moves, but find that your *raison d'être* is not understood by the buyers who have the power to make you a failure or a success. For example, my wife was amazed when she took samples of her well-crafted puppet theatres and designer glove puppets to a leading toy store in London and was told that they were too expensive and that she should go away and have them made of cheaper materials.

She had marketed her company as one that produced high-quality toys, made of solid, durable materials and all hand-crafted. Producing flimsy puppet theatres that would never stand up to the rigours of boisterous play hardly fitted such a marketing scenario. The dilemma then is to decide whether to make a fundamental change in your marketing strategy or persist with what you believe in, convinced that there is a niche-market group of customers out there somewhere.

Don't expect your marketing approach always to match the buying conventions of your potential customers. My wife marketed her puppet theatres, story backdrops and puppets as a matching set. But when she visited one leading store in London, she discovered that there was a buyer for soft toys and a buyer for wooden toys. They insisted on dealing with the theatres and the puppets separately. The result was that the puppets and the theatres were displayed in different parts of the store, losing all the impact of a magical display, had they been combined as intended.

Surprisingly, the best displays of the complete range of puppets and theatres were eventually to be found not in a toy shop, but in a leading chain of shoe shops, which ordered Punch and Judy displays for thirty of its stores throughout Britain to promote children's footwear. This illustrates one of the most enjoyable aspects of marketing, if you believe in your product and remain resolute: as one avenue closes down a new, often unexpected one will invariably open up.

Brochures

Brochures are another overhead cost that can run away with you if you fail to show restraint. It is understandable that every budding entrepreneur should want to produce a highly glossy brochure that does full justice to the excellence of the product or service on offer. But several factors need to be taken into consideration.

The first point is that even modest brochures can be pretty expensive to produce. So the aim should be to keep the information contained in the brochure short and to the point. Don't, for example, include dozens of colour-rich pictures, if one can tell the story just as well. Shop around when selecting a designer and printer for the brochure. There is an enormous variation in charges. Avoid print houses that are used to producing brochures for major companies with household names. Your order will simply be a drop in the ocean for them and they will be inclined to charge you premium prices to offset the nuisance factor.

If you take the trouble, you will almost certainly find a back-street designer who will do a perfecty adequate job and, being a small business operator like you, will often make concessions to get you launched, in the hope that you will become a long-term customer.

Another problem with brochures is that they quickly become out of date and are often not current long enough to justify the high cost of their production. Increasingly, small firms are replacing brochures with slip-page information packs, similar to those produced by PR firms. The advantage of these is that you do not have to produce a completely new brochure every time you expand your product line. You can simply print-off a single page addition and slip it into the pack. Similarly, you can discard the pages illustrating products that have become out-of-date or discontinued. You can make the cover of the information pack look very glossy, perhaps embossed with your company logo, which will give it all the outward appearance of a professional brochure, but inside you can be as flexible as you want, without adding enormously to your marketing costs.

You should also be highly selective when handing out your brochures and information packs. Many people will show interest in your products and you will be tempted to give a brochure to anyone who waxes enthusiastic about them. However, you should always remember that every time you hand over a brochure you are giving away money that may never come back to you in the form of a sale.

Some small firms get around this problem by having a single-sheet price list, produced at a modest price, to hand out to everyone who shows any kind of interest. If in discussion with potential customers, it becomes obvious the level of interest is high, they produce the quality brochure reserved for special clients.

This is definitely a sensible approach to make when you attend a major trade fair. You are likely to have hundreds, if not thousands, of visitors to your stand, but only a small proportion of them will be potential buyers. They will all be only too happy to relieve you of a brochure, which they may be collecting as part of their own market research. Even worse, the brochures may well be screwed up and thrown away after a cursory glance. All the expense will have simply served to fill waste-paper baskets.

The right image

Marketing is the entire process of promoting your product to the buying public, leading ultimately to a profitable sale. That, of course, includes your own enthusiasm for your product which you should impart at every opportunity – on social occasions, not just at official business events. You should always remember that your enthusiasm for your product, and how you express that, is the most important marketing tool you have. If you can talk convincingly about the special qualities of your product or service you are halfway towards making a sale.

But prepare your words carefully and tailor them to the occasion. I remember once deputizing for my wife at the

International Toy and Hobby Fair at Earls Court in London while she went for a coffee break. To my horror, I was approached in her absence by the top buyer of a leading toy chain in America, who showed considerable interest in our display. In my enthusiasm to convey that we had a unique product line with enormous potential, I suspect I overdid the selling job. Our range at that stage was somewhat limited but I mentioned that we eventually planned to produce matching sets of puppets based on a dozen internationally-famous fairy stories.

The American buyer looked at me blankly and asked what I suppose to him was a perfectly logical question: 'Why haven't you?' I immediately realized my mistake. In America, the land where all is possible, you don't talk about what you plan to do; you demonstrate what you have achieved. I feebly muttered something about the fact we were still conducting market research, but it was too late. I could see I had already set off alarm bells in the buyer's mind. Was this a cash-starved small firm that would soon be out of business? Could he take the risk of placing a large order with a company that maybe did not have the resources to fulfil it? What if he advertised the products in his company brochure and the supplier failed to deliver? What would he then say to HIS customers?

Whatever thoughts flashed through his mind, the big order that might have turned Parthenon Toys into a highly successful business never arrived. I was left wondering whether a more carefully prepared statement might have resulted in a quite different result. Had I, in fact, helped to smother the baby at birth? If I could live that encounter over again, I would almost certainly have approached the buyer differently. Whether it would have made any difference, I shall never know.

Market Research

Marketing starts with the market research you should have carried out right at the beginning when deciding which product line or service to provide, as outlined in Chapter 2. The results of your market research should have dictated your marketing strategy. It will have helped you to identify the key elements of your marketing approach:

• *The customers*. Who exactly are they? Where are they located and how can you best reach them? Are there enough of them to sustain your business? It is important to be precise about who your potential customers are. It is not sufficient when selling toys, for example, simply to think of them in terms of all parents of children. What about schools? Why not target children's hospitals? Could the toys be used for psycho-therapy in homes for distressed children. The pool is always wider than you first imagine.

Other considerations help you to narrow down your market. Are the toys so expensive that they can only be afforded by well-to-do parents? Is there any point pursuing outlets which trade primarily by selling cheap imports from the Far East, which your products cannot compete with in terms of price?

If you definitely identify your products as upmarket, how do you reach this segment of the population? Certain areas of the country are known to be popular locations for well-off families. It may be better to target them first. But how? By mailing-shots and mail order catalogues or by approaching toy shops in those specific localities? Possibly a combination of the two, but it is important to concentrate your limited resources on the strategies that are most likely to bring quick returns rather than firing off in all directions and hoping for a scatter-gun success.

Some businesses, such as theme parks, require their customers to seek them out. That calls for an entirely different approach. A fairly heavy investment in advertising will probably be needed to make the business more widely known among the customers who might wish to use it. The main point is that customers are not a homogenous group of people. They all have different tastes and different levels of spending power. You have to make up your mind who you are trying to appeal to and focus your attention on them.

Always remember that the user of the products may not always be the person who makes the purchasing decision. For example, children may fall in love with a particular toy, but if it is beyond the spending range of their parents you are unlikely to make a sale. If it was children who made the spending decision and not their parents, my wife would have become an overnight millionaire, based on the enthusiasm children showed for her puppets when she visited schools as part of her market research.

- *Customer needs*. Don't be too rigid about your product line. It is important to have a clear-cut strategy about the type of products or service you want to provide, but if you consistently receive feedback from customers that they want something slightly different, let them have it. There is a lot of truth in the phrase, 'the customer is king'. They are the people who are going to make the decision about whether or not to buy your product. Their wishes are paramount. In fact, you can often build up valuable new business by providing bespoke products. A small firm is ideally placed to offer this service. It is far more flexible and adaptable than a major company, which is geared up for mass production and carries heavy overheads.

Sometimes you have to make difficult decisions about whether the departure from your standard product line demanded by your customers is in line with the mission of your business. My wife reacted quickly when it became apparent that many customers would like to buy table-top puppet theatres, half the size of the normal products and costing half as much. This was a form of diversification which made a lot of sense and was likely to result in extra sales at a time when it was difficult to sell the more expensive models.

When, however, it became evident there was public demand for a set of Punch & Judy puppets, she had to think long and hard. Punch has a bad reputation for violence and the question had to be asked whether it was a good thing to promote such attitudes in impressionable young children. After considerable reflection, my wife decided that it would be hard to think of any children's fairytale that did not have an element of aggression. It is a tradition going back many centuries and the company was in the business of traditional toys. Production went ahead and Punch and Judy became a best selling line.

● *Overheads*. One of the most important calculations you need to make before setting up a new business is whether you will be able to make enough profit to cover all your overheads, including your own salary and that of any staff you may take on. The first exercise you need to tackle is to estimate how much your raw materials will cost and add to that the costs involved in producing the goods. Obviously, the production costs will be higher if you employ staff or put the work out to contractors or outworkers rather than making the goods yourself. Once you have made that calculation, you probably need to double the figure again to cover your fixed overheads, such as workshop rental, electricity, wear and tear on your company vehicle etc.

What you need to remember is that whatever ex-factory price you put on your product, retailers will at least double that figure to cover their costs. So you end up with a product in the shop that is three times its inherent value (ie the cost of the raw materials and the workmanship). Your product will need to have something special about it to appeal to the ultimate customer.

If, for example, a do-it-yourself enthusiast walks into a toy shop and sees a puppet theatre on sale for a price that seems to be three times its inherent value, he might well go home and make it himself. But if you have incorporated special refinements, such as draw-back curtains and a miniature stage lighting system or perhaps some giveaway puppets for every sale completed, you might just win potential customers over. After all, you will be saving them the time and energy of doing it themselves.

● *Competition*. Your market research should help you to

compare your unique selling points (USPs) against the strengths and weaknesses of the competition. One immediate advantage you will have over your larger competitors is lower overheads. Small-batch production allows you to add refinements which mass producers simply cannot afford to incorporate. You can more easily adapt to changes in the market place and react to the varying demands of your customers. You are in a far better position to produce bespoke products. And obviously the closer you get to meeting the exact needs of your customers the more likely you are to establish long-lasting relationships. Survival, particularly during a difficult economical climate, has a lot to do with keeping your customers happy and forging long-term alliances.

But small firms don't have it all their own way. Large companies have established their name over many years of trial and error. They have already been down many of the blind alleys that may tempt you. They have long-standing relationships with important buyers and often enhance these with expensive free samples and gifts. It is not easy to dislodge an established relationship, particularly as big company sales people are backed up by all the resources and expertise that large corporations have at their disposal.

Buyers are not easily convinced that novelty products will make any impact in the market place. They feel more secure going with the tried and trusted products that have secured their career to date. You may feel you have come up with something that should take the market by storm. But they, like bank managers, are inclined to take a more conservative view.

The important thing is to know who your main competitors are and to be aware of their main assets. If you know exactly what you are up against, you can plan your marketing strategy accordingly. Never under-estimate the big league competition. The reason they have been around for some time is that they have learned the tricks of the trade. They have probably seen off more rival small firms than you have had hot dinners. They have had time to consolidate their position and they will not make way for new upstarts if they see even a small part of their marketing territory being threatened.

Don't look only at those businesses which are similar to yours. Research too businesses offering different products and services to yours, but which may compete for the spending power of your customers. Look for ways in which you can offer that little bit extra, which might make all the difference in attracting a customer.

Questionnaires

A research questionnaire is a useful way to gather and collate much of the information you need to formulate your marketing strategy. Research can be carried out in person, by telephone or by post. Try to ensure that the people surveyed are representative of your target market in terms of sex, age, marital status, occupation etc.

Each method of research has its advantages and disadvantages in terms of costs, time, response rates and accuracy of information provided. But whichever method you use, the questionnaire should be carefully designed.

Questionnaires can be multi-choice, open-ended or closed (yes or no answers). The questionnaire can be structured where questions are asked in strict order, or unstructured where the interviewer can change the order depending on the answers. The questionnaire should be tested to ensure that the questions are correctly phrased, logical and concise.

Gathering information

Research will not always directly involve potential customers. Where location is particularly important to your business, areas of heavy pedestrian or motor traffic can be identified simply by walking around the streets. Talk to other business people to get a feel for locality and its potential.

Be careful to draw the right conclusions from your research. An entrepreneur who decided to set up a car wash centre thought he had found the ideal location adjoining a main road where cars streamed past daily in large numbers. It was only after he had invested a large amount of money in establishing the first of what he hoped would become a chain of such centres that he realized his mistake. The cars travelled past at such high speed that few stopped for a car wash. He would have been better advised to site the centre in a more suburban location, where cars were obliged to travel at lower speeds, and perhaps close to a garage or restaurant where car-owners were more likely to make stops.

Market information can be obtained from many other sources apart from questionnaires. Midland Bank, in its guide to starting a small business, suggests the following:

Libraries have commercial reference sections which contain valuable research material including:
- Market research reports providing information on market sectors, future trends and the main players in the market.
- Trade/specialist directories and databases providing information on companies, their products and services.

Trade associations often have specialist libraries and can provide useful information on your market sector.

Trade publications give information on the competition, recent trends, developments and future prospects.

Visits to *exhibitions and conferences* will enable you to see what competitors are offering and what they feel appeals to customers. Obtain copies of brochures and price lists for comparison.

Yellow Pages, Thomson Directories and local newspapers will list competitors in your area.

Audited accounts of limited companies are available from the Companies Registration Office at Companies House [address given in Appendix A]

Promotion

Once you have identified a demand for your product and arrived at a price customers are prepared to pay, you must now consider how to make these customers aware of your product and generate sales. How you promote your business will depend on the size and location of your potential market, your message and the image you wish to project.

Premises, vehicle and uniform all project images and first impressions are often important. Business stationery, including business cards, order forms, statements, invoices, letterheads and brochures all impart a message about the kind of company you have established.

The best and cheapest form of advertising is word of mouth recommendations from satisfied customers. Midland Bank in its small business guide suggests the following should also be considered:

> *Direct mail and leaflet drop.* Mailing lists can be obtained from specialist organizations. However, response rates are often low, typically two per cent. Leaflet drops can be arranged in target areas of your business.

Tony Randel of Enterprise Plymouth believes mail shots, unless they are very carefully targeted, are a waste of time. Statistics reveal that response rates are rarely above ten per cent – and you will be lucky if you manage to turn more than two per cent of those responses into sales. It is a very simple sum to work out if 0.2 per cent sales is worth the cost of the mail shot.

In the case of targeted mail shots, it is important to contact the potential customers to obtain a name, so that you can personalize your approach. It is advisable to follow up the mail shot a few days later with a personal telephone call.

> *Advertising.* Advertising in local newspapers, magazine, trade publications, cinemas and on local radio will reach a wider

audience. Employing an advertising agency is more expensive than creating your own adverts. One-off advertisements do not have as much impact as a co-ordinated campaign.

Randel advocates using what he calls the 'dripping water on a stone' approach to advertising. He does not believe that the half-page spread in a newspaper every six months or so will achieve the desired effect. He recommends the small single-column add at regular intervals. This, he suggests, will have a subliminal impact on the reader. He cites the example of a small firm that makes gun cabinets. The company's owner advertises in every edition of two well-known hunting and shooting magazines. Apart from going to a game fair every year, that is the only promotional activity he undertakes. It is enough to allow him to capture 60 per cent of the UK market.

Public relations. Positive coverage in the media is free advertising with a high level of credibility because it comes from an independent third party. It takes time to develop relationships with local media and, while you cannot guarantee editorial coverage, it is worthwhile submitting articles about the business and its role in the local community. Topics may include charitable donations, sales promotions and job creation.

Telesales. Telephone sales and door to door selling can be cost-effective in local markets, but may not create the right image for some businesses.

Other forms of advertising include sales promotions, sponsorship, mail order, posters, speaking engagements and entries in business directories such as Yellow Pages and Thomson's Directory.

Randel does not believe small firms use promotional goods as often as they should. It can cost as little as eight pence to produce a pen with your company's name inscribed on it, which is an excellent way to keep your company's name in front of the public. Randel also cites the example of a beer mat that was sent to him by a client company instead of a Christmas card one year. It is still sitting on his desk, long after he threw away all his Christmas cards. He reckons it has led to at least three of his clients being put in touch with the firm in question.

Low level sponsorship is another ideal opportunity to promote the name of your company which a lot of small firms overlook. It is something that Randel strongly recommends: 'I'm not talking about the big league Benson & Hedges type sponsorship of golf matches. But buying a new strip for the local colt rugger team is worth considering. You get your picture in the newspaper and you are also seen as Mr Nice Guy in the community. That's terribly important. OK a rugger strip might cost you £500. Not everyone can afford that. But at a lower level you could consider sponsoring the local darts league. It will cost you all of £30 to £40 for a silver cup and a round of drinks at the end of the season – and your name's in the paper every week.'

Sola Wetsuits succeeded in raising its profile by sponsoring surfing stars who travel the world taking part in major events. The surfers carry the name of the company in bright colours on their wetsuits and are often seen on prime-time TV all over the globe (see page 270).

Another cost-effective way of keeping yourself and your company in the public eye is to become a member of local organizations like the Rotary Club and the local chamber of commerce. Volunteer to give speeches to the local branch of the Women's Institute and other specialist clubs. It is small-scale exposure, but it all helps to keep you in the consciousness of the community, establishing you and your firm as a pillar of that community. It can have a major impact on your trading prospects.

Exhibitions

Taking a stand at an exhibition is time-consuming and can be costly, but it is a popular way for many small businesses to promote their products. Trade fairs can be highly cost-effective, since the company's stand will be visible to a large number of potential customers at a single location. The visitors are usually there because they have an inherent interest in the range of products on display. But like many things, there is an art to exhibiting at trade fairs that inexperienced business owners often learn the hard way.

A computer software company that had not been long in the business decided to demonstrate its unique capabilities at a major international trade fair. Run by a small, but dedicated, team of entrepreneurs, the company was unable to spare the time or the manpower to organize and prepare its stand until the very last moment. As a result, the stand was still being erected late on the night before the opening day. At this very late stage, the firm discovered to its horror that the stand had been designed the wrong shape for the space available. It had to make hasty changes to the design that worked against the main theme of the message the company wanted to put across.

The company also discovered that it had been allocated space that was at the end of a blind alley, well away from the main focus of attention of the exhibition. Even worse, a rival firm that was well established in the software business had a prime position and partially blocked the new firm's stand from general view.

But this was only the start of the software company's problems. With mounting frustration, it discovered that the nearest electricity socket was a long way from where its stand would be positioned. It did not have leads long enough to reach. Without a lot of Heath Robinson re-wiring, it was in danger of not being able to demonstrate the very capabilities it wanted to promote to potential customers.

All these last minute adjustments kept the stand staff up until the early hours of the opening day of the exhibition. When finally they managed to get the stand into some semblance of order, they were tired, dishevelled, and far from alert. The trickle of visitors who did find their way to the company's remote location were met with disgruntled and confused staff who found the eleventh-hour re-design of the stand impractical to work with.

In order to make it fit the available space, the company had abandoned the idea of a section where staff could sit and chat in a relaxed manner to prospective customers. Instead, they had to talk to visitors over the counter. The visitors soon grew tired of having to stand about. Consequently, the software company's tally of orders at the end of the exhibition was negligible and the morale and confidence of its staff had been badly damaged.

Fortunately, not every first-time exhibiter at a trade fair goes through such a nightmarish experience. Those who take the trouble to discuss with the trade fair organizers what they are going to get for their money and how they can best display their products to full advantage are likely to avoid many of the pitfalls.

Comfort in numbers

The cost of taking part in a trade fair can often be reduced by joining forces with trade associations or organizations like the Rural Development Commission (RDC), which set up joint stands at a lower cost. There is also the comfort of being supported by an organization that has long experience of trade exhibitions and of combining resources with the owners of small businesses similar to your own.

The RDC assisted 221 small rural firms to attend exhibitions in the year April 1st 1993 to March 31st 1994. The result was a total of £450,000 in orders at twenty-two shows – sixteen in the UK and six overseas. The exhibiting firms subsequently recorded a further £1.5 million of business in follow-up orders.

David Walker, head of the RDC's sales promotion section, observes: 'Small companies tend to have their main strength in manufacturing expertise, and are weaker at marketing. By taking them to exhibitions we are able to help them meet potential customers and win orders.'

Some nine months to a year before an exhibition takes place, the RDC invites targeted firms to participate as part of a group. The selected firms will have been recommended by one of the Commission's local offices. If the idea appeals, they are given the opportunity to exhibit for three consecutive appearances at the show in question under the RDC's auspices.

A major advantage in exhibiting as part of a Commission group is that it can avoid having to wait in line for years for a place at some of the most prestigious shows. For instance, there is normally a seven-year waiting list for the Nuremberg Toy Fair.

One small company that has benefited from the RDC's support at exhibitions is Snazaroo, which makes and sells high quality face-paint kits. In February 1994, the firm attended the Birmingham Gift Fair for the first time, as one of a group of rural companies exhibiting with RDC support.

The company had already received general support from the RDC in the form of business advice, help with premises and specialist back-up. The owners of Snazaroo, husband and wife team Paul and Lauren Staton, have special reason to be grateful for the assistance they received with the Birmingham show, however. They won orders worth £25,000 at the exhibition, more than 10 per cent of their 1993 turnover.

Sportique Skiboats of Louth, Lincolnshire, a firm set up in 1988 to build dedicated tournament boats for towing water-skiers, has attended the Southampton Boat Show for three years in a row with support from the RDC. In the first year it succeeded in selling two boats. In 1993, however, it sold 12 out of a total of around 40 boats, with two going to export. As a follow-up the firm won a large export order and was able to increase its staff from four to nine people in all.

Mike Keeton, who with his wife Yvonne, founded and owns Skiboats, observes: 'As a young business we could not afford to go to the major shows. We sell a high-priced product and if we were to exhibit at a lesser show, on a cheap stand, it might damage our image and lose us business. With the Commission's help we have been exhibiting in a good international show, with a stand that looks the part.'

The RDC takes an average of six to ten firms to a show, to share a common group stand, although each participant has an individual self-contained company 'shell'. The bulk booking of space and its status as a regular year-on-year participator, gives the Commission the ability to negotiate good terms, which are passed on in the form of a 15 per cent discount.

There is a full hands-on support package for exhibitors, including a meeting with first-time exhibitors, on their premises, and advice with stand design, markting, exporting and PR and packaging at shows. The RDC organizes reduced cost, group-based services, such as freight forwarding of products and promotional materials and translating.

During exhibitions, an RDC marketing consultant spends time with clients and produces a report on their performance as exhibitors. For small firms with slender personnel resources and marketing budgets, the Commission helps with the manning of stands, particularly overseas.

Meet the buyer

Some local councils and trade associations organize meet-the-buyer trade fairs at which major companies exhibit the components that go into their products and invite small firms to put in tenders which might be competitive with the major companies' regular suppliers. There have been many cases where a major manufacturer sends halfway across the world at great expense for components which are being made by an industrious small business just down the road.

Although the government has made efforts to encourage big firms to make more use of small business suppliers – in the defence industry for example – the sad truth is that most large firms still depend heavily on bulk suppliers. These can offer them enticing discounts, with which small firms cannot possibly compete. Most of the contracts major firms put the way of small firms tend to be the crumbs rather than the hoped-for bonanza.

Key concepts

There are four key concepts that Tony Randel emphasizes in his Enterprise Plymouth seminars, which sum up the message this chapter has tried to convey:

1. *The world will not beat a path to your door*. 'Only two people will – the people you owe money to and the people who want to sell you something. Marketing is about getting out and doing it. It's not about sitting back and hoping.'

2. *The difference between marketing and sales*. 'There is a lot of muddled thinking about this. Marketing is creating an environment or an atmosphere in which a sale can be made. You have got to tell people what you are doing before they will even think of coming to you to buy something. You've got to project the message somehow or other.'

3. *Marketing is more of an art than a science*. There is no guaranteed way of making a sale. There are plenty of wrong ways to go about promoting your product or service. There is no single right way. 'You cannot do it scientifically. You cannot guarantee that a prescribed mixture of media advertising and sponsorship, for example, will ensure success. You have got to suck it and see. You mustn't be hide bound. The most successful marketeers are those who are a bit original in what they do without being gimmicky.'

4. *If you personally can't sell, don't try*. If you are not a salesman by instinct, not only will you fail to get the order you will actually lose the order that someone more skilled than yourself would get. 'I think I'm quite a good marketeer, but I am a hopeless sales person. I get a knot in my stomach.'

The Chartered Institute of Marketing

The Chartered Institute of Marketing (CIM) is a leading source of information and advice for companies of all sizes. Founded in 1911 and awarded a Royal Charter in 1989, it is the representative body for some 24,000 members and over 30,000 registered students worldwide, the majority of whom are practising marketing and sales professionals. It provides a comprehensive range of activities, services and benefits, including the following:

- *Education and personal development.* As an examining body for over sixty years, the Institute's certificates and diploma are internationally recognized qualifications available via a worldwide network of educational institutions and distance learning providers.
- *Training.* The Institute is a market leader in the provision of specialist marketing, sales, strategy and management training with over 8,500 delegates trained annually. It has a strong portfolio of residential courses, many of which are held at its high quality purpose-built facilities in Berkshire, together with non-residential seminars and courses which can be tailored to clients' needs.
- *Information.* The CIM's pedigree as a specialist marketing information provider is well recognized through its library/information service, INFOMARK.
- *Recruitment.* The CIM's 'Executive Resourcing Service' specializes in the recruitment of senior marketing and sales executives at home and abroad.
- *Consultancy.* The CIM offers professional marketing advice through some 350 listed and vetted consultancy practices.
- *Europe.* As a founder member of the European Marketing Confederation (EMC), CIM maintains close links with other representative bodies on the continent.

KEY POINTS

- Don't confuse advertising with marketing.
- Marketing is everything concerned with producing the right product or service at the right time at a price the customer is prepared to pay.
- Your marketing strategy can only be decided after careful market research.
- Niche products require an entirely different marketing approach.
- Take into account your own overheads and the retailers' mark-up when pricing your goods.
- Consider whether expensive brochures and high-quality packaging are really essential to sell your products.
- Never under-estimate the 'big league' competition.
- Trade fairs can be a very cost-effective way to reach potential customers, but be selective about the ones you decide to attend.

CASE STUDY
MAID, Part 2

Having successfully raised the finance to launch MAID, providing a computerized database to serve the advertising industry (see page 108), Dan Wagner faced a marketing crisis. With the company haemorrhaging between £45,000 and £80,000 a month, he needed to do something drastic to persuade customers to sign up. Only one sale – to the advertising agency BBDO – was made in the first three months of the company being launched. After six months the number of clients had risen to a mere five – far short of that needed to make the venture viable. The target was four sales a month, but it was to take one-and-a-half years to achieve that goal.

With the future looking grim, Wagner persuaded his fellow directors to let him attend an information technology trade show in New York. While there, he went around trying to sign up customers. To his amazement he clinched deals with four American clients within as many days. He was astounded by the enthusiasm he encountered. He found a much higher degree of acceptance in the US where on-line information systems were far more widely understood at the time than in the UK.

Within a few days of returning from the US, Wagner was back on a plane to New York again, together with his sales director. Operating with one telephone between them, they conducted an intensive six-week sales drive, making six presentations a day to prospective clients. They reaped a rich harvest of new signings. Recalls Wagner: 'The Americans liked our youthfulness. We were going into offices and people were latching on immediately to the value of the service.'

Michael Mander, a director of merchant bank Hill Samuel and non-executive chairman of MAID, was in awe of Wagner's audacity: 'I was quite frankly amazed when he would arrange to see the presidents of some of the largest US corporations and, as a young whipper-snapper, make a very competent presentation.'

The American market needed concerted attention and Wagner and two fellow directors took turns to man the New York office they opened in May 1986 overlooking Central Park. By November of the same year US orders were accounting for 46 per cent of MAID's sales.

Shortly after setting up in the US, MAID had attracted sufficient attention to warrant an article in *Business Week*, even though the august American magazine does not normally feature start-up companies until they have achieved several years of profitable growth. Within days of the article appearing, Wagner received two firm bids for MAID from US companies. One offer was in excess of $5 million from one of the world's leading on-line information providers.

Wagner was highly tempted, but such a grand offer only served to underscore what a potential gold mine he had launched. Says Wagner: 'I had a meeting with three executive vice-presidents of one of the biggest companies in the world. The fact they showed that much interest gave me even more confidence that we had an excellent product and that we were on to something very big. So it was almost to their detriment that these three high-level executives were meeting me in their boardroom. Had they sent a lowly accountant along, more in line with the size of the investment, I would probably have accepted their offer.'

The American impetus gave MAID the boost it needed and previously reluctant British companies soon followed suit. By the autumn of 1988 MAID's turnover was running at around £70,000 a month and the following year the company came close to breaking even.

Exclusive contracts had been signed with most of the leading UK marketing information providers and MAID was supplying in excess of 40,000 full text reports and information from more than 600 publications worldwide – and all accessible at the touch of a modem keyboard.

Wagner is convinced that the critical factor that led to such rapid growth was the system of charges. He introduced up-front subscription fees right from the beginning which at the time was frowned on by other data providers: 'We were selling subscriptions to the service even before customers got access and then they were required to pay per minute for what they used.'

Once customers discovered how efficient the system was, the cost was no deterrent. MAID was soon achieving an annual renewal rate consistently over 90 per cent. The high take-up rate was no surprise to Wagner because he believes the exclusive deal he pulled off with publishers such as the Economist Intelligence Unit, Reuters, Euromonitor, Keynote, Mintel and Frost & Sullivan helped him to tie up the market – and not just in the UK. He recalls: 'We had a very strong policy of signing up new publishers and we soon covered Europe and the US, almost in a monopoly-type way and the rest of the world – Japan, Australia –in a fairly comprehensive way. Some bits and pieces were available on other systems, but as a comprehensive database MAID was at least fifteen or twenty times larger than the nearest rival.'

MAID's future looked even more secure as its customer base became extended across a wide range of users, including corporate subscribers like Johnson & Johnson, Whitbread, McKinsey, *The Daily Telegraph* and the Ford Motor Company. Other users included the DTI and the French Embassy. By the end of 1992 only about 25 per cent of its customer base was in advertising, the original target for MAID.

Wagner considers MAID fortunate to have faced so little competition in its formative years: 'Nobody else thought of it because delivering on-line information was a very new market. Those already in the market were primarily involved in real-time financial systems, which were huge loss-makers. It was a very off-putting area to get involved in unless you were naïve, twenty and didn't see anything else going for you. I thought I could break the trend and do it cheaply. Actually that was what I was able to do. It only cost £1 million to get this business in profit. Most businesses in this field take years and years and many millions before they go into profit.'

CHAPTER 9

Exporting

Too many small businesses adopt a very blinkered attitude to marketing. They tend to confine their trading initially to the region they operate from, in the mistaken belief that it is the best policy to expand the market in easy stages as the business builds up. What they are inclined to overlook is that if they don't generate enough sales, they won't have a business for very long. Achieving the volume of sales necessary to sustain a viable business often means casting a very wide net.

This is even more true at a time of recession, as the owners of the Henry Hedgehog brush company discovered (see page 208). If they had taken the advice they were given to keep out of export markets until they were firmly established locally, their company would almost certainly not be around today. Similarly, the Somerset company of Middleton Leisure ensured its survival through the recession by exporting vigorously all over the world. The body care specialists export some 90 per cent of their total turnover to nineteen countries, including Taiwan and Malaysia. The company's export business took off after two appearances at the Hong Kong Health and Beauty Exhibition.

Testing the local market is obviously a sensible first step. Henry Hedgehog's owners initially discovered there was a demand for their products by setting up a stall at a local craft fair. Similarly, Pauline Ralph received encouraging feedback when she visited local souvenir shops to sound out reaction to a prototype thatched cottage music box she had made and hoped would be the basis of a successful business. Once she had received a positive response, she wasted no time expanding both nationally and internationally. Her company was soon exporting to numerous countries and among the many different styles of music box she subsequently produced was a range of New England miniature houses specifically for the US market.

The most successful small businesses are often those that go for export markets at an early stage in their development. Some jump in at the deep end right from the word go. Valerie Burrell built up her successful knitwear company almost entirely on export orders. Shortly after setting up her company, she went to a meeting of a local export association. One of the officials was about to visit the US to show buyers samples of products made by some of the association's members. He took some of Burrell's knitwear with him. They were a sell-out and her business took off immediately, almost exclusively on the basis of export orders.

It is understandable that many start-up entrepreneurs fight shy of going for export markets. If there are problems attached to finding the right home market, they are multiplied many times when it comes to exporting. When things go wrong a long distance from a company's base, it can be a nightmare trying to sort them out, unless the company has an agent located abroad. Building up a healthy export market can make all the difference to a company's growth pattern, but achieving overseas sales can be fraught with dangers.

There are three main factors first-time exporters need to get right if they are to succeed. These are: finding the right market for a particular product; ensuring the product is priced right for overseas; and making sure that you are going to get paid at the end of the day.

Failing to do the research

The most common mistake made by first-time exporters is that they fail to do the necessary market research. They assume that because their products are selling well on the home market, they will automatically achieve good sales abroad – in France, for example. But there may already be a French manufacturer making similar products that sell at a cheaper price. You need to look at the market as a whole and consider which products are likely to be acceptable in the countries you are targeting. If you are making grandfather clocks, for example, China would probably not be a very rewarding market. It would probably be better to target the American market or Germany, for example.

On the other hand, it can be very rewarding if you do manage to break into a new market which on the face of it doesn't offer much prospect. A firm that makes vehicles for recreation parks succeeded in selling a consignment of go-karts in China – not the most promising market for such a product. There is a great sense of achievement in conquering unlikely markets, but they obviously should not be what you depend on for the survival of your company.

In the first instance, it would be prudent to opt for a 'soft market' to gain confidence. The Netherlands, Germany, Denmark, Norway and Sweden are generally recognized to be countries that are pro-British and therefore less likely to be 'a hard sale'.

France, by contrast, is a notoriously difficult market to break into, partly because it insists on the use of the French language for labelling, invoices and contracts. It is sometimes possible to break into difficult export markets via your existing home country customers. Parthenon Toys, had been supplying rag dolls to Conran's London store for several years. When the store decided to open a branch in Paris, there was a request for Parthenon Toys' glove puppets and rag dolls to be supplied to France. It was an effortless entrée to a new export market.

A comprehensive range of information about the peculiarities of different export markets can be obtained from Overseas Trade Services, operated jointly by the Department of Trade and

Industry and the Foreign and Commonwealth Office. Its services are outlined in detail later in this chapter.

Pricing the product right

Inexperienced exporters also tend to overlook that they require bigger profit margins for their products to be successful in export markets. They believe naïvely that if they price at £75 a product that has cost them £50 to make they will make a tidy profit. They grossly under-estimate the cost of getting their products on to foreign markets outside the EU. Observes George Raybould, an exporting consultant: 'Just take selling to the American market. You've got to pay American import duty, plus customs clearance charges, plus the cost of shipment and delivery to the customer over there. To cover that, your £50 product probably needs to sell for £200.'

Getting paid

Many first-time exporters are so ecstatic about winning a substantial overseas order, they don't stop to think how they are going to get their money. They rely on the goodwill of the foreign customer. Such vagueness can be fatal. Companies who put too much faith in verbal promises often end up going out of business. Cautions Raybould: 'You've got to decide whether you want the buyer to pay before the goods are shipped or afterwards. If it's afterwards, is it thirty days after the date of shipment or the date of the invoice, or what? Is the customer going to provide an irrevocable letter of credit?'

A letter of credit is a document which is issued by the customer's bank to you as the exporter and it states the nature of the goods, when they have got to be shipped by and the documents that need to accompany them. Provided you ship the goods by the date specified and you have provided the necessary documents, in good order, by the expiry date of the credit, you have a 99 per cent guarantee of getting paid.

All the evidence shows that a letter of credit is the best way to ensure payment. Provided it is confirmed by your bank, it is irrevocable, which means it cannot be cancelled. There used to be revocable letters of credit, whereby the customer could refuse to accept the goods, but this is very rare today.

It is important to realize, however, that the overseas bank is not acting on your behalf. It is there to protect the interests of your customer. If there is a minor error in the documentation, it will often be used as an excuse to delay payment. The bank will probably charge between £25 and £50 to open the letter of credit in the first place and a further one per cent of the invoice value or a minimum charge to negotiate the agreement. It is not worth entering into a letter of credit for orders valued less than £250.

For higher value orders, however, it is a prudent way to deal with export business. It means that the value of the invoice is set aside as credit. As soon as the documents arrive at the foreign bank notifying it that the goods have been despatched, the money is released and should arrive in your bank account within about seven days.

If the goods are being despatched by a long-haul merchant ship there is every likelihood that the payment will arrive in your bank account prior to the customer receiving the shipment. If the goods are being air-freighted, of course, it is most likely the customer will be in receipt of them before you have got your money.

Some companies bypass their own bank and deal directly with the foreign bank to reduce the charges involved. But most small business owners feel safer having their own bank in on the deal.

The owners of Henry Hedgehog adopted a prudent policy from the outset. They asked all their new customers to pay for orders prior to delivery. Once they have established that the customer is trustworthy, they relax their payment terms.

Most of the large clearing banks run an exporter's scheme similar to a factoring service, which guarantees a high percentage of an invoice value as soon as it is despatched (see page 220).

Middle East Markets

Despite the availability of such safeguards, many inexperienced entrepreneurs rush into exporting without considering the risks they are taking. The market which has a special fascination for many is the oil-rich Middle East, with its inflated reputation for turning entrepreneurs into millionaires overnight. There is a widespread misconception among inexperienced Middle East-bound business people that the area represents easy pickings and that big profits can be made without much investment in time, money or energy.

What many businessmen tackling the Middle East for the first time tend to overlook is that it has become a buyer's market. According to one consultant familiar with the area: 'The decision-makers in the Middle East realize that to a large extent they were ripped off in the late 1970s and are now much more stringent in their commercial dealings. Also, a lot of major developments have already been done.'

A survey among business people who regularly travel to the Middle East concluded that cultural empathy was the most important prerequisite for operating there successfully. Any businessmen venturing into the Middle East for the first time who does not bear this in mind is very likely to return home empty handed.

A principal pitfall is the failure to recognize that Middle East people have an entirely different concept of space and time to Westerners. Tying Middle East businessmen down to a fixed appointmnt can be a nightmare. Newcomers touring the Middle East are advised to try to stick to a schedule, but not to fret if things go awry. It is not unusual to arrive for a firm appointment with a Middle East executive only to find he is not even in the country. Advises a regular visitor: 'Be patient. It is absolutely vital. They don't intend to be rude and it is very easy to lose your cool when you're tired from travelling.'

Once having got an appointment, the visiting businessman will often be horrified to discover that he has to conduct his transactions in a room full of people. It is not unusual for a Middle East executive to hold court with a whole group of hopeful visitors at the same time. Insisting on a private meeting will only antagonize the host, from whom it is hoped to secure a contract.

Middle East concepts of courtesy and respect can be very confusing to outsiders. Suggests the consultant: 'Don't confuse courtesy and hospitality with sincerity. The visiting businessman will do well to assess what he has achieved at the end of each day. The host country's friendliness may leave him with a comfortable feeling that things are going well, but he should ask himself whether he has really made any progress.'

The Middle East novice will soon be disabused of the popular view that business can be done there out of a suitcase. The big orders nearly always go to those who have on-the-spot facilities and give the impression of a degree of permanence. To obtain contracts it is necessary to have constant follow-up. Middle Easterners are notorious for failing to answer letters or respond to faxes and telexes.

Many Middle East veterans regard it as essential to have a local agent. He will be able, among other things, to keep the businessman informed about new projects before they are publicly announced. He will also have inside knowledge about who the key decision-makers are when it comes to major contracts.

The agent will be familiar with the ever-changing regulations in each country. The sudden introduction of a regulation that makes it mandatory to submit all proposals for public sector work in Arabic, for example, can cause havoc to the businessman caught unawares.

Customs regulations, too, are frequently changed. For example, if a country's government feels that sufficient quantities of a certain range of products are available within the region, it can ban their importation overnight. A good agent will alert the businessman to such dangers.

Choosing the right agent is very important. The Middle East is swarming with people who offer their services as agents. Many of them lack the contacts and influence that they claim. It is best to check with the British Embassy or the local expatriate community before making a decision.

Bribes and Commissions

The issue that most troubles newcomers to the Middle East is the vexed problem of bribes and commissions. Middle East veterans draw a clear distinction between a commission and a bribe. It is generally considered to be above board to pay a commission for information to ensure that your tender does not get overlooked. It is inadvisable, however, to offer a bribe to ensure that a contract is guaranteed to the exclusion of other competitive tenders.

It should always be remembered, however, that Middle Easterners are all traders by nature. Wheeling and dealing, as anyone who has visited the markets of Cairo on holiday will testify, is in their blood.

Authority is centralized in most Middle East companies. The head of a firm usually insists on meeting business contacts personally. By the same token, Middle East executives expect to deal with chiefs, not underlings. They are usually not interested in negotiating with business representatives who lack authority to make decisions. And although they take their time in awarding contracts, they expect the goods to be delivered tomorrow once an agreement has been reached.

A new, highly educated generation of Arabs are appearing on the scene, who give the impression that the differences between the Middle East and the Western world are disappearing. The knowledgeable executives are given positions of great authority in their firms because it is regarded as undignified to make them climb up through the ranks as business graduates tend to do in the West. It is important to remember that although they may have degrees from Harvard or the London School of Economics, they will almost certainly lack practical experience.

Language Skills

Many small firms fail to take full advantage of exporting opportunities because of a lack of language skills. There is the famous story about the auditors who were going through a company's affairs after it had gone into liquidation. They came across a letter written in German. When translated, it turned out to be the largest order the company had ever received and would probably have saved it from closing down if only someone had been able to understand German.

It is unrealistic to expect the members of a small firm to be skilled in all the languages of potential export markets. But there is no shortage of translation agencies prepared to assist for a modest fee.

A number of studies have highlighted the fact that British companies operate at a disadvantage when it comes to language ability compared to their European counterparts. For example, a survey of 1,500 small and medium-sized companies in seven European regions published by the London-based Centre for Information and Language Training and Research showed that nearly a third of all Britain's smaller exporting businesses face language barriers. This compared with fewer than one in five companies in Spain – the EU country with the next highest degree of language difficulties.

Such difficulties result in loss of trade. Even if it is fairly small, it adds up to a significant national loss when taken across the country as a whole, both in terms of revenues and jobs. For this reason, the Department of Trade and Industry launched in 1994 a National Languages for Export Campaign, with the aim of overcoming language and cultural barriers in international trade.

It is not difficult to understand why the UK lags so far behind its overseas competitors when it comes to language skills. In the past, UK companies traded largely with Commonwealth countries and the United States, and English was almost always used. Modern languages were taught in our schools as academic subjects, mostly to study literature, rather than to communicate verbally.

But today over 60 per cent of the UK's exports go to non-English speaking countries, with Germany as our biggest export market. Looking to the future, the greatest prospects for growth lie in the Pacific Rim, East Asia, South America and Eastern Europe – virtually all non-English speaking. Teaching methods in schools have already changed, but it will take a good many years for those changes to work through the population and affect trade in any significant way.

Increasingly, small firms are turning to export markets to ensure their long-term viability and face communications problems – in meetings, attending exhibitions, with correspondence and trade literature, advertising locally, hiring agents, carrying out local market research, negotiating, travelling around the world or just establishing a good rapport with potential and existing clients. Cultural differences, particularly in the Pacific Rim and other East Asian markets, can pose special problems for British business people working in, or visiting, the region. A real commitment to overcoming these obstacles is essential if small business owners want to succeed in foreign markets.

Starting Point

In April 1994 National Languages for Export Week focused attention on the value of linguistic and cultural competence to international trade. It was intended as a starting point for galvanizing local business communities, and especially small to medium-sized firms, into action. Several national events were held together with a calendar of local events organized by local chambers of commerce.

During the week, the country's first Languages for Export

Awards were announced for those exporting firms, employees, language trainers and educational institutions deemed to have made an outstanding breakthrough in overcoming language and cultural barriers.

In addition, short guides to language issues were prepared and the DTI offered a subsidized language audit service to encourage companies to review their specific needs. A national database of language providers was distributed through business support organizations to help UK companies to make an informed choice about their language needs and those they employ.

The database is administered by the National Business Language Information Service, which is located at the Centre for Information on Language Training and Research (CILT) in London.

Overseas Trade Services

Overseas Trade Services is designed to help businesses break into new export markets. Operated jointly by the Department of Trade and Industry and the Foreign and Commonwealth Office, it can, for example, help small business entrepreneurs to obtain information on a specific market – its business culture and potential competitors. It can also help to promote a firm's product or service overseas and assist in finding a local agent. Its wide range of services includes financial support for trade missions, overseas trade fairs, store promotions and seminars.

In 1992/93 around £177 million, including Foreign Office costs overseas, was spent by Overseas Trade Services on help for exporters. Part of this expenditure was devoted to the *Trade Fairs Support Scheme*. Each year this offers financial help to some 7,000 Britons who take part in over 300 selected overseas exhibitions, as members of groups sponsored by trade associations or chambers of commerce. The Silver Crane Company, manufacturer of decorative tinware, has used the scheme to exhibit at several overseas exhibitions. The 1993 New York Gift

Fair produced a large number of enquiries for the company, many of them subsequently converted into valuable orders.

The *Outward Missions Scheme* assists a further 2,000 or so Britons who travel abroad each year with Overseas Trade Services' help. The scheme gives a company financial support for its first three missions to any one market (five to Japan). A wide range of publicity and promotional services is offered to mission participants, from a free 'curtain-raiser' press release sent to the local press before the group arrives, to a 'Made in Britain' illustrated leaflet in the relevant language, printed for companies' own use.

Overseas Trade Services also provides a number of information schemes. The *Export Data Services*, for example, are designed to enable businesses to carry out preliminary desk research in the UK before entering an overseas market, and to keep up-to-date with new export opportunities.

One of the services, *Export Intelligence*, has been used with great success by Midland Cosmetics Sales which, after trying for several years, finally broke into the US market.

If a business requires details of the opportunities for its products, processes or services in a specific target market, the *Market Information Enquiry Service* can be of help. This service – based on information provided by specialists in Britain's diplomatic posts overseas – was used by cutlery manufacturer Richardson Sheffield to gain an insight into the mechanics of the Japanese knife and scissor market.

A British product or service which is new to a specific overseas market can be promoted at any time by a *New Products from Britain* press release, another service on offer. For example, two American specialist magazines reprinted a *New Products from Britain* story about the limited edition porcelain dolls made by Marianne Haben Ltd., which resulted in a large number of enquiries from US collectors.

Many companies choose to take part in an *Overseas Stores Promotion*. British Museum Connection, which produces and markets replicas and giftware on behalf of the London museum, recently took part in a promotion organized by the Lotte department store in Seoul, Korea. Financial support is given by Overseas Trade Services to the participating stores to help defray their expenses.

Help is also available through the *Export Representative Service* for companies wanting to appoint an overseas agent. In addition, the *Export Marketing Research Scheme* gives professional advice and financial support for marketing research conducted in-house or by consultants; the *Overseas Status Report Service* assesses the suitability of a proposed overseas agent or of companies with whom a company plans to do business; the *Inward Missions Scheme* provides financial support for group visits to the UK by overseas buyers; and *Overseas Seminars* enable firms to present their products or services to a target audience.

Five additional services have been introduced in selected markets on a pilot basis: help for Britons in arranging a programme of visits in an overseas market; provision of a market expert to accompany the visitor during the business calls; guidance for British exporters exploring overseas investment opportunities; management of overseas seminars; and monitoring of the display of company literature at overseas trade fairs.

The Overseas Trade Services' network of 197 offices worldwide had some 2,000 staff in the UK and overseas whose aim is to help British businesses realize the vast potential of overseas markets. To obtain advice or general information on all services, firms should contact their nearest DTI regional office or the export departments of the Scottish Office, Welsh Office or Industrial Development Board for Northern Ireland.

PROFIT

The Rural Development Commission (RDC) operates the Programme for International Trade (PROFIT) to help rural businesses adapt to the new trading conditions created by the removal of trade barriers in the European Union. The programme was introduced by the RDC in 1990 as a practical programme to help small firms face up to the challenge of the single European market. Now that the single market is in place, PROFIT continues as a service for eligible firms to be briefed on European or export trade matters.

Export Clubs

Export clubs, supported by the DTI, provide another useful support group for inexperienced exporters. There are around eighty export clubs throughout the country. They are non-profit making organizations which meet informally so their members can exchange export ideas. The DTI helped establish the Export Clubs' Advisory Committee, which debates exporting issues at an annual conference. Part of its aim is to encourage small and medium-sized businesses to start exporting by explaining the opportunities the European single market represents.

One active export club is the International Business Club in Bristol, set up under the auspices of Bristol Chamber of Commerce. Geoffrey Coates, its chairman, observes:

'One of the main objectives of the club is to provide a focus for all business people connected directly or indirectly with international markets, covering the whole range of activities associated with promoting and actively seeking overseas business.

'We aim to provide a forum for the exchange of views, problems and concerns of participating members and to use this forum for liaison with official bodies, such as the DTI. Many organizations now seem to be involved in offering export advice and the export clubs have an important co-ordinating role to play.'

Active Exporting

The DTI has entered into partnership with local chambers of commerce in a number of regions to promote the idea of more active exporting. For example, it has joined forces with Bristol Chamber of Commerce to provide a service that identifies export markets and customers for local companies. Called *Active Exporting*, the initiative has benefited a large number of smaller firms by developing trade links worldwide, from the United States to the Middle East.

It is run by Viv de Silva, the DTI's export development adviser for the South West. In one year alone de Silva and his researchers visited ninety-three small and medium-sized firms in the region to carry out free export audits. Over thirty companies have commissioned Active Exporting to research markets in foreign countries. As a result a number of the firms have visited potential customers overseas and several have gone on to win thousands of pounds worth of orders.

After a free export audit, de Silva agrees with the company which countries it wants to target. With the help of British Embassy commercial officers, international chambers of commerce and his own contacts, he then produces data on potential customers and, in some cases, arranges introductions between the organizations. He maintains that there are a huge number of small British firms with the potential to export, but which hold back because they are uncertain about what is involved: 'Many firms have got excellent products and services for which there is an overseas market but don't think they have the ability to sell them. In fact, with services like ours available to businesses, there is little that they have to do themselves. We help with initial research, administration, shipping, customs – in fact almost everything that a company would need to do. We look for agents and distributors who are hungry and technically competent to represent our companies.'

Because Active Exporting receives funding from the DTI and

the chamber of commerce, it provides its services at very modest fees, charging around a third of private consultants' fees. The service is also available to small firms which are not members of the chamber of commerce.

One company that has benefited from the services is S M Gauge Co. Ltd., a specialist supplier of pressure gauges and thermometers, which has developed a growing export trade since approaching Active Exporting.

Having asked de Silva to explore potential overseas markets, the firm was provided with a list of suitable agents. After preliminary discussion between de Silva and a potential Saudi agent, S M Gauge's partners, John and Tim Sheppard, flew out to the Middle East for a personal visit. Within months the company was receiving large orders.

This has led to discussions about a long-term joint manufacturing venture with the Saudi company and to a further exploration of new export markets concentrating on Pakistan, Abu Dhabi and Bahrain.

Pipetech, a small firm specializing in repair kits for the exhaust pipes of competition dirt bikes, was keen to sell its products in California, the world-centre of off-road racing. Keith Stone, the company's owner, was convinced there would be a market there for his products, but was not sure how to go about selling them. He talked the idea over with de Silva, who carried out a survey of the US market and produced a list of fifty companies that were interested in the product. Stone then visited the United States and made contact with a firm which had tested demand for the kit at a major trade fair. The US firm then agreed to manufacture the kit under licence and distribute it worldwide.

Exporting Livewires

Livewire, the organization sponsored by Shell UK that encourages young people to set up in business, has introduced an exporting initiative together with brewery giant Bass. It gives young entrepreneurs the chance to get into exporting by offering specialist advice and training, including an organized trade mission to the Continent.

The Export Challenge is a further development of the support for the Livewire network for young businesses started by 16 to 29 year olds (see page 74). According to Sandy Ogilvie, Livewire's UK director, the scheme aims to fill a gap in the market: 'It's often thought that exporting is a preserve of big business when, in fact, smaller firms enjoy some important and valuable advantages when it comes to overseas trading.'

Livewire is operating the scheme through its network of local co-ordinators. The scheme was piloted in four areas in 1994 – Chester, Cardiff, Birmingham and Staffordshire. Up to twenty youngsters were selected to join a trade mission to one of four European cities: Amsterdam, Antwerp, Hamburg and Paris and they were given support by Livewire's European partner agencies which provided business facilities and assistance in developing overseas sales contacts.

Export Award for Smaller Businesses

Smaller firms are experts in carving out a niche in overseas markets where large companies often fear to tread. Recognizing this fact, the government has entered into an initiative with the private sector that encourages and rewards small business exporters who adopt aggressive exporting campaigns. The Export Award for Smaller Businesses (EASB) is open to any independent firm which employs less than 200 people and which can demonstrate a substantial growth in export earnings of more than £100,000.

Each of five main winners receive £5,000 in prize money and professional advice, presented at a luncheon ceremony at the Savoy Hotel in London. In addition, certificates of merit are awarded to companies whose exporting performance is considered highly commendable by the judging panel. Each winner also receives £1,000, for a purpose approved by the sponsors to be used for the benefit of all employees, and a commemorative plaque and certificate.

EASB is the only government-sponsored award geared specific-ally to *small* business exporting. (The Queen's Award for Exporting Activity is open to companies of all sizes.) It examines the past performance of entrants and judges them on how well they have achieved consistent growth. It also actively encourages certificate of merit winners to enter again in the following year.

The adjudication panel largely comprises private sector bodies which are experts and practitioners in the field – including the Confederation of British Industry, the Trades Union Congress, the Institute of Export, British Invisibles and the British Chambers of Commerce. The current sponsors are: The British Overseas Trade Board, which is the principal adviser on export promotion and trade policy matters to the DTI and the Foreign and Commonwealth Office; Kompass British Exports, which provides two Kompass International editions chosen by the winners and also covers the administration costs and acts as award administrator; Grant Thornton, chartered accountants, who provide up to £2,000 of professional advice to each winner and Midland Bank, which provides £2,000 for each winner to be spent either on the acquisition of further export skills or investigating and developing export markets.

Pointers to success

Every small business has its reasons for exporting and its own way of doing so. However, the experience of EASB winners shows that the most successful ones have demonstrated the following characteristics:

- a strategic rather than an *ad hoc* approach
- a sensible spread of countries, markets and products
- non-reliance on only a few markets, in case of collapse
- market research and staff training

- effective technical back-up and distributor support
- an awareness of foreign customs, language and invoicing
- attendance at trade fairs and use of government schemes
- imaginative and novel ways of penetrating new markets

Winners

Among the winners of the 1993 EASB awards was DeSurvey Ltd. from Birkenhead, which provides engineering design services to the offshore and international petrochemical industries. It was founded in 1976 by the present managing director, Ron Curnow. Its prime markets are mainland Europe and the Middle East.

The company gained the award on the back of export earnings which at £6.25 million had doubled in two years. Since then the company has gone from strength to strength, achieving overseas sales that represent over 90 per cent of its total business. Curnow has five tips for exporting small firms:

- You have to know your customers' company, where they are, what branches they have and what are their main objectives.
- Always be prepared to take an overseas trip if your customers want you to.
- Get properly up to speed on foreign as well as UK legislation – particularly import duties, visa customs, transportation, taxation and insurance.
- Talk clearly – if not in your customer's language, then in clear, concise English.
- And lastly, show an interest in the country itself – its current affairs, sport, politics and customs. It makes a real difference.

Another 1993 EASB winner was Mayflower Glass Ltd. of East Boldon, Tyne and Wear, which manufactures sculptures in Borosilicate glass. Harry Phipps, its founder and chairman, has produced glassware for the laboratory and scientific industry for more than thirty years. In 1984 he decided to diversify into producing ships in bottles. Since then, business has grown and grown. According to David Timmis, the company's managing director:

'The EASB has a unique kudos. Unlike the Queen's Award, there are only a handful of winners each year and this means we see ourselves as being in exclusive company. Also unlike the Queen's Award, it provides a financial prize. In Mayflower's case, we were able to distribute this on the shopfloor and help finance a highly successful trade mission to China.

'We place great emphasis on language facility and trading in foreign currency. We speak more than seven languages fluently and produce brochures in Spanish, Italian, Portuguese, Japanese and Dutch.'

Donald Russell Ltd., another 1993 EASB winner, is a specialist exporter in prime quality Aberdeen Angus beef, Scottish lamb and smoked salmon. It exports to over twenty-two countries and lists among its clients the famous Raffles Hotel in Singapore, the Hilton International chain, and hotels and restaurants at Euro Disney.

Export earnings represent over 90 per cent of the firm's total sales. Since winning the award the company has set up plans to diversify into other Scottish food products, such as venison, game, chicken and wild mushrooms, and has expanded its factory and opened a new sales office.

Other exporting competitions

The TECs, chambers of commerce and a variety of other organizations stage exporting competitions throughout the country which can reap rich rewards in prize money for the winning small firms.

For example, Devon & Cornwall TEC makes £1,000 awards to businesses that submit outline export ideas considered to be the most practical and with the greatest potential for business growth. The prize money is intended to help the winning businesses to prepare a plan to develop their export idea.

In addition, each of the twenty-four successful businesses annually are eligible to win one of twelve further prizes of £15,000 to help implement their export plan. Apart from the prize money, winners enjoy the prestige associated with being recognized as a leading exporter and the high profile resulting from media coverage.

Newton Abbot-based Vander Ltd., a Devon company that makes waterproof clothing, used the £15,000 it won in Devon & Cornwall's TEC's 1993 export competition, to research the single European market and to draw up a comprehensive plan for its approach to exporting. As a result orders flowed in from Holland, Austria, Germany and Ireland.

Stuart Barker, Vander's commercial director, said: 'We used the export initiative award to research markets in the Netherlands, Austria, Ireland, Norway and Canada. We are able to see that the quality and performance of our products are superior to those produced in mainland Europe. We need to plan for future expansion, so as to be able to meet the needs of European markets as they come out of the recession.'

Vander has seen its workforce grow steadily since the company was set up by managing director Hugh Anderson and his wife ten years ago and now employs around seventy people. The company's garments are made from the highest quality materials and have been worn in some of the world's harshest climates. Sherpas who accompanied Rebecca Stevens, the first woman climber to reach the summit of Everest, were protected by Vander coats.

KEY POINTS

- Exporting at an early stage can save a small firm from going under, especially during a recession.

EXPORTING

- Products that sell well on the home market may not find a ready market abroad. Do your research.
- Gain confidence by opting for a 'soft' export market.
- Take account of export charges when pricing your products for overseas markets.
- Avoid payment problems by insisting on an irrevocable letter of credit.
- It is a misconception that the Middle East represents easy pickings and big profits for very little investment in time, money or energy.
- Language skills are a great asset for exporters.
- A wide range of programmes to assist small firms to break into new export markets is available from Overseas Trade Services.

CASE STUDY
Henry Hedgehog

When David Eke and his wife Delicia set up a small business producing hedgehog boot wipes in 1989, they were advised not to attempt exporting until they had established a solid home market. But when they exhibited for the first time at a major giftware fair in Birmingham, foreign distributors fell in love with their bristly products and the orders came flooding in. They would have been foolish not to take advantage of the overseas demand.

In the early part of 1991, with the recession biting hard, the couple were thankful that they had ignored the advice to hold back on exporting. Around 90 per cent of all they produced was being sent abroad. Exports saved the company. Explains Delicia: 'Like everything else we've done, we just used our gut reaction and went straight to Europe. It was fortunate for us that we did because in early 1991 our home sales dropped dramatically. We merely concentrated more on our European markets.'

European sales kept the Henry Hedgehog company alive until the market picked up again in the UK. Export sales subsequently dropped back to around 70 per cent of production and the company, which operates from a converted poultry unit in a small Avon country village at the foot of the Mendips, was able to maintain turnover at around the £200,000 mark.

David Eke, a former agricultural broker, stumbled on the hedgehog idea more than thirty years ago. It occurred to him that the stiff brushes used for cleaning out milk churns could be adapted to make a boot wipe, particularly useful to farmers with muddy footwear. Years later he resurrected the idea and when his wife took some prototypes to a local craft market in Bath they sold out within two hours. Then in a twelve-week period before Christmas, they sold 1,500 brushes at the market. This was not just a flash in the pan. David distributed more prototypes among thirty farmers he had traded with during his time as a broker. 'They all ordered more of them for friends. I thought that was a good test.'

That led to the idea of exhibiting at agricultural shows and craft fairs held all over England. By now David and Delicia had got the bit between their teeth and they spent a year renting exhibition space at ninety different shows – about two a week.

David was making all the brushes himself, originally in his garage, but after about three months the couple managed to rent a cellar in a big country house that was equipped with a lathe and some band-saws. This enabled them to step up production to keep pace with the growing demand. The brushes were supplied by another company. Henry Hedgehog simply added a base, a handle and the hedgehog features. The idea to diversify the range mainly came from people who visited their stands at the craft fairs. Some ideas were scrapped when they failed to sell well, but the original Henry Hedgehog has since multiplied into a range of around sixteen products, including boot jacks, book ends and door stops.

Throughout 1989 David and Delicia were swept along on the crest of a wave. But then business dried up. Says David: 'We had worked hard all year. We were on a high and thought "great, everything up until November has paid all our expenses, so December is ours". But December didn't happen. We lost money on every show we did.'

The company had been selling exclusively to the buying public. The two founders quickly realized that to generate more sales they had to reach a wider customer base – and that meant selling to the retail trade. But they were uncertain how to go about it. They sought the advice of the Rural Development Commission (RDC) and were advised to exhibit at the leading UK giftware trade shows. The RDC helped with both the financing and the preparation for these events. The first was the Torquay Gift Fair. It was a baptism of fire. Confesses David: 'We went to Torquay thinking we knew what to do. We came away thanking God it wasn't a big show. We didn't know how to display our products properly; we didn't have the right paperwork. We looked very amateurish really.'

Nevertheless, they managed to secure orders worth £4,000. Their next target was the annual Spring Gift Fair held at Birmingham's National Exhibition Centre – the mecca for giftware buyers. An association of Westcountry craftware manufacturers had some spare space on their stand and offered it to Henry Hedgehog. It was a turning point for the Avon firm.

The company took £10,000-worth of orders at the Birmingham show and the couple were overwhelmed by the enthusiasm of overseas distributors. They received about twenty orders directly from giftware shops on the Continent and thought they had hit the big time.

There followed, however, what David describes as a 'comic cuts' exercise: 'I thought that if we boxed up all the orders for the Continent I could probably get them in the back of the Volvo and go over to France, Belgium and Germany and deliver them personally. We could then meet the customers and cement our relationship with them.'

The next move was to find out what documents were required to export the goods to Europe. David rang Customs & Excise and was told that he could pick up the necessary forms from the local Avonmouth office. This he did but he found the questions on the form baffling so he sought the advice of the Bristol Chamber of Commerce, which informed him that the forms were out of date. The questions on the new forms were even more baffling.

Delicia went to the local airport to find out if a freight company could be of any help. The company she approached advised them not to deliver the goods personally, pointing out that delivery vans are often delayed for long periods at custom points. She was also told that if they had failed for some reason to deliver the goods destined for France they would have to take them to Belgium and that would need another set of documents. The complications were manifold. The simplest solution was to leave it to an experienced international carrier. Says David: 'All we have to do is produce four export invoices, ring up the courier, tell them the weights and away it goes. It saves a lot of hassle. A lot of newcomers to the business think that exporting is difficult. We have been surprised how easy it is.'

The exporting push was masterminded with the help of a marketing consultant made available to the Avon company under the DTI's Enterprise Initiative scheme. He surveyed all the company's customers and carried out a complete breakdown of which products were selling well. Points out David: 'We had a lot of facts and figures in our files, but we weren't necessarily using them correctly. He got reports back from all our customers about what they thought of the products and the prices, which was a big help. He also made us realize that we needed to produce a better finish on our products, particularly if we wanted to do well in export markets.'

CASE STUDY
Tidco Croft

Selling sand-making machines to the Middle East may sound an unlikely venture, but Somerset firm Tidco Croft has managed to do just that.

The firm, which sells Barmac rock-crushers, has sold machinery that grinds rocks into sand to the Saudi Arabian construction industry which cannot use the fine-grain sand found locally.

This overseas sales coup is one of many which the firm has pulled off, with support from the DTI's Overseas Trade Services (OTS). Exports are now a major part of the firm's operations and make up nearly 80 per cent of total sales.

The exports boom took off in 1992 when the firm approached the DTI, which jointly operates OTS with the Foreign and Commonwealth Office. Until 1992 exports had been limited to Europe and had mainly been in response to enquiries. Tidco Croft approached the DTI after deciding to target the Middle East proactively. Peter Hobbs, international sales administrator, explains: 'I knew the Middle East well and recognized the sales potential but we needed some help making initial contacts there for our range of crushers. We gave DTI information on our products and the types of customers we were seeking and asked them for market information reports on selected Middle Eastern countries. We soon got back from them some excellent reports with full details of potential customers.'

Hobbs put this information to use when the firm participated in an outward trade mission to Saudi Arabia, supported by the DTI and Bristol Chamber of Commerce. He wrote to the DTI's list of contacts to let them know that Tidco's technical support manager, Tony Kingston, would be in the country and available for technical and commercial discussions. Adds Hobbs: 'By the time he got there, potential customers were queueing up to meet him and discussions opened immediately over a deal for a machine worth £100,000.'

The same strategy of combining an approach to DTI contacts with an outward mission was later used to target customers in Oman and the United Arab Emirates and resulted in the sale of ten machines in those territories. The firm subsequently used the same approach in Yemen in search of further sales successes.

Existing and potential Middle Eastern customers were kept up to date on Tidco's activities and products by mailshots of the firm's brochures and magazine which are distributed by their overseas agents and by Tidco direct.

The DTI helped Tidco in the difficult task of finding agents by providing lists of possible candidates in various countries. Warns Hobbs: 'Any firm exporting should be wary of rushing into agreements with agents who approach them. You should see the agent in operation on their own territory and find out as much as possible about them. If you really want an agent you should get details of as many as possible which is where the DTI can help by providing such information.'

Hobbs' other tip for firms considering overseas trade is to get to know the customers' country: 'Every country has a different way of doing business and a different culture and it is vital to understand how a country does business if you hope to sell a product to them. You can do this by spending time there. That time can turn out to be well invested if you make sales as a result.'

This approach has worked for Tidco which has an annual turnover of around £3 million and now exports to many different countries as far afield as the Middle East, western and eastern Europe, the eastern Mediterranean and Africa. The firm has also made overseas contacts by taking part in OTS inward trade missions and has hosted visits by Foreign and Commonwealth Office representatives from posts around the world.

CHAPTER 10

Administration and Red Tape

Once they have succeeded in raising the finance to set up their companies, many small business entrepreneurs neglect their ongoing requirements for liquidity. They often confuse profit with cash, whereas you can be extremely profitable but short of cash. It is important to look after cash flow because you can make a lot of money this year, but still be short of cash next year. Liquidity is an essential requirement for the ongoing development of the business.

This is an area that can cause a lot of confusion among inexperienced small business entrepreneurs. They often boast that they are ploughing profits back into their companies and have no need of business loans. What they are actually doing is buying capital items out of revenue and decreasing their working capital. In fact, they ought to be financing those fixed assets through long-term loans.

Such misguided entrepreneurs eventually find themselves running out of cash. They haven't recognized that as their turnover increases so does their liquid requirements, basically to cover stock and debtors. Trying to support a growing turnover on an inadequate amount of working capital invariably leads to overtrading. The severity of the problem will depend on the kind of business the entrepreneur is running – whether he is in a cash-generating trade or he is giving several months' credit to his customers.

214

Overtrading

Overtrading means you are taking on far too much business for the capital you've got to support it. It becomes an inverted triangle. You have a very small capital base with a large turnover. You only need one small problem or hiccup to knock the whole pyramid over. The idea is to increase the capital base on which to support an ever growing turnover. That's either done by retaining profits or by injecting outside capital or bringing in venture capital.

Late Payments

One source of funds small businesses often overlook is their own customers. Many small firms apply for extra funding from banks or venture capitalists while they have large sums due to them. The problem is that larger customers are often reluctant to pay their debts within a reasonable period of time, especially in a recessionary climate. Cash-starved small firms could often solve the problem overnight if they could get access to money owed them more quickly.

The advantage to the larger companies of not paying their bills until they absolutely have to is obvious. At any given time, they will have vast sums owing to numerous suppliers. The longer they can retain that money in their bank accounts, the more interest they can earn on it, taking the pressure off their own cash flows. As one financial expert puts it: 'No one is going to thank a group treasurer for paying early when he could have had the money invested on the money market.' At the last count, Britain's small firms were owed £50 billion in overdue debts. On average they are waiting eighty-one days for payment from date of invoice.

British companies have the worst record for late payment in the whole of Europe, according to a survey by Europe's largest debt collection group Intrum Justitia. This depressing discovery is supported by another survey conducted by Robin Teverson, a

Liberal Democrat. A report based on this maintains that late payment is such a serious problem that it is holding back the pace of economic recovery. It also identified bigger companies as the chief culprits. Teverson asked some 600 businesses whether late payment was affecting their cash flow. The response was indeed alarming: 'Over half said the late payment of debts by their industrial customers had threatened the future of their businesses. There is even greater concern for the future. Again, over half stated that their investment plans had been cut back for the same reason.'

Industrial blackmail

Many of the businesses have standard credit terms of thirty days, but often their customers are taking up to three months or longer. Nan Palmer, a director of Print World UK Ltd, in Callington, Cornwall, claimed that it was 'industrial blackmail. Many of the big firms say that if we don't wait for them to pay, we won't get their business.'

The survey painted a bleak picture of big companies holding their smaller suppliers to ransom. Observed Teverson: 'The evidence shows that it is the big companies up country that are holding back payments. It means that our small companies are financing their expansion – for free.'

It is easy to point the finger of blame, but the problem is not always as straightforward as it seems. The managing director of a chemical company acquired in a management buy-out discovered that the firm he inherited was several months behind in its payments to its small business suppliers. Morally, he felt compelled to redress the situation, but to do so would have cost him in the region of £575,000, which would have put the viability of his newly-acquired firm under threat. He was unable to do what his conscience dictated.

In such circumstances, of course, it becomes a vicious circle. Everyone is late paying everybody else. But it is the small businesses at the end of the line that suffers most – sometimes fatally.

Undeterred by the moral implications, the larger companies play on the fact that the smaller firms cannot exist without their patronage and therefore are unlikely to do much about it. It is very difficult for a small firm, desperate to get business, to adopt an aggressive stance towards the very providers of its livelihood.

Self-Regulation

The Department of Trade and Industry, under pressure from small firms lobbying groups, has been reviewing its policies towards late payments. Up until now it has resisted calls for there to be a statutory interest payment slapped on overdue bills. This solution has already become law in a number of other European countries. John Langhorn, UK managing director of Intrum Justitia, points out that countries such as Sweden, Finland and Norway, which have the most extensive legislation on late payment, have the shortest overdue payment periods. But in true British fashion the UK government has rejected statutory measures, such as the right to charge interest on overdue accounts, in favour of a policy of self-regulation. It has only gone so far as to publish a code of conduct which appeals to the conscience of persistent late payers.

One of the arguments against legislation put forward by the government is that it could penalize small firms as well as the large ones. It points out that small firms are also guilty of late payments and would probably be in a less favourable position than their bigger counterparts to absorb any financial penalties resulting from legal prosecution.

The truth, most likely, is that late payment is contagious. If the bigger companies fail to pay their bills on time, the small companies have insufficient funds to pay their suppliers and everyone blames everybody else. There seems little prospect of a resolution of the problem in the immediate future. Even if a bill is drawn up to penalize the worst offenders, there is no guarantee it will ever reach the statute book.

Pressure is, however, mounting on the government to introduce statutory interest charges on erring companies. The latest body to enter the argument is the British Chamber of Commerce (BCC), which represents more than 200,000 businesses. It has joined the chorus of calls for action on what it says is an 'endemic culture' of late payment of bills. BCC leaders argue that late payment is jeopardizing the UK's economic recovery by restricting the growth of the primary small businesses on which so much depends. The BCC supports its argument with the results of a survey showing that 94 per cent of almost 700 sample companies had suffered negative effects from late payment. As many as 71 per cent said they knew of at least one company that had gone out of business because of it.

Factoring

Increasingly, small firms are turning to factoring to solve the problem. This enables them to obtain up to 80 per cent of the value of an invoice immediately it is despatched. The service doesn't come cheap and many small businesses see it as an extra financial burden they are unprepared to pay. Others, however, see it as a solution that is well worth the price.

Factoring does more than improve a small firm's liquidity. It can smooth a firm's cash flow and help it forecast financial progress more accurately. It can do away with the necessity for a sales ledger and credit control team, thus saving the wages' bill. It also provides an in-built insurance for bad debts, and for exporting firms it reduces the hassle involved in collecting debts from overseas customers.

The UK market for factoring has grown rapidly in the past twelve years, achieving an average compound increase per year since 1981 of around 20 per cent. Despite, or perhaps because of, the recession, the industry continues to grow. In 1993 the eleven members of the Association of British Factors & Discounters provided 11,000 businesses with over £1.6 billion in finance – 34 per cent more than the UK's venture capitalists.

According to Michael Bickers, writing in the January 1994 issue of *Director* magazine, there are a number of reasons for the comparatively recent awakening of interest in factoring. Higher interest rates generally have meant that the cost of credit has increased and trade debtors are taking increasingly longer to pay. This, in turn has put a great strain on working capital with the result that the management of working capital, especially that of credit control, has taken on a level of priority not previously experienced by industry. More recently, the banks' general reluctance to lend to small businesses at previous levels has meant that even more companies are turning to factoring.

Domestic Factoring and Discounting Services

Many small firms have between 20 and 25 per cent of their annual turnover tied up in trade credit. Factoring and invoice discounting help companies to turn their major current asset – unpaid invoices – into working capital.

The great attraction of factoring and invoice discounting is flexibility, providing a range of services that can be tailored to meet individual requirements. The basic services, however, fall into the following categories:

● *Invoice discounting* is suited to companies that want finance in exchange for their invoices, but little else. Clients maintain full control over their sales ledgers and remain responsible for chasing slow payers.

In an invoice discounting relationship, companies send out their invoices, duplicating them to the factor. On receipt, the factor makes an immediate cash payment of up to 80 per cent of the approved invoice value. The balance is due when the customer pays.

• In the case of *full service factoring*, factors assume responsibility for both the administration of the sales ledger and credit management. This ensures that the ledger is kept up to date, that the collection of outstanding debts is handled in an efficient and diplomatic manner and that finance is released. Full service factoring can be offered with or without credit protection (non-recourse or recourse factoring).

There are two types of full service factoring. With *non-recourse factoring*, factors provide 100 per cent credit cover against bad debt losses, thereby protecting profit margins, and it is at clients' discretion how much they draw down on at any one time. In the case of *recourse factoring*, factors assume responsibility for both the administration of the sales ledger and provide credit management; but credit protection is not provided. Recourse factoring tends to be used by businesses with a larger spread of customers or those already utilizing credit insurance.

International Factoring Services

Business globalization and the crumbling of trade barriers has led to the development of a number of financial packages for exporters wishing to sell their goods overseas, as well as for importers seeking to minimize their exposure to trade risk.

In addition to the full range of services offered in the UK domestic market, export services will usually include:

• Advice on trading terms in export markets.
• Local collections and assistance with the resolution of disputes.
• Protection against exchange risk when invoicing in a foreign currency.
• Swifter transfer of funds to the UK.
• Expert local knowledge of overseas buyers' creditworthiness.
• Financial facilities available in sterling or major currencies.

How much does it cost?

Factoring firms claim that their services are extremely cost-effective, providing finance when it is needed and sales ledger and credit control functions. All of this would otherwise have to be paid for in increased staff and overhead costs.

Charges for factoring are made in two ways: a fee for the services and a separate charge for the finance made available against sales, geared to current base rates. The service fee varies between 0.5 per cent and 2.5 per cent of gross annual turnover. For example, a company with a £500,000 turnover could pay a service fee of around £6,000.

The principal charge for invoice discounting is a discount charge linked to established base rates which is comparable with overdraft rates. In most cases, a fee is charged to cover the administration of the agreement – normally between 0.2 per cent and 0.5 per cent of turnover.

The charges for factoring and invoice discounting should be set against the many services and benefits that they provide, from a reduced administrative burden to the flexible provision of finance. Taken together, the service package that factoring and discounting provide is highly competitive – an important element in the rapid growth of factoring and invoice discounting in the UK market.

Associations

There are two main organizations that supervise the professional standards of factoring firms. The Association of British Factors and Discounters (ABFD), formed in 1976, comprises twelve of the UK's largest factoring firms representing over 90 per cent of the market for factoring and discounting services. ABFD's contribution to the enterprise economy is illustrated by the fact that around 70 per cent of its members' clients have turnovers of less than £1 million.

The other organization in this field is the Association of Invoice Factors, whose ten members represent mainly independent factoring companies not aligned to the major clearing banks in the UK. Founded in 1978, this association includes among its members both independent finance companies and financial subsidiaries of industrial concerns.

A list of the members of both associations, together with contact numbers is provided in Appendix A at the end of this book.

Terminology

In recognition of the difficulty that many businesses encounter with much of the terminology surrounding the industry, some factors are now avoiding use of the terms 'factoring' and 'invoice discounting'. For example, Kellock Factors and Griffin Factors now refer to their services as 'Cash-flow' and 'Cash-flow Finance' respectively, and RoyScot Factors uses 'Cashflow Management'.

Small businesses have been put off from considering factoring by the perceived high costs involved. It is widely regarded as a last-resort lending mechanism and is still one of the least used means of raising finance among small firms. However, economic constraints are causing an increasing number of small firms to consider factoring as an option.

Michael Bickers in his *Director* magazine article lists the following pros and cons:

The Pros:

- Provides business finance for working capital requirements, thereby eliminating or reducing cashflow problems;
- Attractive balance sheet or substantial net worth not required;
- Funds are provided in proportion to sales, reducing the risks of overtrading;
- Relieves companies of the burdens of credit control and maintenance of the sales ledger.

The Cons:

- The service is perceived to be expensive;
- Loss of control of the sales ledger. A third party has access to all your customers in respect of the issue of debt;
- Image — factoring is associated with last-resort-lending. Will it be seen as a sign of financial weakness by suppliers?

Finance for Swimsuits

When the two directors of a sportswear business achieved a breakthrough by obtaining the major order they had always dreamed of from a leading mail order firm, they were immediately faced with the problem of how to finance the deal. The order for 23,000 swimsuits was far larger than anything they had handled before and they badly needed additional finance to pay for machinery and materials.

Their solution was to opt for the NatWest credit factoring scheme, which guaranteed them 70 per cent of the value of the invoices on despatch. The service didn't come cheap at an initial 1.5 per cent of sales, but the directors saw it as their only means of survival. 'It took all the worry out of it,' said one director. 'We didn't really have much choice. We couldn't have got the money any other way.'

More Profit

Some experts argue that factoring should simply be regarded as another form of borrowing. Observes one financial adviser: 'It's a help because it cuts out the waiting time, but you pay heavily for that and it never improves the gearing of the company, because it actually increases the borrowing.'

The banks have utilized factoring as a means of getting more profit out of their organizations, because whereas banks used to provide certain cover for debts under a floating charge, their degree of control over the debtors was virtually non-existent. Factoring organizations, often subsidiaries of the major clearing banks, can actually take over the ledger. They are then much more able to monitor closely a company's debtor profile and lend against it than in the case of the traditional clearing bank operation.

Factoring has the distinct advantage that the amount of finance made available to the user tends to increase as the business expands. This is because the user can claim a proportion of the outstanding debts. This contrasts sharply with an overdraft facility which is usually for a fixed amount agreed in advance with a bank. Another advantage is that factoring companies often keep a black list, which encourages big firms to pay up on time to avoid any adverse effect on their credit rating.

Credit Control

Not everyone believes it is necessary to resort to factoring to control the bad debts problem, however. Some experts believe a lot can be achieved by more efficient credit control. 'The name of the game is not debt collection; it's cash flow,' suggests one expert. 'What many small companies fail to realize is that debtors are the easiest form of finance they can put their hands on.'

Instead of looking at the issue in this way, most small firms behave like bad bankers. They lend money to their customers through selling goods and services on credit. They earn no interest on what they have lent. They don't seem to grasp the point that sales are not really sales until the customer has actually paid. The transaction remains a free loan while the cash is outstanding. Big companies regard living off such free loans as fair game in business life.

A lot of blame rests with the small business entrepreneurs themselves. Many of them do not bother to set up efficient systems for keeping on top of outstanding debts. There are a number of well-established guidelines for avoiding debts:

224

- Establish a systematic procedure. Where possible, send invoices out the same day as the goods or services are despatched.
- Ensure that invoices are properly prepared; that they carry an order number and bear the name of the person who normally deals with them.
- Check that invoices and correspondence are properly addressed.
- Make sure that customers understand the terms and conditions of payment at the time the order is discussed. Remember to state them clearly on all necessary documents.
- Challenge any terms of payment you consider unfair and liable to harm your business – 'No payment for ninety days' for example. Be sure you know what you are letting yourself in for.
- Develop a proper collecting procedure. Send out statements on time, for example.
- Don't be afraid to ask for the money once it becomes due. Don't let an old debt became a bad debt.

It might be a good idea to offer a settlement discount for early payment or to charge interest for every month payment is overdue. But both should be made clear in the terms of payment. Administering such schemes, however, can sometimes give more problems than they solve.

Small firms that rely on one or two major companies for their income are particularly vulnerable to the problem of bad debts. One solution is to bring the big companies out of their environment and down to your level. With a little research it should not be difficult to find out the name of the financial director of a guilty big company. Telephone him at home, apologize for the disturbance, but explain how vital prompt payment is for the survival of your business.

If you are supplying him with good quality products, it will not be in his interest for you to go out of business, but, more importantly, he will not wish to be contacted at home again and will probably make every endeavour to ensure you are paid on time in future.

Henry Hedgehog, the small business run by David Eke and his wife Delicia (see page 208), has made a special effort to keep on top of bad debts. Most of its customers pay within sixty days. Those who fail to keep to agreed payment terms find the label of a credit protection company attached to their second statements. This invariably does the trick. The company insists that all the customers get the same treatment, even if they are stores with household names. 'If it upsets them, so what? If they don't pay on time, we don't want them.'

Delicia, who comes from a banking background, keeps an equally tight control of the company's cash flow. She maintains: 'You should always keep your cash flow statement up to date at the end of the month, because then you know where your money is.' But when there are problems with cash flow, she advises: 'Always tell your bank precisely what's happening as it happens, not after it's happened.'

She insists that small business operators should always keep in touch with reality and always live within their means. Never be lulled into a false sense of security: 'You might be able to kid a lot of people, but never try to kid yourself. If you're getting a bit tight on cash flow and you've got orders for next month, they're orders for next month, not this month. Don't sit down and think: "We shall be all right". You've always got to be on top of your financial situation and be honest with yourself. If it's tight, don't go out and buy new machinery; make do with the old.'

Keeping records

You will need to keep records for your own sake, but NatWest advises in its guide to business start-ups that they should also be kept for legal reasons to support your VAT and income tax payments and claims. If you are a limited company you must also send in a copy of your annual report and accounts to Companies House and keep records of board meetings and transactions in your company's shares.

If you are a sole trader or a partner, the tax rules are different, but you will need to produce complete financial records unless your annual turnover is under £10,000.

If you plan to keep information about people electronically, for example on a computer or word processor, you need to consider registering your business under the Data Protection Act 1984. This act restricts computer users by making them register and meet with the Data Protection Principles.

Tax Liabilities

By deducting your business expenses from your gross profit you can reduce your tax bill – another important reason for keeping proper records. If you are a sole trader or in a partnership, you pay income tax. If you form a limited company, you are obliged to pay corporation tax on the profits your company makes. You are also required to pay income tax on your wages. This will be paid by PAYE (Pay As You Earn) since you are an employee of the company.

Value Added Tax (VAT)

Each year, the government sets a level of turnover and if your business exceeds this level you must apply for VAT registration. In some cases, it can make sense to register even if you are below the prescribed level.

Paying VAT is a straightforward process if it applies to all your supplies. You charge VAT on certain goods and services and send the money you collect to Customs and Excise every month or three months. In turn, you may be charged VAT on goods and services you need to run your business, such as materials, legal fees, telephone bills and so on. If so, you can claim it all back.

In practice, you simply take the second 'outgoing' total from the first 'incoming' total. Then you pay or claim the difference. VAT regulations change constantly, so you need to keep up to date with developments.

Customs and Excise take a firm line with businesses that pay late or do not register when they should.

Quality Standards

Another burdensome area of administration that is increasingly being imposed on small firms is British Standard 5750 (BS 5750) and its international equivalent, ISO 9000. Many small firms regard the quality standard BS 5750 as too onerous and unnecessary, but since many of the larger firms among their customers are demanding compliance with the standard as a condition of doing business, small firms have little option but to commit resources to it.

BS 5750 started out with the ambitious aim of revolutionizing UK management by concentrating on quality in all the aspects of operating a business – a worthy goal, but an additional burden small firms are finding hard to bear.

In an article published in the December 1992 issue of *Director* magazine, Matthew Rock maintains that now large companies have started to drive the quality issue through their supply chains, the weaknesses of BS 5750 are becoming apparent. 'While medium-sized companies are benefiting from the discipline, smaller firms are hurting,' he observes.

Rock notes 'signs of inertia and disillusionment everywhere.' He cites a *Director* survey of private businesses in which 58 per cent of a thousand respondents were neither applying for nor considering BS 5750. Of these, 63 per cent considered BS 5750 accreditation would neither assist in the development of their company nor provide new business opportunities.

A NatWest quarterly survey of small businesses found similar anxiety. 'Many small firms are concerned that certification under BS 5750 will raise costs without improving quality,' it deduced. 'Others fear that they will be forced out of business because they cannot afford certification. Ninety-five per cent of the comments derived from the survey were negative.'

The concern voiced is echoed by Ro Pengelly, employment affairs policy chairman at the Federation of Small Businesses, who goes even further: 'BS 5750 does not bring benefits to any company under twenty employees.'

Pengelly points to a threefold problem. In her view the standard is 'over-complicated, over-expensive and being forced upon us'.

Rock points out in his article that BS 5750, which emerged from the Ministry of Defence's Def Stan 0521, was originally designed for large suppliers to the defence industry. Since it was written in 1979, BS 5750's remit has become wider and it has been actively marketed to non-manufacturing companies. It was also taken as the model for the European and international versions of the standard – EN 29000 and ISO 9000 respectively.

Many small businesses complain that, given this large-industry history, it is not surprising that it is inappropriate to their needs. The issue of coercion is leading to much hostility because increasingly, large companies are insisting that suppliers, whatever their size, should be accredited.

The process of making BS 5750 a more appropriate quality standard for smaller firms began in earnest in early 1994 when findings of a pilot study were revealed. Conducted by the Small Business Research Trust, it was the forerunner of a survey issued at random to 30,000 smaller firms. The study, aimed at assessing the problems small firms face with the standard, received the backing of Lord Strathclyde, then small firms minister. It found that small businesses doubted that BS 5750 could help them improve the consistency of their quality. Rather, they saw the standard as a marketing tool to keep existing customers and obtain new ones.

Welcoming the research, John Cammell, board member of the British Standards Institution, said: 'The problems of smaller firms in implementing BS 5750 must be addressed . . . The challenge is to make the standard more user-friendly and ensure its application is simple for small firms.'

Assessment and registration

Despite all the controversy, an increasing number of large firms are insisting that their small business suppliers are registered for BS 5750 as a guarantee that they are dealing with an organization that gives high priority to quality assurance. In the circumstances many small firms are obliged to seek assessment and registration via the British Standards Institution.

To be registered by BSI means that your firm has been independently assessed by a team experienced in quality assurance and the technical conditions that apply in your industry. The team is chosen by BSI in agreement with the company undergoing assessment. The team's size depends on how big your company is, the product or service for which you wish to be registered and the complexities of the technologies involved. A BSI representative will call on you, on request, to explain the assessment procedure and to advise you on the requirements of BS 5750.

The first essential for assessment is that you are operating a quality system which you consider meets the requirements of BS 5750. You will be asked to send the system documents in the form of your quality manual to BSI for checking to see that all the appropriate parts of the standard are covered.

Registration will commence when the assessment team is satisfied that you are implementing your accepted quality system and you have agreed to the required level of audit tests.

The BSI Kitemark

Your customers will often want to know not only that you have a first class quality system to BS 5750 standard but also that your finished products are up to the BSI Kitemark which carries the assurance that products comply with national or international standards.

The Kitemark is BSI's registered certification trade mark, which you can be licensed to use if BSI is satisfied that you produce goods consistently to the required standards.

Commercial benefits

BSI argues that meeting its quality assurance standards can result in tangible commercial benefits:

● BSI certification is a first-class marketing tool. The certification marks and symbols can be used on publicity, packaging and company literature.

● Major buyers like the Ministry of Defence already accept BSI certification and registration as proof of quality and technical expertise.

● Your customers are much less likely to ask for their own special assessments – thus saving everyone time and money.

● The cost of lost orders, reworking, extra handling, scrapped production, wastage, senior executive time – all these will come down once you are operating BS 5750.

● Better quality performance will improve customer satisfaction and lead to increased sales, competitiveness and profitability.

● As more British standards become harmonized with international ones, BSI certification will be an increasing help to you in export markets.

Red tape

There is no question that significant progress has been made over the past decade in reducing the red tape burden on small firms, releasing them to concentrate on their prime function of creating new wealth and jobs. But the view persists that there is still much more to be done in this area. A recent survey by the Federation of Small Businesses shows that more than 40 per cent of small firm owners are spending around one day a week dealing with such matters as cash flow, business plans and debt. Some 18 per cent spend more than a day on administrative issues.

Ian Handford, the Federation's policy group chairman, points out: 'Time spent on paper work (albeit necessary) is valuable time spent away from the pivotal function of business owners, namely wealth creation. Government proposals to tackle late payment and to abolish the statutory audit for small incorporated companies must be introduced as soon as possible to release some business owners from unnecessary and time-consuming paperwork exercises.'

The Federation survey also showed that 60 per cent of small firms are now faced with increased legislation and administration costs as a result of the European single market. Only five per cent saw greater turnover opportunities arising from trade barriers being lowered throughout Europe.

KEY POINTS

- Small firms often confuse profit with cash and neglect their ongoing requirements for liquidity.
- Trying to support a growing turnover on an inadequate amount of working capital invariably leads to overtrading.
- Many cash-starved small companies are suffering from late payment of bills, particularly where their larger customers are concerned.

- Factoring provides 80 per cent of the value of an invoice immediately it is despatched.
- An efficient system of credit control can help to reduce bad debts.
- Keeping good records helps you to run your business more efficiently and is required to support your VAT and income tax payments and claims.
- Many small firms resent having to comply with quality standard BS 5750, but large company customers are increasingly making it a condition of contract.

CASE STUDY
Gibsons of Bournemouth

In 1987 Gibsons of Bournemouth, a supplier of designer dresses to small fashion boutiques all over Britain, enjoyed a 30 per cent surge in sales at a time when many UK clothing firms were going under. Recalls Richard Proctor, Gibsons' owner and managing director: 'We had stopped going to trade shows and indulging in other extravagant things as part of a cost-cutting exercise, so our prices had become competitive and our customers were buying a lot more.'

This runaway success could well have been Gibsons' undoing if Proctor had not taken the precaution of enlisting the aid of RoyScot Factors (now known as Royal Bank of Scotland Invoice Finance). The company had become a victim of its own success – the more business it generated, the more it needed to go back to the bank to raise extra cash to finance the growth.

In common with many clothing companies, Gibsons was faced with an enormous gap between the time it ordered materials and when it received payment for the finished goods. It was in the invidious position of having to buy fabric in April to produce dresses and suits that would not be paid for until the following winter, even though the garments were delivered in time for the autumn season, and Proctor found himself in a classic dilemma: 'How do you finance production of next season's garments when you haven't yet received payment for the current season?'

He had grown tired of the tedious treadmill of repeatedly revaluing property he owned to provide security for yet another top-up of his overdraft.

Factoring provided a tailor-made solution, and he embraced it with unqualified enthusiasm. Instead of having to wait up to six months for payment, he was able to receive 80 per cent of the value of the invoice from the factoring company within 48 hours of it being despatched. Enthuses Proctor: 'The level of orders that

234

you receive is reflected later on by the amount of money you get in. The great advantage of factoring is that it allows you to bring that forward by many months – virtually to the moment you actually write the invoice.' Also in a business where the personal touch can be important, he did not wish to run the risk of his customers being upset by indelicate demands for them to pay up. He says: 'Our customers are scarcely aware that we use factoring, although we do state the fact on our invoices.'

He points out that he only pays 2.5 per cent over base rate for whatever he borrows against the value of an invoice. This, he argues, is no more costly than the overdraft facility he has with the Royal Bank of Scotland. And he only draws out as much money as he needs, which means it is a lot more flexible than a straight loan. On top of this, however, Gibsons pays an additional charge to the factoring company of 0.65 per cent of annual turnover. Companies that also use factoring for chasing overdue payments can be charged up to two per cent of their annual turnover, but Proctor decided to retain control over his own sales ledger since he already had a computerized system operating when he opted for factoring.

Another consideration that persuaded him to retain credit control in-house was that he supplies about 300 dress shops 'from the tip of Cornwall to the north of Scotland'. Handing over the administration of such a diversity of customers to a factoring company would inevitably be costly.

Proctor finds the charge he does pay is reasonable for the service the factoring company provides: 'What you get for that money is the facility to draw on finance when you need it. Secondly, you get something I think is very important to small businesses. That is the sort of discipline that a large company such as ICI might apply to its sales ledger, but which the average small business usually doesn't have – the discipline of making regular checks on which customers' payments are overdue and seriously thinking about when to take action against them.'

The discipline is imposed on Gibsons by the fact that the

factoring company can claim back the money it has advanced on any invoice that is not paid within three months. 'There is considerable pressure on us to collect the money, which is a useful discipline. A small business doesn't normally have one person whose sole job it is to chase overdue accounts as many big companies do and it is the sort of thing that can very easily be overlooked.'

CHAPTER 11

Picking the Right Staff

As your company grows you will almost certainly need to take on more staff to help you cope with increased production and the mounting administrative load. But think twice before you decide to take on additional full-time staff. There are a number of alternatives that achieve the same ends without placing such a heavy burden on your overheads.

You can, for example, sub-contract part of your production. The danger here, of course, is that it might not be easy to find a contractor who will make such a good job of the work as you do. Your sub-contracted consignment will almost inevitably be only a small part of the outside firm's work load. It would be very surprising if the sub-contractor took as much pride in, or knew as much about, your product as you do. You need to feel confident that this will not affect the quality of your products or services to the extent that you are likely to lose customers.

Outworkers

Some manufacturing procedures are highly suited to outworkers. These mostly relate to products that require a high degree of manual labour and individual care. All over the country there are women who, for one reason or another have to be at home but who still retain such skills as typing or sewing. If you produce a prototype that needs to be mass-produced, such outworkers, costing you nothing in overheads, are an ideal solution to your problem. You simply deliver them the materials for the job and keep a close watch on quality. They find it convenient to work at home, putting their skills to use and earning some extra money, while at the same time being able to look after their family responsibilities.

My wife's designer glove puppet business was built up by employing a network of such outworkers. An artistic designer produced the prototypes for the puppets; my wife shopped around for the raw materials and made regular visits to her network of outworkers to supply them with their materials and to pick up the finished articles. This left time free for her to concentrate on marketing and product research. She did not have to concern herself with finding expensive factory space or with buying sewing machines. The outworkers were already equipped with them.

Outsourcing

As the recession took hold outsourcing became the name of the game for large companies. Desperate to reduce their overheads and at the limit of staff cutbacks, they turned increasingly to outside specialists and consultants to provide their basic needs. The small firm entrepreneur, however, does not need to be under economic pressure to realize the advantages of keeping a slim workforce in the early growth stages of a business.

There is a real danger that as a small firm starts to take off the founders can become carried away by success and make hasty decisions about acquiring more sophisticated resources and hiring additional staff. Often extra hands are needed to meet a seasonal or cyclical upsurge in demand. It is all too easy in the first flush of success to take on extra staff at the height of a seasonal upswing, only to find these new staff members surplus to requirements when things tame down again.

Interim management

Increasingly, this problem is being overcome by resorting to the compromise of interim management. Temporary clerical staff, brought in at peak times to help cope with the administrative work load, is a practice that has been around for a good many years. Interim management applies the same principle to people with management skills.

It has become more popular during the recession for two reasons. One is that companies want to keep their work force lean until the economy picks up. The other is that there have been a huge number of redundancies and there has probably never been a time when so many talented managers have found themselves hunting, often in vain, for work.

The interim manager is attached to the hiring company simply for the duration of the assignment. When it has been completed he or she goes off in search of another project. Unlike consultants, interim managers become an integral part of the company for the duration of the assignment and to all intents and purposes they become a member of the staff, although everyone knows their tenure in the job is likely to be short-lived.

The idea behind interim management has been around on the Continent for some time. The Dutch-based Boer and Croon Group and Swiss-owned Egon Zehnder International set up a European company, Executive Interim Management (EIM) over twenty years ago. Its London office, opened ten years later, has a cadre of carefully selected senior-level interim managers on its books. Says Robert Mark, who runs EIM's London office: 'Our people have to go through an intense vetting programme, including reference checks and most of them are fairly well-known figures. They are always highly experienced blue-chip people in an age bracket of between forty-eight and fifty-five. They are usually unwitting victims of mega-mergers and the like.'

To co-ordinate the approach of the growing number of interim management companies setting up in the UK, the Association of

Temporary & Interim Executive Services (ATIES) was founded in January 1990. The ten members include offshoots of the consulting group P-E International and accountants Ernst & Young.

Charles Russam, whose Dunstable-based interim management company GMS Consultancy is a founder member, is the association's vice-chairman. Research conducted by GMS estimates that the market for independent consultants in the UK is around £70 million to £100 million a year and ATIES' members are reckoned to have somewhere between a 12 and 15 per cent share of the available business.

Russam believes interim management has been slow to develop in the UK because there are so many misconceptions about it: 'It's non-traditional; companies think they are being asked to take on other people's cast-offs; that it's out of work people trying to fill in; they don't believe that interim managers can come up to speed quickly enough.'

But he also believes interim management is about to become a fast-growth market, 'primarily because lots of executives want to do it; they're being released by their companies at a much younger age. Forty is too old these days. A lot of people in their mid-forties say to themselves: "I've reached a high position; I've got some skills; the children have flown the nest; I haven't got much of a mortgage; I'm not going to play this political rat race any more." ' There are also significant advantages to companies in using interim managers to sort out one-off problems rather than turning to more traditional management consultants. Says John Skinner, an interim manager with Barton Interim Management (BIM): 'For the period of an assignment, I become a member of the company's staff rather than an off-line adviser. When a consultant goes in he is purely an adviser and doesn't get his hands dirty very often.'

Nicky Cutts, BIM's chief, who used to run an international headhunting operation from Amsterdam, but is now UK-based, adds that by becoming a temporary member of the company's management team, the interim executive's loyalty is attached to the client rather than to the consultancy firm that sent him. She also argues that interim management firms have access to a greater range of talent and specialized knowledge than most consultancies.

Another advantage interim managers have over ordinary consultants, she points out, is that they are cheaper. They normally cost between a half and two-thirds less than consultants. Some assignments last only a few days, though the average is around three months.

BIM evolved out of Cutts' headhunting work. She found she was talking to an increasing number of executives who were looking for part-time or project work. She adds: 'On the other hand, I was getting a number of companies – often quite small – who wanted help they couldn't afford on a full-time basis. A typical example is a small company that needs more financial help than a firm of accountants can give it. It can use a financial director one day a week. This financial director would be far too highly qualified for the job as a full-time position, but he can help perhaps five or six small companies in this way. There are no pension schemes or holiday entitlements to worry about. Once the interim manager has done the job, he leaves; there are no redundancy problems. So it's cost-effective and it's time-effective.'

Another example of where interim management can be an ideal solution is when a company wants to relocate and finds that part of its management team has decided against moving with it. The company can take on a temporary manager to tide it over.

But where do interim managers come from and what attracts them to temporary assignments? John Skinner suggests that two key qualities are required of a successful interim manager: 'Basically, there's got to be an appetite to get something good out of a company situation in a short time. You've got to get into it and within days have worked out in your head what you're going to do. The other quality is keenness to solve problems and get through them quickly, because both of these characteristics have an effect on the time involved, which is, of course, the essence of interim management.'

In general, Skinner finds that he can settle quite rapidly into an interim management assignment and usually manages to avoid any resistance from permanent members of the client company suspicious of his role. He adds: 'If the managing director has done his job right, the way is paved. In other words, it is so glaringly obvious to everybody that help is needed that they have no option but to accept you.'

Non-executive directors

Another way to help you shoulder the increasing burdens of a growing company is to consider inviting a non-executive director to join your workforce. This can be a very flexible arrangement. The non-executive director can put in as much time as you require and as much as he or she can afford to give. It can be a mere two days a month or four days a week, for example, depending on how much work needs to be undertaken. The input can also vary according to the peaks and troughs of business cycles.

The non-executive director will normally be chosen according to his or her expertise in a skill your company lacks or in which it has a particular weakness. The real advantage is that a non-executive director is usually someone with a long-standing business background and plenty of experience of the kind of problems a small business is likely to encounter. The non-executive director will normally also have good contacts in the business world, which can stand the small firm in good stead and lend it considerable credibility.

In some cases venture capital groups and other lending organizations will only invest in a small firm on the understanding that a nominated non-executive director becomes part of the board. They insist that an experienced business practitioner be appointed to keep a safe watch on their investment and to prevent a small firm going too far down a dangerous path before taking remedial action.

Recruitment

Of course, if your company really is growing rapidly and looks likely to continue to expand into the foreseeable future, stop-gap solutions such as those described above will not be the answer. You will need to recruit full-time staff who are going to become a permanent part of your workforce and grow with your company – and you hope make a long-term contribution to its success.

Needless to say, those you select for a more permanent role in your company need to be chosen carefully. If you do not have a particular person in mind, such as a friend or relative, you will have to search the job market for a person with the skills and experience you require. The Midland Bank, in its guide to starting a small business, advises that this can be done through your local job centre or careers office, by advertising in a local newspaper or through an employment agency. The latter is usually the most expensive way.

You should have a clear idea of what the job involves, the skills and experience required of the jobholder, and what salary and benefits you are prepared to offer. If you advertise the job you should also include details about your business and when and how to apply. You must always bear in mind that it is illegal to advertise a job and then select people in a way that discriminates against a particular sex or race.

You should obtain background information about each inter-viewee by asking them to forward a completed application form and curriculum vitae (CV) before the interview. The interview is a fact-finding mission for both parties, so outline the nature of the job and your business in greater detail. If possible test the applicant's skills – for example, the typing, dictation and shorthand skills of a secretary.

243

The employer's responsibilities

If employees earn more than the minimum weekly wage, you must deduct income tax under the PAYE system as well as their national insurance contributions from their wage or salary.

You must notify the local Inland Revenue Office and Department of Social Security that you are employing someone. You will be told how to calculate the income tax and national insurance contributions and how you should pay these amounts to the Inspector of Taxes.

You should also take out employers' liability insurance to cover your business against accidental damage to employees and/or their property.

Employees contracted to work for more than sixteen hours a week must be provided with a written Statement of Terms of Employment. This sets out the name of the employer, employee and the job title. It should also contain a job description and details of hours of work, amount and frequency of pay, sick pay arrangements, holiday entitlement, pension rights, disciplinary regulations, grievance procedures and the period of notice required to end employment.

Each year you must complete a P60 certificate of pay, tax and national insurance contributions; a P35 year-end payroll summary; and a P14 year-end return for employees.

Three other important aspects of becoming an employer are outlined in NatWest's business start-up guide:

Health and Safety
Make sure you are in line with the Health and Safety regulations which lay down minimum standards for fire precautions and other safety issues. Contact your local Health and Safety Executive for advice and information which will help you set up and maintain safe and legal working conditions for employees.

Trade Unions
Make sure you know about the various laws which safeguard your employees' rights to choose whether to join a trade union.

Dismissing an Employee

Should it come to the worst, tread carefully. Talk to your solicitor first and follow the legal procedure exactly. Any employee is entitled to the period of notice set out in the terms of employment, or at least one week's notice if they have been employed for more than a month. You can only sack someone on the spot if you can prove they are guilty of some gross misconduct, like theft. Even in extreme circumstances, sacking on the spot should be your last resort. Even after giving due notice, you should still think carefully before dismissing anyone. Statutory compensation for unfair dismissal can be costly.

Training

Research shows that 88 per cent of firms with more than 500 employees have training plans, but in businesses with fewer than twenty-five staff that figure drops to less than 17 per cent. The disparity occurs mainly because small firms cannot afford to send employees on training courses.

Comments David Lavarack, head of small business services at Barclays Bank: 'The major gap now is the skills gap across the whole range of management skills. People end up being a jack-of-all-trades in small companies. But it is unreasonable to expect that people will have all the necessary skills. What you need is accessible pieces of information.'

A solution of sorts was offered in 1994 when Barclays joined the Clydesdale and Co-operative Banks in backing a new Department of Employment initiative for training loans for small firms.

The small firms training loan is targeted at all businesses that have fewer than fifty employees. It covers the cost of hiring a consultant to explain what the training requirements are and also helps to pay for replacement of staff while employees are being trained.

Speaking at the launch of the training loans, Lord Henley, the employment minister said:

'Our shopfront to the world is filled with small businesses striving for competitiveness, and that effort is never-ending. In this tough environment we in government work hard to ensure that we offer small businesses all the help we can.

'Small firms employ over one third of the working population of this country – that's around nine million people – and their success is crucial to the prosperity of our economy. Between 1989 and 1991 [the latest figures available], for example, they generated 350,000 new jobs.'

Commenting on the insignificant amount of training taking place in small firms, the minister added: 'I can understand how a small business can think of training as a luxury it cannot afford. Often hampered by cash restraints, and faced with the difficulties of releasing key staff, small businesses can lack the knowledge to identify what training is needed or how to plan it. The new training loans plan to tackle these problems head on.'

The loans are available to cover the costs of training consultancy as well as the cost of training a small company might want to undertake. Key features include:

- loans from £500 to £125,000;
- repayments deferred for up to thirteen months. During this time the loan is interest free for the small business;
- loans available for up to 90 per cent of the course fee and the full costs of books and other training-related expenses up to an overall average of £5,000 per trainee;
- up to 90 per cent of the cost of hiring training consultants can be loaned to a maximum of £5,000;
- cost of temporary replacement for workers undergoing training, where necessary, may be included in the loan.

Alongside the banks, Training and Enterprise Councils (TECs) and their Scottish equivalents, Local Enterprise Companies (LECs) play a central role in the success of the training loans. It is a condition of the loan that the TEC or LEC must give its endorsement. In return for fulfilling this role, the Department of

Employment pays TECs and LECs £500 for every successful applicant approved by the bank.

At the launch of the scheme, Lord Henley set a target to have 3,000 training loans, amounting to around £30 million, by the end of March 1995.

KEY POINTS

- There are a number of alternatives to taking on extra full-time staff.
- Some manufacturing procedures are highly suited to out-workers.
- Interim managers operate on a similar basis to temporary clerical staff. They join a company for a limited period to deal with a short-term problem.
- Non-executive directors can introduce new skills, experience, and important contacts to a small firm.
- Be aware of your statutory responsibilities as an employer.
- Loans are available to small firms wishing to send their staff on training courses.

CASE STUDY
Torex Hire

Ben Longrigg, who runs Torex Hire, a chain of tool hire stores with a turnover of £4.5 million, faced a problem. A decision to diversify into the hire of modular self-erect marquees was foundering on the company's inability to manage the manufacture of the marquees.

With the peak summer months fast approaching, there was nobody in Longrigg's management team he could spare, or who had the right experience, to supervise the new activity. The limited number of marquees he aimed to produce did not justify setting up a whole new division.

Just when he was beginning to think there was no way out of the problem, Longrigg came across Barton Interim Management (BIM), an organization that leases out executives on a temporary basis to solve exactly the kind of short-term problem Longrigg faced.

John Skinner, a former production and distribution manager on BIM's books, was taken on by Torex Hire for several months to oversee the manufacture of the marquees. It proved to be an ideal solution to Longrigg's problem:

'The great advantage of interim management is that you can get someone to devote the whole of their time absolutely non-stop to doing the particular project you have in mind. When you're on a fairly tight time scale, that concentration is a tremendous help.

'I believe there are a great many companies that need this kind of expertise. The fact is many companies struggle on trying to do things themselves when there is expertise and management available if they only knew.'

CHAPTER 12

Expansion, Selling off & Selling out

For many entrepreneurs it is the creative challenge involved in building up a new company that gets their adrenaline going. Once the company has been established and it becomes a routine matter of managing its day to day affairs, their enthusiasm tends to wane. They would prefer to sell out and begin the exercise all over again.

Others, once having been through the baptism of fire, yearn for a less traumatic life, and are prepared to hand over the baton to someone else. For example, after initial disquiet, Tom Ketteringham felt a sense of relief to see the ultimate financial responsibility for Martek, the company he had built from scratch, pass into other hands (see page 45). The worry and the heartache of constantly having to seek funds to keep his company going, distracted him from what he was best at – making things.

It was his inventive skills that brought Martek to life, but he did not relish the lonely task of nurturing his brainchild for the rest of his working life. When his Swiss suppliers gained financial control, he was only too happy to let them take on that task. It has given him the peace of mind to experiment with more inventive ideas, which are the life blood of Martek's expansion. The transition has been assisted by the fact that the new owners have been relatively hands-off in their management approach.

Similarly, Graham Sadd and his partners, shed no tears when the Graphics Technology Group (GTG), the software company they had struggled to keep alive, was finally sold off to Ventura Software, a subsidiary of US giant, Xerox. A total of £1 million had been invested by 3i and the British Technology Group (BTG) to fund the company's growth and keep it independent. But even that was not enough to meet the development and marketing costs of a breakthrough software package for the desk-top publishing industry (see page 265). In September 1992 GTG's directors bowed to the inevitable and sold the company to Ventura.

Transition

Sadd and his partners had recognized a universal truth about creating a new company. The secondary growth phase requires a different approach from the start-up phase. It invariably takes small business entrepreneurs time to grasp this fundamental fact and indeed they often simply fail to recognize they have moved into the new phase. The realization often comes too late. They cling to the old way of doing things, because that is the way that has led to success up to now.

Once a small business finds a winning formula, the growth rate can be surprisingly rapid. Entrepreneurs who started experimenting with raw materials in a back garden shed can find themselves a few years later touring enormous factories, buzzing with activity and churning out products at a phenomenal rate.

It is sometimes hard to believe that so much has happened so quickly. Before he knows it, the entrepreneur can wake up one morning and find that he is no longer the custodian of a small business, but the chief executive of a medium-to-large company that promises to join the ranks of the country's more successful industries.

The transition often creeps up on unsuspecting entrepreneurs and the problems it poses can be almost as threatening as the dangers that engulfed them in the early stages of setting up the company. One of the hardest things for successful entrepreneurs to accept is that they cannot for ever keep control of all aspects of running their expanding firms. After all, they conceived the company. They were the ones who nurtured it through all the growing pains. It is easy for them to be convinced that nobody else, not even their closest and most loyal employees, can understand as they do what really makes the company tick.

But inevitably the day will come when they will start to lose control. It will become physically impossible for them to keep track of all the developments taking place. There will simply not be enough hours in the day. Because, however, the employees have become accustomed to all the major decisions being channelled through the founder-entrepreneur, they will have grown up in a climate in which personal initiative has not necessarily been encouraged. It will take a clear signal from the company's owner to convince them that things have changed. Without such a signal, employees will feel stifled. Their ability to grow with the company will become stunted. Their personal potential will never materialize or they will feel compelled to join a company where their talents will perhaps be more fully appreciated. In either case, it can be a serious loss to the original business at a time when it needs the support of all its employees.

Fortunately, most entrepreneurs see in time the dangers of hanging on to absolute power too long. It may take one or two minor crises to bring it home to them, but eventually they will wake up to the realization that their company is in a different league and requires a different style of management. It is time for autocracy to give way to professional management.

This does not imply that the company has been badly managed up to this point. Indeed, if it was not being run efficiently it would probably never have survived so long and some would argue that a good dose of autocratic management is appropriate for a small business in the early stages of its development.

What has basically happened is that the company's operations have grown so vast that each division, whether it be marketing, finance, production or public relations, has become a mini-business in its own right and requires to be run as such by someone who has the authority to make decisions without having to refer back to the top man all the time.

Once the founder-entrepreneur realizes this, a crucial decision needs to be made. Is there sufficient managerial talent within the company that can be relied on to share the load? Or is it necessary to go outside the company and hire 'professional' managers with a proven track record?

Making the decision

Making a wrong decision can be calamitous. If the company owner demonstrates a lack of faith by recruiting outside talent, the existing staff will be demotivated and their goodwill may well be forfeited, something that can have serious repercussions for the future development of the company.

If, on the other hand, the entrepreneur decides there are sufficint skills within the company's own ranks and that the only way to fulfil the potential of the existing team is to put it to the test, that could also mean gambling with the future of the company. Irreparable harm may be done to a business it has taken years to build up.

There are, of course, no pat answers to this dilemma. The founder-entrepreneur will have to use his own judgement. It is certainly true to say that some people never shine until they are given authority. The only way to find out if they have what it takes to succeed is to plunge them in at the deep end. The company owner might also be influenced by the knowledge that 'professional' managers can be an anathema to the true entrepreneur who often operates more from experience and instinct than by pragmatic management. The entrepreneur may simply find it impossible to work with professionals and may be left with little choice but to fall back on home-grown talent, even if there are some doubts about the capabilities of those concerned.

It was just such a dilemma that faced Gerry Hazlewood,

founder and former chairman of Westwood Engineering, a leading garden tractor manufacturer that has since been acquired by the Ransomes Group. Hazlewood began by bending pieces of metal in a garden shed to make simple rotary mowers some twenty-five years ago. The company ultimately had a turnover of more than £17 million before being absorbed by Ransomes.

Prior to the takeover, Hazlewood had been experiencing nagging doubts about the way the company was being run. One morning he woke up and realized in a blinding flash exactly what the problem was. For a company of its size, employing 330 people, he was still playing too much of a hands-on role in management. Because he had built Westwood from scratch, he knew every inch of it and his influence was all-pervasive. Inevitably, he was cramping everybody else's style. In addition, he was trying to handle more jobs than it was physically possible to cope with.

As a result, there were signs that some areas of the company were becoming neglected. In trying to grapple with the problems of rapid growth, for example, the company's quality control procedures were not as effective as they might have been. Westwood had reached that classic stage in its development when it was crying out for a more professional approach. Hazlewood later admitted: 'I could see I was actually stopping the company from progressing.'

Believing strongly that identifying a problem is three parts towards solving it, Hazlewood decided no half-measures would do. Having resolved to take more of a back seat in the running of the company, he handed over the managing directorship to his 32-year-old sales director and promoted his works manager and purchasing manager to the rank of director. He announced that in future the company would be run by this triumvirate.

Hazlewood remained chairman until the takeover, but to underline his resolve to withdraw from the day-to-day running of the company, he vacated his spacious office and moved to a back room away from the centre of operations.

Coinciding with the shift in managerial control, Hazlewood made a magnanimous gesture which left other industrialists aghast. He gave away a quarter of the company's shares to thirty-five of the most loyal employees. Typically, Hazlewood made the decision on impulse. He later recalled: 'When I came to work in the morning, I had no intention of doing it. I had never thought about it before.' But he did not believe it would have been sufficient to hand over management control without backing it up with a stake in the company: 'I don't think that would have been honest. That was the value I placed on them. They had supported me so fully. I had really been the administrator of their efforts.'

Adapting to changes in the market

Not only does the management style of a company have to change as it matures; the management has to recognize changes in the market place and adapt accordingly. What was once a winning formula can suddenly become out of fashion because of shifting social patterns or a major change in economic circumstances.

Plymouth-based Sola Wetsuits, for example, realized when the recession set in that it had to change direction to survive. Sales of its fashionable wetsuits slumped as the amount of disposable income people had to spend shrank dramatically. But just when things looked particularly bleak, one of the company's directors became aware of new legislation that made it compulsory for oil rigs and certain ocean-going vessels to be equipped with inflatable survival suits.

Sola made adjustments to its production facilities and cashed in on a market that filled the gap resulting from falling sales in its traditional product lines (see page 270).

Surviving the recovery

Many small firms may find that surviving the recovery is as

perilous as struggling through the recession. James Bethel, writing for the Small Business Focus Page of the *Sunday Times*, points out that past recoveries have been peppered by company failures as the economy emerges from recession, and over-borrowed firms find that the demands for greater working capital are too great to stomach. Overtrading, warns Bethel, is a common trap: 'The pattern is classic and lethal: with their finances already stretched after the long recession, companies suddenly find they have to find new money to finance higher stocks of raw materials as business picks up. Their rising overdrafts break existing bank agreements and the banks take the opportunity to appoint receivers to a business which they now believe has a value. For businesses in this condition, one bad debt can spell disaster.'

Cash flow problems are exacerbated when companies lose sight of their margins and profits in their rush to sign new contracts after years of denuded order books. Christopher Wheatcroft, the partner responsible for owner-managed businesses at accountants Touche Ross, told Bethel: 'Businessmen just do not appreciate how much extra working capital they will need to survive the recovery.'

How to stay in business

Terry Bard of the London Enterprise Agency suggests the following measures to avoid over-trading in an economic upturn:

- Improve your terms of trade by extending the terms of credit you receive and reducing the credit you give.
- Rent, lease or hire fixed assets instead of buying them. This avoids increasing commercial lending and allows greater financial flexibility.
- Refuse tough orders; ration production by raising prices.
- Consider factoring your debt to improve cash flow. You receive most of the money and pay a factoring agent's commission of one to three per cent (see Chapter 10).

- Companies reluctant to hand administration to third parties can receive cash immediately for their invoices (in return for a commission) through invoice discounting (see Chapter 10).
- Consider a new partner who can inject fresh capital. Business angels are attracted by tax incentives (see Chapter 6).
- Speed up the financial money-go-round by reducing stocks and debtors.
- Re-negotiate bank overdrafts for term loans and equity investments which are more appropriate for financing capital investment as repayment can be scheduled to suit revenues.

Going public

For a growing number of small business entrepreneurs flotation on the stock market is the only true measure of success. It represents to them the coming-of-age of their company – proof that it has reached a stage of maturity and is ready to join the senior league of enterprise. A stock-market listing is more than simply joining the ranks of the big players, however. Going public provides the opportunity to market a company's shares to raise capital and for other shareholders to obtain a return on their investment.

For many years the most popular way of achieving that goal was via a flotation on the Unlisted Securities Market (USM), a second-tier market for small-to-medium-sized firms. The USM was established in 1980 for companies which for one reason or another were unable, or did not wish, to obtain a full listing on the Stock Exchange.

The requirements for a USM listing were far less stringent than those for a full listing. The average cost was considerably cheaper than a full listing and a company could qualify for the USM without having to release more than 10 per cent of its shares, whereas 25 per cent of a company's equity has to be in the hands of the public to achieve a full stock-market listing.

The success of the USM exceeded most expectations. In the first five years around 400 companies joined it and £1 billion was raised. It turned numerous small business entrepreneurs into millionaires and there have been surprisingly few failures.

Despite its success, the USM is to be phased out in 1996 as a result of EU regulations which virtually eliminate any differences between the USM and the official list of the Stock Exchange. News of the USM's demise prompted criticism of the Exchange, which was accused of a lack of concern for smaller companies. In response, Sir Andrew Hugh Smith, Exchange chairman, set up a working party to investigate whether a successor to the USM was needed and what form it might take.

Much of the debate revolved around whether a second market should continue to be operated under the Stock Exchange umbrella or whether a credible alternative should be developed, for example, using brokers, market makers, accountants, solicitors and other advisers.

In September 1994 a successor to the USM was announced by the Stock Exchange to be known as the Alternative Investment Market (AIM), targeted at small, fast-growing firms. The aim was to provide an opportunity to trade shares in these companies without all the cost and bureaucracy which come with a full Stock Exchange listing.

The plan was to have AIM up and running by June 1995, but firms were able to apply to join from January 1995. AIM operates under Rule 4.2 of the Stock Exchange regulations, which was designed to allow the occasional trading of shares in unquoted companies without having to provide the same level of disclosure as with a full listing. In 1993 264 companies traded their shares under Rule 4.2 and as the deadline for the closure of the USM grew closer interest in the scheme heightened.

Entry rules for AIM are looser than for the main market with firms only having to produce a prospectus or similar document plus audited accounts. Some market participants expressed concern at the exchange's decision to allow companies to come to the market without a sponsor – a broker or bank. Others, however, took the view that by making the rules more flexible, companies will avoid the huge professional fees that have deterred many from seeking a listing in the past. As one stockbroker put it: 'The great thing for small companies will be that at last here is a way around the big problem of getting a prospectus out without lining the pockets of a bunch of bankers, accountants and lawyers.'

Company directors are responsible for the accuracy of information while firms have to provide figures at the half year and full year and announce price sensitive information promptly. Trading in shares is subject to the same level of regulation as the main market.

At the same time, the Stock Exchange set up a smaller companies panel to lobby on behalf of smaller firms.

Reasons for floating

While all this turbulence has been taking place, there has been no sign of a fall-off in the number of companies wanting to float, even though some of the listings have been temporarily postponed due to the volatility of the stock market itself. More than 165 new companies went public in 1993, raising £5 billion and this figure was exceeded by a large margin in 1994.

Like all business transactions, planning is the key to a successful flotation, but first you need to be clear about your reasons for going public. According to Ian Robinson, corporate finance partner at the Bristol office of accountants KPMG Peat Marwick, writing in the August 1994 issue of *Business South West* magazine, these can include:

• *Cashing in on success*. Shareholders can turn part of the paper value of their shares into cash at an attractive price and in a tax efficient way with the added bonus of still retaining both shareholder and management involvement;

• *Finance*. Through a flotation companies can build a

stronger capital base that will widen the options for future fund raising exercises to achieve strategic expansion of the business;

• *Status*. Despite certain notable failures there remains undoubtedly a certain sense of corporate achievement when management successfully launches strategic expansion of the business;

• *Competitive position*. A public company is better able to respond to competitive threats than a private company, whether this is in expansion through acquisition and the access to additional capital or through further finance for organic growth;

• *Employee motivation*. A public company is better able to motivate managers and employees through share schemes which enable them to see the success of their efforts reflected in the value of their stake through the quoted share price.

John Wakefield, director of stockbrokers Rowan Dartington, suggests that there are two compelling reasons for a company to undergo the arduous process of a flotation:

'First and from a corporate point of view, a stock-market quotation enables the company to raise equity capital on which it can in turn raise (or pay back) debt to finance further growth; and secondly, and perhaps even more compelling for the individual shareholders, it enables them to unlock a significant part of their investment while at the same time retaining an equity investment which, if the company's rate of progress goes according to plan, should continue to grow in value and significantly outperform inflation.

'I can think of no more compelling reason for a company to float than the desire of its shareholders to become very rich. And very often there is an overlap between the corporate objectives to achieve future growth and the individual aspiration to unlock wealth because it is a proven fact that, without wishing to decry the achievements of those companies whose rate of growth has come from steady development of their own core business, spectacular rates of growth can only be achieved through selective acquisition. A stock-market quotation gives the growing business access to the institutional investors with the deepest pockets.'

Wakefield points to another important aspect of a stock-market quotation: 'It enables the workforce to be properly motivated through attractive share option schemes which enable them to participate in the company's success in a tangible way reflected in the company's share price. The combination of access to capital, liquidity and employee incentive is a potent one which many companies find irresistible, given the right market conditions.'

Planning for a share listing

The planning for a share listing must begin well before the flotation as there may need to be fundamental changes to the business structure or management to improve the public profile. It is not unreasonable, or indeed unusual, Ian Robinson of KMPG Peat Marwick observes, to begin the process some two to three years before the contemplated date.

The more detailed timetable leading up to the flotation itself is often six months and sometimes up to a year. The first stage will be the selection of the advisory team of sponsors, brokers, reporting accountants, solicitors and public relations people. This is a critical decision because of the need to have a strong team in place that will work well together during what can be, at times, an arduous process.

Robinson suggests that the typical areas that a company has to review as part of its planning process are:

● To consider shareholder investment intentions after the flotation;
● Whether the company is sufficiently large for a proper market to develop in its shares;
● Whether the trading record of the company is attractive to

potential investors. The company must normally have a trend of increasing profit. An erratic profits performance needs careful explanation;

- Prospects – whether there is confidence that the company will continue to increase its profits;

- How investors will judge the board and the rest of the management team. Management must be aware of the additional responsibilities of a quoted company. Additionally, the board must seek the appointment of non-executive directors in accordance with the Cadbury code and the selection of the right non-executives can be a lengthy process;

- Whether the company has an acceptable capital and legal structure. Changes may be needed to simplify the structure before flotation to aid the potential investor's appreciation of the company. This is particularly the case with companies that were created as management buy-out structures in the late 1980s as they involved complex share structures which need to be unravelled before a flotation can be achieved;

- Whether the company is capable of complying with the requirements of the Stock Exchange.

Prospectus

The main requirement is for a prospectus (called Listing Particulars) which contains all the information about the business to enable prospective investors properly to evaluate the shares and the company's prospects. The personal circumstances of the existing shareholders, who may be selling a substantial number of shares and who will want to achieve this in a tax efficient way, will also be an important consideration.

It is the responsibility of the sponsoring brokers or merchant bank (if there is one) to take the principal lead in producing the Listing Particulars in conjunction with the company's professional advisers, who will include reporting accountants and solicitors.

John Wakefield of Rowan Dartington advises that the Listing Particulars should give details of the company's trading record for at least the past three years, its share capital and the number of shares it proposes to issue, as well as its management team.

In addition to containing this core information, the Listing Particulars must also be a selling document and seek to persuade the prospective investor, who has very many competing claims for his or her cash, that he should invest in this particular company. Adds Wakefield: 'It must achieve all this without being in any way misleading and must satisfy the requirements of the Stock Exchange as well as general company law. The sponsor will be assisted in this process by commissioning a Long Form Report from the company accountants which will investigate the company's corporate history since formation, especially its recent trading performance, the market in which it operates and will probe the management's claim about its position within that market and its future prospects.'

Timetable

Ian Robinson warns that the detailed timetable leading up to the eventual impact day will put a considerable demand on management time in order to provide the necessary data to ensure the success of the listing. This commitment to the project should not be under-estimated, he insists, and efforts should be made to share the responsibility for the ongoing management of the business amongst the members of the board who are not involved in the flotation on a day-to-day basis. The chairman, chief executive and finance director will normally bear the greatest responsibility for the flotation.

The main steps during this final process are:

• Selection of a co-ordinator within the business who will monitor the allocation of responsibilities;
• Preliminary review and assessment by the reporting accountants;

- Investigation. If a Long Form Report is required from the reporting accountants (as will be usual), this will take about six weeks to prepare. The report is a confidential document prepared for the information of the sponsors and directors;
- A preparation of Listing Particulars and other documents including statement of indebtedness and adequacy of working capital;
- Draft copies of the Listing Particulars and other legal documentation must be submitted to the Stock Exchange sufficiently in advance to allow time to deal with any comments. In practice it is always advisable to submit drafts six weeks before impact day so that problems can be dealt with at an early stage;
- Listing Particulars and other supporting documents must be lodged in final form with the Stock Exchange at least forty-eight hours before the hearing of the application for listing;
- Listing particulars must be approved by the Stock Exchange prior to their publication.

One advantage of a public listing is the higher profile it affords a company, which often results in a rapid increase in the level of business. MAID, the on-line information service provider (see pages 108 and 183) that floated in March 1994, saw its subscriber base boosted by more than 25 per cent in the first half of the year. There was also evidence that existing subscribers were making more frequent use of the service.

In the six months to June 1994 MAID achieved a rise in pre-tax profits from £207,000 to £440,000. Hoare Govett, MAID's broker, predicted a pre-tax profit of £1.2 million for the whole of 1994.

Dan Wagner, MAID's founder and chief executive, was quick to refute suggestions in the press that his prime motive for floating the company was to make him personally rich, even though it made him a millionaire several times over: 'If that was my motivation I would have sold at least some of my shares. In fact, I am looking to buy more shares when dealings open. We have only just started.'

Wagner told Judi Bevan of the *Sunday Telegraph* that as far as he was concerned the personal wealth he had gained from the flotation was completely irrelevant: 'I've had a nice salary, a nice car, a nice time. As long as I can have lunch somewhere nice, buy some clothes and go off on holiday without worrying too much about the cost, that's what matters. Obviously, we all have financial problems and actually I am always in debt personally. I don't think that will ever change.'

He had a similar riposte for Prufrock of the *Sunday Times*, which also questioned whether he was likely to stick with the company now he had made his fortune: 'We are just getting going. I would be crazy to cash in now. We know the sort of profits there are down the line.'

KEY POINTS

- Once they have established a small firm, some entrepreneurs are happy to let others take over the financial burden of ownership.
- They would prefer to concentrate on what they are best at – being creative.
- The secondary growth phase of a company requires a different approach to the start-up phase.
- As a company grows the entrepreneur will need to delegate some of the control.
- Deciding whether to bring in new management or promote from within is not always an easy choice.
- It is important to adapt to changes in the market place.
- Surviving an economic recovery can be as hazardous as struggling through a recession.
- Be clear about your reasons for opting for a stock-market flotation.
- A public listing can result in a higher profile and a rapid increase in the level of business.

CASE STUDY
The Graphics Technology Group

Graham Sadd is fond of catching out his acquaintances with a trick question. Who, he asks, are the world's top publishers by volume? The answer, surprisingly, is not Rupert Murdoch or any of the other famous media barons. They figure, according to Sadd's research, well down the league table, after the Jehovah's Witnesses, the US government and IBM.

Sadd poses the question in order to underscore the point that corporate publishing is an enormous – some would say – untapped market. When you think about all the brochures, booklets, annual reports, price lists and product manuals most major companies produce each year, it is not so difficult to believe.

Desk-top publishing has revolutionized the way all this corporate literature can be produced and in 1988 it was just beginning to take off. Software packages were already available, but Sadd and his two colleagues spotted a hole in the market. He recalls: 'The new wave of desk-top packages were all very good at taking information from word processors, but there was absolutely no way you could access databases. Yet it was obvious that the majority of information depositories were held on mainframe databases.'

They decided to provide the electronic link between databases and desk-top publishing and the Graphics Technology Group (GTG) was formed. Its directors decided their mission in life was to become a top quality OEM (original equipment manufacturer) in the corporate electronic publishing business. Sadd and his colleagues knew it would be a long haul. To fund the development process they continued providing an electronic publishing consultancy. Adds Sadd: 'Every time we got a consultancy job, we stopped everything on software development to do that in order to pay the rent and to finance the development costs.'

Operating under the constraints of this stop-go procedure, it took three-and-a-half years to finalize the desk-top package. At the time, GTG was crammed into a tiny building. It was then that a car company came along with a potentially lucrative, but near-impossible, task – a tender for supplying trucks to the MOD. Sadd and his colleagues knew that they would have to organize the work like a military operation.

It took the best part of four weeks working through the night to complete the twenty volumes of the tender, each of which contained around 200 pages. Recalls Sadd: 'We were taking three-hour sleep breaks. By the last week we had representatives from the motor manufacturer down with us proof-reading things on the screen. They slept on the floor and when we needed them to proof-read something we kicked them awake.'

In early 1989 it became obvious that GTG could not survive on its earnings from the consultancy work alone. Sadd decided to approach the local branch of 3i to seek some venture capital. He knew he would have his work cut out. Says Sadd: 'A venture capital company decides on whether it is going to invest in you in the first ten minutes. They then spend the next six months looking for reasons why they shouldn't. If they can't find any, they carry on with the investment. But I was convinced GTG had a very strong hand. We could actually go to 3i with an established management team with disparate complementary skills and with a very focused target market of corporate electronic publishing. We knew where we were going and we had a product.'

The confidence proved to be well-founded – 3i agreed to invest £500,000 in GTG in a sequence of tranches in return for a 25 per cent equity stake. The infusion of capital allowed GTG to strengthen its specialist staff and to appoint some high-powered salesmen. But the payback from all this expensive manpower was slow to materialize. Sadd believes in hindsight he did not give sufficient attention to directing the new staff. It was a very painful management learning exercise.

It soon became apparent that GTG was failing to perform to

plan. It could see a lot of investment disappearing into a black hole. Recalls Sadd: 'I would maintain we reacted very quickly to that by cutting back very hard to plug that black hole. That, of course, stops the revenue going out, but you are not replacing it with a revenue earner. So you've got to restructure the whole of the remaining part of the business to compensate for that. We were wearing at the time three hats and we suddenly ended up with five hats in order to be able to do that. We weren't performing to plan and that made things very difficult. We had to argue our case very much with 3i.'

The consolation was that development work on the software package, which GTG called *DataBase Publisher*, was going well. GTG had not yet struck any OEM deals, but was confident enough to test out the market for the software package under their own imprint to see what the reaction would be. The immediate future brightened further when GTG landed a £100,000 deal for its software with a major distributor. This was enough to encourage 3i to continue investing.

The drama was far from over, however. On one fateful day, Sadd and his management team were expecting the latest tranche of 3i money to be transferred to the company's bank account when the telephone rang. It was the distributor to say it would be sending back the software that GTG had supplied. The deal was off. The distributor was in financial trouble.

GTG was in a terrible dilemma. If it informed 3i of the loss of this major order, it was quite likely the venture capital group would put a stop on further payments. On the other hand, 3i would find out sooner or later, and if it felt GTG had been less than honest, the relationship would have been soured. Says Sadd: 'We got straight on to the telephone to 3i, because in the end you've got to have the confidence of the financial institutions you are dealing with, and there was no way we were going to withold the information from them.'

The bad news caused 3i to hesitate momentarily, but three weeks later it wired through the outstanding funds. GTG, however, still wasn't out of the woods. In fact, by the middle of 1990 it was technically insolvent. It had to seek professional advice as to whether it could legally carry on trading. GTG was advised by 3i to sell off the company or at least some of its assets as a damage-limitation strategy, even though by then it had signed a potentially lucrative joint venture marketing agreement with IBM.

Sadd regarded the advice as 'sensible' and set about looking for a buyer. But while attending a technical conference and exhibition in Nice in the South of France he mentioned his company's dilemma to a journalist from the *Financial Times*. A subsequent article deploring the way companies such as GTG were starved of venture capital struck a sympathetic chord and 3i offered to help to find another source of investment.

GTG was introduced to the British Technology Group (BTG) at the end of 1990 but it took until August 1991 for BTG to put £500,000 investment capital at GTG's disposal. But even this was not enough to meet the development and marketing costs. By September 1991, GTG's directors had bowed to the inevitable and decided to sell the company to US-based Ventura Software, a subsidiary of Xerox.

GTG had been marketing its products through the American software house and the sale of the company's assets was unavoidable in Sadd's view: 'It was always our best option, but we would have preferred to have waited another year or two, as indeed would have Ventura. But 3i and BTG were not really in a position to provide us with more funding to weather the financial storm.'

Sadd and his fellow directors, who all joined the management of Ventura, had few regrets at having to sell their brainchild to a foreign company. Says Sadd: 'It meant we could play on a bigger stage than we were able to do before. Ventura didn't just absorb the product. It recognized that the asset was in the people. That had very much been a condition of the sale.'

Ninety per cent of GTG's staff were relocated to Ventura's

European headquarters in Slough, a short distance from GTG's former head office in Maidenhead. Sadd was made a vice-president of Ventura and managing director of the US group's European operations.

CASE STUDY
Sola Wetsuits

Pride of place in the reception room of a fast-growing company at Ocean Quay, Plymouth, is taken up by a model wearing one of the firm's colourful red, white and blue wetsuits, embrazoned with the entwined rings of the Olympic Games. It is a visible symbol of the marathon struggle Sola Wetsuits & Leisurewear has experienced to reach the peak of its market against considerable odds.

It originally won the order to supply wetsuits to the yachting contestants in the Seoul Olympics in 1988 in competition with more than forty other manufacturers. Its products were so highly regarded that the order was repeated for subsequent Olympic events.

The small Plymouth company achieved this pre-eminent niche in a highly competitive market by sticking to quality when many of its rivals succumbed to the temptation to cut corners and use cheaper materials in an effort to survive the recession. That, combined with strict production controls and an ongoing diversification programme has seen the company expanding steadily when the reverse may well have been the case.

Now, with a workforce of around fifty people, an annual production rate of some 40,000 wetsuits and a turnover of several million pounds, chairman Stuart Hutchins can look back with some amusement at the inauspicious birth of Sola in 1985.

Hutchins was originally sales manager of another leading Westcountry wetsuit manufacturer. He, together with Ross Winmill, now Sola's managing director, was largely responsible for that company's annual turnover going from just under £300,000 to £1.5 million in three years.

When Hutchins and Winmill decided to form their own wetsuit company and were prepared to put a considerable amount of their own capital into the venture, they thought it would be an easy matter to raise additional finance from a high street bank. They were confident their track record would speak for itself. But they met with rejection after rejection.

The banks did not believe in their ambitious business plan that predicted sales of £200,000 in the first year of operation. In the event, Sola achieved a turnover of £213,000 in its first year and reached the £1 million mark within three years. But that was only after Hutchins and Winmill had finally persuaded NatWest to put up the additional capital to make the project viable.

With the two marketing men working flat out to break into the sportswear market, Sola soon outgrew its original premises in Plymouth. They moved into their existing factory in 1987 and became a shining example of the enterprise culture.

As the recession began to bite, however, it became obvious that the leisurewear market was in decline and Hutchins and Winmill realized that if they did not devise a diversification plan all their steady progress would come to a halt.

At around the time of the Piper Alpha disaster in the North Sea, regulations were introduced requiring all oil rigs and ocean-going vessels of a certain size to be equipped with survival suits. This seemed like a golden opportunity for Sola as it was obvious the demand for this equipment would explode as the deadline for the new regulations approached. Recalls Tony Raftery, Sola's financial director: 'We earmarked an opening in the market because the legislation actually came into force in July 1991. Prior to that, Department of Transport surveyors were at the ports checking that the safety regulations were being fulfilled. There was a massive demand which we were able to supply and it helped us through the recession.'

Indeed, demand was so brisk that Sola had to install a new mezzanine floor at its Plymouth factory in 1991 that added a further two and a half thousand square feet to its production area.

The venture took Sola into a completely new area of technology. The suits, which are made of a high quality fire retardant material known as Neoprene, are understandably required to meet stringent safety standards. In addition, the suits have to be made in such a way that in an emergency they can be donned within two minutes over all types of clothing. It cost Sola £20,000 just to get the Department of Transport's approval for its suits.

As part of the approved procedure, survival suits had to be sent to Canada where they were tested on the world's only operating thermal manikin. This has electrodes attached to various parts of its anatomy which calculate to a fine degree whether the suits are capable of maintaining core body temperatures in an emergency situation.

The survival suits became 25 per cent of Sola's production capacity at the peak of the demand, but that has since dropped back to about five per cent as customers have steadily met with the legal requirements. Even though Sola went on to get approval for its designs in Holland, Russia, Spain, Norway and Sweden, it had to face the fact that this was a limited market and that it needed to come up with a new diversification plan if it was to continue to grow.

By this time Sola's image was already one of a company that supplies quality products to the top end of the water sports market. Part of this was achieved through imaginative marketing and by sponsoring world class surfers and body board champions. But the vast majority of its outlets were UK retailers. The time seemed ripe to sail into new waters – Europe in particular.

An export manager was appointed who has been rapidly building up new markets on the continent from his base in Holland. Says Raftery: 'In the past we've approached Europe in a half-hearted fashion. We decided that's where the expansion lay and we've gone all out to achieve it.'

Having come through the worst of the recession, Raftery is optimistic about the company's future: 'Every year we're getting stronger from the management point of view; the teamwork is getting better; we've got a more organized sales force now. Hopefully within a year or two we will be a complete supplier to the water sports industry. There will be no reason to buy from anyone else and we will get dealers who are a hundred per cent Sola stockists.'

The only brake on Sola's progress is the high cost of advertising, particularly in European water sports magazines. Hutchins wishes the government would come up with a scheme to help underwrite such costs rather than focusing on programmes to offset the costs of consultancy work. 'A couple of years ago one of our rival brands in Australia got 80 per cent of its advertising costs paid for by the government. What a fantastic promotion!'

Hutchins stresses, however, that without the support of NatWest, which kept funding Sola through the worst of the recession, Sola would have had a job to survive. 'NatWest deserves a pat on the back,' he insists. That is an unusual accolade at a time when many small businesses are bemoaning the lack of interest being shown in them by the high street banks. For Sola Wetsuits, that is a thing of the past.

APPENDIX A

Small Business Contacts

INTRODUCTION

The Centre for Small and Medium Sized Enterprises, Warwick Business School. Contacts: Prof David Storey – Tel: 01203 523692 and Dr Robert Cressy or Marc Cowling – Tel: 01203 523741.

CHAPTER TWO

Patent Office/The Trade Marks Registry, 25 Southampton Buildings, London WC2A 1AW. Tel: 0171–438 4700.

The Chartered Institute of Patent Agents, Staple Inn Buildings, High Holborn, London WC1V 7PZ. Tel: 0171–405 9450.

The Institute of Trade Mark Agents, 4th Floor, Canterbury House, 2–6 Sydenham Road, Croydon CR0 9XE. Tel: 0181–686 2052.

The British Franchise Association, Thames View, Newtown Road, Henley-on-Thames, Oxon RG9 1HG. Contact: Brian Smart, executive director. Tel: 01491 578049.

National Westminster Bank, NatWest Tower, 25 Old Broad Street, London EC2N 1HQ. Contact: Peter Stern, head of franchise section. Tel: 0171–726 1793.

Midland Bank plc, Business Sector marketing, Griffin House, Silver Street Head, Sheffield S1 3GG. Tel: 0114 2529037.

Companies Registration Office, Companies House, Crown Way, Maindy, Cardiff CF4 3UZ. Tel: 01222 388588.

CHAPTER THREE

3i plc, 91 Waterloo Road, London SE1 8XP. Tel: 0171–928 3131.

Centre for Management Buy-out Research, Institute of Financial Studies, University of Nottingham, University Park, Nottingham NG7 2RD. Contact: Ken Robbie. Tel: 0115 9506101.

CHAPTER FOUR

Association of Independent Businesses, Independent House, 26 Addison Place, London W1 4RJ. Tel: 0171–371 1299.

Confederation of British Industry (CBI), Centrepoint, 103 New Oxford Street, London WC1A 1DU. Tel: 0171–379 7400.

Federation of Small Businesses, 32 St Anne's Road West, Lytham St Annes, Lancashire FY8 1NY. Tel: 01253 720911.

Forum of Private Business, Ruskin Chambers, Drury Lane, Knutsford, Cheshire WA16 6HA. Tel: 01565 634467.

Small Business Bureau, Curzon House, Church Road, Windlesham, Surrey GU20 6BH. Tel: 01276 452010.

Business in the Community (BiC), 277a City Road, London EC1V 1LX Tel: 0171–253 3716.

National Association of Shopkeepers and Self Employed, Lynch House, 91 Mansfield Road, Nottingham NG1 3FN. Tel: 0115 9475046.

Association of British Chambers of Commerce, 9 Tufton Street, London SW1P 3QB. Tel: 0171–222 1555.

The Rural Development Commission (RDC)

Head Offices:
Dacre House, 19 Dacre Street, London SW1H 0DH. Tel: 0171–340 2900.
   141 Castle Street, Salisbury, Wiltshire SP1 3TP. Tel: 01722 336255.

Durham, Cleveland, Northumberland:
Morton Road, Yarm Road Industrial Estate, Darlington, Co. Durham DL1 4PT. Tel: 01325 487123.

Cumbria, Lancashire:
Haweswater Road, Penrith, Cumbria CA11 7EH. Tel: 01768 65752.

Humberside, Yorkshire:
Spitfire House, Aviator Court, Clifton Moor, York YO3 4UZ. Tel: 01904 693335.

Gloucestershire, Hereford and Worcester, Shropshire, Staffordshire:
Strickland House, The Lawns, Park Street, Wellington, Telford, Shropshire TF1 3BX. Tel. 01952 247161.

Derbyshire, Leicestershire, Lincolnshire, Nottinghamshire:
18 Market Place, Bingham, Nottingham NG13 8AP. Tel: 0115 9839222.

Cambridgeshire, Essex, Norfolk, Suffolk:
Lees Smith House, 12 Looms Lane, Bury St Edmunds, Suffolk 1P33 1HE. Tel: 01284 701743.

Kent, East Sussex, Isle of Wight:
141 Castle Street, Salisbury, Wiltshire, SP1 3TP. Tel: 01722 336255.

Dorset, Somerset, Wiltshire:
3 Chartfield House, Castle Street, Taunton, Somerset TA1 4AS. Tel: 01823 276905.

Cornwall, Isles of Scilly, Devon:
27 Victoria Park Road, Exeter, Devon EX2 4NT. Tel: 01392 421245.

Association of County Councils, Easton House, 66A Eaton Square, London SW1W 9BH. Tel: 0171–235 1200.

Department of Trade and Industry (DTI)

Department of Trade and Industry, Ashdown House, 123 Victoria Street, London SW1E 6RB. General enquiries: 0171–215 5000. Business in Europe: 0117–9444 888. Innovation Enquiry Line: 0800 44 2001. Environmental Enquiry Point: 0800 585 794.

DTI North East:
Stanegate House, 2 Groat Market, Newcastle-upon-Tyne NE1 1YN. Tel: 0191–235 7223.

DTI North West (Manchester):
Sunley Tower, Piccadilly Plaza, Manchester M1 4BA. Tel: 0161–838 5000.

DTI North West (Liverpool):
Graeme House, Derby Square, Liverpool L2 7UP. Tel: 0151–224 6300.

DTI Yorkshire & Humberside:
25 Queen Street, Leeds LS1 2TW. Tel: 0113 2338272.

DTI East Midlands:
Severns House, 20 Middle Pavement, Nottingham NG1 7DW. Tel: 0115 9596324.

DTI West Midlands:
77 Paradise Circus, Queensway, Birmingham B1 2DT. Tel: 0121–212 5118.

DTI South West:
The Pithay, Bristol BS1 2PB. Tel: 0117 9272 666.

DTI South East:
Bridge Place, 88–89 Eccleston Square, London SW1V 1PT. Tel: 0171–215 0888.

DTI East:
Building A, Westbrook Centre, Milton Road, Cambridge CB4 1YG. Tel: 01223 346772.

Scotland:

The Scottish Office, Industry Department, Magnet House, 56 Waterloo Street, Glasgow G2 7BT. Tel: 0141–242 5675.

Wales:

Welsh Office, Industry Department, New Crown Building, Cathays Park, Cardiff CF1 3NQ. Tel: 01222 825400.

Further information on Regional Selective assistance and Regional Enterprise Grants:

Department of Trade and Industry, Investment, Development and Accountancy Services Division, Kingsgate House, 66–74 Victoria Street, London SW1E 6SW. Tel: (RSA) 0171–215 2565, (REG) 0171–215 8459.

European Investment Bank, 68 Pall Mall, London SW1Y 5ES. Tel: 0171–839 3351.

European Loans Unit, Barclays Bank plc, PO Box No 256, Fleetway House, 25 Farringdon Street, London EC4 4LP. Tel: 0171–489 1995.

Association of District Councils, 26 Chapter Street, London SW1P 4ND. Tel: 0171–233 6868.

The Employment Service, Rockingham House, 123 West Street, Sheffield S1 4ER. Tel: 0114 2739190.

Scottish Enterprise Agency, 120 Bothwell Street, Glasgow G2 7JP. Tel: 0141 248 2700.

Welsh Development Agency, Pearl House, Greyfriars Road, Cardiff CF1 3XX. Tel: 01222 222666.

English Tourist Board, Thames Tower, Black's Road, London W6 9EL. Tel: 0181–846 9000.

Scottish Tourist Board, 23 Ravelston Terrace, Edinburgh EH4 3EU. Tel: 01031 332 2433.

Welsh Tourist Board, Brunel House, 2 Fitzalan Road, Cardiff CF2 1UY. Tel: 01222 499909.

Northern Ireland Tourist Board, St Anne's Court, 59 North Street, Belfast BT1 1NB. Tel: 01232 246609.

Livewire, Hawthorn House, Forth Banks, Newcastle upon Tyne NE1 3SG. Tel: 0191 261 1910.

The Prince's Youth Business Trust, 5 Cleveland Place, London SW1Y 6JJ. Tel: 0171–321 6500.

CHAPTER FIVE

National Westminster Bank Small Business Services, Level 10, Drapers Gardens, 12 Throgmorton Avenue, London EC2N 2DL. Contact: Ian Peters, Head of Small Business Services. Tel: 0171–920 5555.

British Venture Capital Association, 3 Catherine Place, London SW1E 6DX. Tel: 0171–233 5212.

3i Group plc, 91 Waterloo Road, London SE1 8XP. Tel: 0171–928 0058.

CHAPTER SIX

Business Marriage Bureaux

Bedfordshire TEC. Contact: Graham Moores. Tel: 01234 843100.

Blackstone Franks Chartered Accountants. Tel: 0171–250 3300.

Calderdale & Kirklees TEC. Contact: Alastair Graham. Tel: 01484 400770.

Capital Connections. Tel: 01254 301333.

Capital Exchange Ltd. Contact: Nigel Lacy. Tel: 01432–353760 or 01730 814733.

Cornwall Enterprise Board. Contact: John Berry. Tel: 01872–223883.

Daily Telegraph Business Network. Tel: 0171–538 7172.

East Lancashire TEC. Contact: Peter Davies. Tel: 01254–61471.

Gloucestershire Enterprise Agency. Tel: 01452 501411.

Hilling Wall Corporate Finance. Tel: 0171–495 1302.

H W Fisher Chartered Accountants. Tel: 0171–388 7000.

Informal Register of Investment Services. Tel: 01422 361507.
Interim Management. Tel: 0171–404 6772.
Investors in Hertfordshire. Tel: 01727 852313.
LINC (London Enterprise Agency). Contact: Fiona Conoley.
   Tel: 0171–236 3000.
Milton Keynes Business Venture. Tel: 01908 660044.
Principality Finance Management. Tel: 01792 474111.
South & East Cheshire TEC. Contact: Liz Davis.
   Tel: 01606–847009.
TECHINVEST. Tel: 01606 737009.
Venture Capital Report. Contact: Lucius Cary.
   Tel: 01491–57999.
VentureList. Tel: 01483 458111.
WINSEC Corporate Exchange. Tel: 01621 815047.

CHAPTER SEVEN

The Rural Development Commission, 141 Castle Street,
   Salisbury SP1 3JP. Tel: 01722 336255.
ADAS, Oxford Spires Business Park, The Boulevard, Kidlington,
   Oxon OX5 1NZ. Tel: 01865 842742.

CHAPTER EIGHT

The Information Centre of the Advertising Association, Abford
   House, 15 Wilton Road, London SW1V 1NJ. Tel: 0171–828
   2771.
Chartered Institute of Marketing, Moor Hall, Cookham,
   Maidenhead, Berkshire SL6 9QH. Tel: 016285 24922.
Direct Marketing Association, Haymarket House, 1 Oxendon
   Street, London SW1Y 4EE. Tel: 0171–321 2525.
Institute of Public Relations, The Old Trading House, 15
   Northburgh Street, London EC1V 0PR. Tel: 0171–253 5151.

Institute of Practitioners in Advertising, 44 Belgrave Square, London SW1X 8QS. Tel: 0171–235 7020.

Institute of Sales Promotion, Arena House, 66/68 Pentonville Road, London N1 9HS. Tel: 0171–837 5340.

Market Research Society, 15 Northburgh Street, London EC1V 0AH. Tel: 0171–490 4911.

CHAPTER NINE

The Export Award for Smaller Businesses

Sponsored by:

British Overseas Trade Board, Kingsgate House, 66–74 Victoria Street, London SW1E 6SW. Contact: David Hoggett, joint directorate. Tel: 0171–215 4919. Fax: 0171–215 2863.

Kompass British Exports, Windsor Court, East Grinstead House, East Grinstead, West Sussex RH19 1XA. Contact: Karen Viney, product manager. Tel: 01342 326972. Fax: 01342 335 747.

Midland Bank, 2nd Floor, St Magnus House, 3 Lower Thames Street, London EC3. Contact: Rob Bolton, Trade and International Banking Services. Tel: 0171–260 5397. Fax 0171–260 9998.

Grant Thornton, The Quadrangle, Imperial Square, Cheltenham, Glos. GL50 1PZ. Contact: Patrick Brooke. Tel: 01242 222 900. Fax: 01242 222 330.

Supported by:

AEEU, 110 Peckham Road, London SE15 5EL. Contact: Mel Barras, national organizer. Tel: 0171–703 4231. Fax: 0171–701 7862.

British Chambers of Commerce, 4 Westwood Business Park, Coventry CV4 8HS. Contact Steve Baker, export executive. Tel: 01203 694492. Fax: 01203 694690.

The Institute of Export, Export House, 64 Clifton Street, London EC2A 4HB. Contact: Ian Campbell, director general. Tel: 0171–247 9812. Fax: 0171–377 5340.

Confederation of British Industry, Centre Point, 103 Oxford Street, London WC1A 1DU. Contact: Dr Ian Peters.
Tel: 0171– 379 7400. Fax: 0171–240 1578.
(Entry forms available from DTI regional offices, the sponsors and Kompass British Exports, the award administrator)
The DTI's 'Business in Europe' has a telephone hotline – 0117 9444888 – for enquiries about new opportunities in Europe.
The National Business Language Information Service, Centre for Information on Language Training and Research, 20 Bedfordbury, London WC2N 4LB. Contact: Penny Rashbrook.
Tel: 0171–379 5131.
The Languages for Export Campaign, the DTI, Contact: Robert Holkham. Tel: 0171–215 4857/8146.

CHAPTER TEN

Association of British Factors and Discounters

Information Office, 1 Northumberland Avenue, Trafalgar Square, London WC2N 5BW. Tel: 0171–930 9112.
ABFD Members:
Alex Lawrie Factors Ltd., Beaumont House, Beaumont Road, Banbury, Oxon OX16 7RN. Tel: 01295 272272.
Barclays Commercial Services Ltd., Aquila House, Breeds Place, Hastings, East Sussex TN34 3DG. Tel: 01424 430824.
Close Invoice Finance Ltd., Southbrook House, 25 Bartholomew Street, Newbury, Berkshire RG14 5LL. Tel: 01635 31517.
Griffin Factors, 21 Farncombe Road, Worthing, West Sussex BN11 2BW. Tel: 01903 205181.
Hill Samuel Commercial Finance Ltd., Boston House, The Little Green, Richmond, Surrey TW9 1QE. Tel: 0181–940 4646.
International Factors Ltd., PO Box 240, Sovereign House, Church Street, Brighton, Sussex BN1 3WX. Tel: 01273 321211.
Kellock Ltd., Abbey Gardens, 4 Abbey Street, Reading, Berkshire RG1 3BA. Tel: 01734 585511.

Lombard NatWest Commercial Services Ltd., Smith House, PO Box 50, Elmwood Avenue, Feltham, Middlesex TW13 7QD. Tel: 0181–890 1390.

Royal Bank of Scotland Invoice Finance Ltd., Exchange Court, 3 Bedford Park, Croydon, Surrey CR0 2AQ. Tel: 0181–686 9988.

Trade Indemnity-Heller Commercial Finance Ltd., Park House, 22 Park Street, Croydon, Surrey CR9 1RD. Tel: 0181–681 2641.

UCB Invoice Discounting Ltd., Wren House, Sutton Court Road, Sutton, Surrey SM1 4TE. Tel: 0181–307 7744.

Venture Factors Ltd., Sussex House, Perrymount Road, Haywards Heath, West Sussex RH16 1DN. Tel: 01444 414199.

Association of Invoice Factors

Jordan House, Brunswick Place, London N1 6EE. Tel: 0171–248 4901.

AIF Members:

Anpal Finance Ltd., PO Box 37, Kimberley House, Vaughan Way, Leicester LE1 9AZ. Tel: 0116 2516066.

Bibby Factors Ltd., Kenwood House, 77a Shenley Road, Boreham Wood, Herts WD6 1AG. Tel: 0181–207 1554.

Bibby Financial Services Ltd., 105 Duke Street, Liverpool L1 5JQ. Tel: 0151–708 8000.

Gaelic Invoice Factors Ltd., Finlay House, 10–14 West Nile Street, Glasgow G1 2PP. Tel: 0141–248 4901.

KCH Ltd., The Computer Centre, Benmhor, Campbeltown, Argyll PA28 6DN. Tel: 01586 54488.

London Wall Factors Ltd., Barkhill House, Shire Lane, Chorleywood, Herts. WD3 5NT. Tel: 01923 285199.

Maddox Factoring (UK) Ltd., Argent House, 1 Progress Business Centre, Whittle Parkway, Slough, Berkshire SL1 6DQ. Tel: 01628 668706.

Metropolitan Factors Ltd., 4 Heath Square, Boltro Road, Haywards Heath, West Sussex RH16 1BL. Tel: 01444 415081.

RDM Factors Ltd., Fairfax House, 461–465 North End Road, London SW6 1NZ. Tel: 0171–386 7233.

Ulster Factors Ltd., 7 North Street, Belfast BT1 1NH. Tel: 01232 324522.

British Standards Institution, Milton Keynes MK14 6LE. Tel: 01908 221166.

Glossary of Terms

Assisted Areas: Areas of industrial decline, designated by the DTI. Projects in these areas may be eligible for Regional Enterprise Grants or Regional Selective Grants.

BS 5750: The quality assurance standard obtainable through the certification and assessment services of the BSI (British Standards Institution).

Business Plan: A plan setting out the objectives of the business and how they are to be achieved.

Business Angel: A private investor who injects capital into fledgling small firms.

Business Expansion Scheme (BES): A government scheme that offered income-tax relief to private investors prepared to invest in promising new companies. It was replaced by the Enterprise Investment Scheme (EIS) at the end of 1993.

Development Area: A DTI Assisted Area (see Assisted Areas).

Development funding/capital: Venture capital after a company has become established, to fund an expansion of the business.

Enterprise Investment Scheme: A replacement for the BES. This scheme allows income relief to investors in genuinely risky small firms. Investors who back EIS companies can offset any losses against income or capital-gains tax after five years.

Equity: A shareholding in a company.

Exit: The route by which venture capitalists realize their original investment, usually as a result of a flotation or corporate purchase.

Factoring: The purchase of the trade debts owed to a business by a factoring company. This provides short-term financing and may include the administration of the businesses' sales ledger by the factor who will be responsible for credit control and the despatch of statements.

Financial Services Act 1986: The regulations which govern the conduct of investment business in the UK.

Flotation: Term used to describe the entry of a company to the stock market, whether by an offer for sale, placing or introduction.

Franchising: The means by which business owners (franchisors) grant a licence (or franchise) to other entrepreneurs (franchisees) to start up replicas of a successful and proven business concept. The Body Shop is one of the best-known examples.

Gearing: Broadly, the ratio of debt to equity in a company's capital structure.

Incorporated: Limited company status.

Institutional investor: An investor investing other than in a private capacity – normally a financial institution such as an insurance company.

Interim managers: Managers who are attached to companies for a limited period of time to run specific non-core activities.

Intermediate Area: A DTI Assisted Area (see Assisted Areas).

Invoice discounting: Similar to factoring, but confidential. The customer should be unaware that the invoice has been discounted.

Irrevocable letter of credit: A banking procedure for ensuring exporters receive payment for despatched goods.

ISO 9000: The international quality assurance standard.

Leveraged buy-out: Similar to a management buy-out or buy-in but without the same degree of direct equity participation by the managers. The term 'leverage' is another name for gearing.

Livewire: A nationwide organization that helps young people start and run businesses.

Loan Guarantee Scheme: A government scheme that guarantees a proportion of a bank loan for a viable business that lacks security.

Lobbying groups: Pressure groups that press for reforms to reduce the amount of red tape involved in running small firms.

Local Enterprise Agencies: A national network of more than 300 agencies committed to the economic development of their areas through the provision of help to new and existing small businesses.

Management buy-in: An arrangement whereby a team of outside managers purchases a business with funding provided by a group of financial backers.

Management buy-outs: An arrangement whereby the management of a company purchases the business with funding provided by a group of financial backers.

Marriage bureaux: The intermediary agencies that bring together small firms seeking investment and private investors (sometimes known as business angels).

Mezzanine finance: A form of finance falling between equity and debt, typically used in a management buy-out. Frequently unsecured, it usually carries interest at a higher rate than secured loans.

One-Stop-Shops: Regional agencies that act as a single focus for business development schemes and form part of a national 'Business Link' network.

Outworkers: Local craftsmen and women who operate from home. Work is sub-contracted out to them, avoiding the costs of full employment for growing small firms.

Overdraft: A flexible form of bank lending. The advantage is you only pay for the funds you use, making it a suitable means to fund working capital.

Prospectus: A document offering shares or debentures in a company to the public for subscription or purchase.

Rachet: An incentive arrangement whereby a number of trigger points for future profits are set such that the managers get a bigger share of the equity if the company performs well and a lesser share if it performs badly.

Regional Enterprise Grants: DTI grants, broken down into regional investment grants and regional innovation grants (see Assisted Areas).

Regional Selective Assistance: Regional financial assistance from the DTI (see Assisted Areas).

Rural areas: The RDC defines rural areas as regions in England that lie outside towns with a population of more than 10,000. Rural areas account for some 85 per cent of the total area of England and for around 20 per cent of its population.

Rural Development Commission (RDC): The agency that offers incentives for small businesses that create jobs in rural areas and help to halt rural economic decline.

Seed capital: Venture capital used to bring a research idea to the development stage.

Sensitivity analysis: Analysis of the sensitivity of predicted

---

results to changes in the underlying assumptions of a business plan.

Service industries: A sector of the economy that provides services as opposed to manufactured products.

TECs: Regional training and enterprise agencies are private-sector led partnerships in the local community, whose role is to devise and deliver quality training and small business support. They have taken over a number of employment schemes and advisory services previously provided centrally by government.

Teleworking: Operating from home or remote from an employer or customer, using information technology equipment.

Term loan: A loan for a fixed amount with a fixed repayment schedule, normally from a bank.

Unincorporated: A form of business which is not a limited company – normally a sole trader or a partnership.

Unlisted Securities Market: A means for smaller firms, which are unable to meet the stringent requirements of a full-listing to gain access to the Stock Exchange. The USM is being phased out in 1996 and replaced by the Alternative Investment Market (AIM).

Venture capital: Funds invested into a company in return for a share in the company's equity.

Working capital: The cash resources a company needs to operate as a going concern on a daily basis.

Index

INDEX

British Chambers of Commerce (BCC) 203, 218
British Coal Enterprise (BCE) 148
British Dalcon Plastics 65
British Franchise Association (BFA) 28–31
British Institute of Management 118
British Invisibles 203
British Museum Connection 197
British Overseas Trade Board 203
British Standard 5750 4, 71, 228, 229–31, 233
British Standards Institution (BSI) 230
British Technology Group (BTG) 26–7, 250, 268
British Telecom 118, 135–6, 152
British Venture Capital Association 91
brochures 163–5
budgets 101–2
bureaucracy 2, 4, 52, 72, 232
Burrell, Valerie 14, 187
Business and Enterprise Services 68
Business angels 114–31, 256
business ethics 8, 30, 39
Business Expansion Scheme (BES) 3, 111, 127–8
Business in the Community (BiC) 25–6
Business Links 5, 26, 61, 79
business plans 3, 57, 67–9, 75–6, 97–107, 138, 156, 232
business rates 71–3
Business South West 258
Business Start-up Schemes 68
Business Week 184
buy-ins 19, 48; management buy-ins 52–9, 95; BIMBOs 58; VIMBOs 58
buy-outs 19; management buy-outs (MBOs) 9, 50–3, 57, 89, 95, 216, 261; BIMBOs 58; VIMBOs 58

Cadbury Code 261
Cairo 193
Calderdale 117
California 201
Callington 216
Cammell, John 230
Canada 22, 206, 272
Candover Investments 57
capital, access to 3; development 91; equity 46, 259; fixed 62; growth 92; investment 24; loan 83; own 56; raising 61; seed 16, 42, 50–1, 96; share 262; working 48, 57, 214, 219, 222, 232, 255, 263
Capital Exchange Ltd 117
Cardiff 202
Career Development Loans (CDLs) 69–70
Caribbean 139
Cary, Lucius 42, 116, 121–2
cash flow 10, 15, 82, 99–100, 102–3, 106, 125, 214–15, 218, 222, 224, 226, 232, 255; forecasts 102–3, 106
catalogues 158
CBI News 57
Centre for Information on Language Training and Research (CILT) 194, 196
Centre for Management Buy-out Research 56–7
Centre for Small and Medium Sized Enterprises 87
Chalice Foods 22, 39–44, 161–2

Chartered Institute of Marketing (CIM) 181
Cheadle 54
Cheshire 117
Chester 202
China 188, 205
Chubb Locks and Safe Ltd 129
CINVen 27
City of London 46, 85
Clutterbuck, David 51
Clydesdale Bank 66, 70, 245
Co-operative Bank 70, 245
Coates, Geoffrey 199
commissions 193–4
Commonwealth 195
communications 43
Companies Act 1985 92
Companies House 33, 172
Companies Registration Office 172
competition 8, 19–21, 37, 159, 169–72, 182, 259
Confederation of British Industry (CBI) 57, 61, 203
conferences 71
Conoley, Fiona 119–20
Conran's 188
consultants 5, 7, 61, 181, 238, 240–1
conversions 140–1, 153
Coopers & Lybrand 58
copyrights 36
Cornerstar Design Company Ltd 76, 80–1
Cornix Ltd 137
Cornwall 45–6, 117, 139, 216, 235
CoSira 142; *see also* RDC
Country Landowners' Association 142
County NatWest Ventures Ltd 52, 55
Coventry 139
Cranfield School of Management 7
credit control 218–25, 233
credit management 220
Cumbria 154
Curnow, Ron 204
Curran, Stephen 57
customers 9, 12, 41, 167–9, 182, 204, 231
Customs & Excise 5, 210, 277–8
Cutts, Nicky 240–1
CX Monthly 117

Daily Telegraph 185
Data Protection Act 1984 227
debt 72, 103, 215, 232, 255–6, 259, 263; bad debts 86, 114, 218, 244–5
delegation 251, 264
Denmark 188
Denton, Baroness 88–9
Department of Social Security 244
Department of Employment 117, 245–7
Department of Trade and Industry (DTI) 26–7, 60, 62–6, 69, 79, 88, 92, 102–4, 106, 118, 141, 185, 188–9, 194, 196, 198–200, 203, 211–13, 217
Department of Transport 271–2
depreciation 101–2
deregulation 3
de Silva, Viv 200–1
DeSurvey Ltd 204

291

INDEX

INDEX